EXPECTING Twins?

A complete guide to pregnancy, birth & your twins' first year

PROFESSOR MARK KILBY DSc MD MB BS FRCOG

JANE DENTON CBE, FRCN

with Debbie Beckerman

Quadrille
PUBLISHING

Contents

INTRODUCTION

Twins are fascinating and throughout the ages, in all cultures and across societies, they have evoked immense interest about how and why twinning occurs, their development from conception onwards and their relationships with each other, their families and the rest of the world.

The aim of *Expecting Twins?* is to provide clear, comprehensive information about twin pregnancies and how to care for babies in the first year. We hope it answers the myriad questions that parents have about the pregnancy and caring for twins and provides a guide through every stage. We want parents to feel well informed, so that their anxieties are minimised, they can be confident about making the choices and decisions that suit them and they are able to enjoy this precious time.

Twins are very special in so many ways, but on hearing the news of a twin pregnancy, most parents experience mixed emotions as they start to consider what lies ahead. Numerous questions about the pregnancy, how to feed two babies, how to cope with the practicalities and how much more it will cost can make the prospect seem overwhelming. Tremendous developments in medical knowledge and techniques also mean we can now much better manage twin pregnancies and births, significantly reducing the risk for the mothers and babies at this crucial stage. Recent advances in neonatal care mean that many more babies born preterm now survive.

Through explaining clearly how the undoubted risks for the mother and babies can be reduced and how to prepare for the challenges of parenting twins, we hope to help minimise the problems and dispel many of the myths.

My personal interest and involvement with multiple birth families arose through meeting and then working with the inspirational Elizabeth Bryan. Elizabeth was a consultant paediatrician who devoted her whole career to learning more about twins and their families and, most importantly, how to help them. She was closely involved with Tamba and the Twins and Multiple Births Association, and founded the Multiple Births Foundation in 1988 to provide direct professional support to parents and information and training for professional colleagues. Her work and wealth of experience have transformed how we support multiple birth families today and form the cornerstone of this book.

JANE DENTON

The beginning

The conception of twins is a fascinating and complex feat of nature. This chapter will explain how conception takes place, specifically, how a twin pregnancy occurs. The different types of twins are also explained.

CONCEPTION

A complex sequence of events involving the interaction of hormones has to take place during a woman's menstrual cycle in order for ovulation to be possible. Sperm have to go through a long and hazardous journey to reach and fertilise an egg, during which most do not survive.

The female cycle

The average length of a woman's cycle is 28 days, but there can be considerable variation within that, and a cycle that is between 23 and 35 days and is regular (it happens every month) is considered normal. Ovulation takes place fourteen days before menstruation begins. In a 28-day cycle, therefore, ovulation typically occurs on Day 14; however, once again, there is considerable variation, and also if a woman's cycle is shorter, longer or irregular.

A baby girl is born with about three million eggs. By the time she reaches puberty, this number has reduced to about 400,000 and during her reproductive lifespan a woman will only release about 400 eggs. Each month about twenty eggs start to develop inside their individual fluid-filled sacs (follicles). Usually only one egg per cycle fully matures and is released from the follicle, although occasionally there may be two or more. Therefore ovulation takes place from only one ovary per cycle.

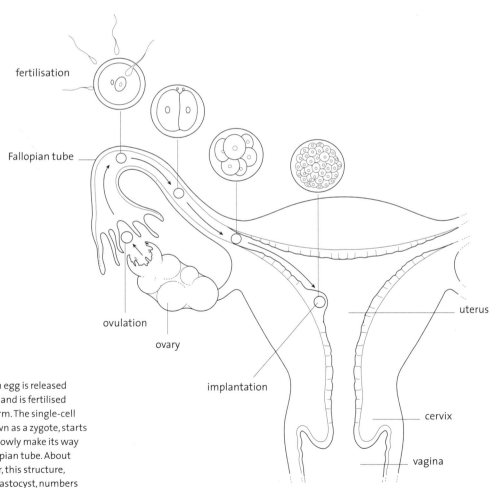

fertilisation

Fallopian tube

ovulation

ovary

implantation

uterus

cervix

vagina

Fertilisation An egg is released from the ovary and is fertilised by a single sperm. The single-cell structure, known as a zygote, starts to divide and slowly make its way down the Fallopian tube. About eight days later, this structure, now called a blastocyst, numbers about 100 cells and implants into the endometrium.

The female cycle

DAY

0

Day 1

Follicle-stimulating hormone (FSH) is produced, which allows the follicles containing the eggs to grow. Each egg is surrounded by cells that feed it and produce oestrogen.

7

Days 7–9

Oestrogen levels continue to rise, causing the endometrium (the lining of the uterus) to thicken, and less FSH is produced.

Days 11–12

Rising oestrogen levels indicate that one follicle is ready to burst. Luteinising hormone (LH) is produced that enables it to do so about 36 hours later.

14

Day 14

The egg is released from the ovary (ovulation).

Day 14 onwards

The cells from the ruptured follicle form a cyst-like swelling called the corpus luteum, which produces the hormone progesterone, causing the body temperature to rise by about 0.2°C. The rising level of progesterone thickens the endometrium and produces the nutrients required to maintain a pregnancy. It also switches off production of FSH and (if fertilisation has not taken place) of LH, so that the corpus luteum withers away within 48 hours of ovulation. The mature egg starts to make its way down the Fallopian tube, propelled by cilia (microscopic hairs) that line each tube.

21

Days 24–28

If the egg has not been fertilised during that cycle, levels of oestrogen and progesterone start to fall within a few days of ovulation. By Day 24 they are below the levels required to maintain a pregnancy, the egg and the thickened endometrium start to disintegrate and, by Day 28, menstruation begins.

28

CONCEPTION

Male reproduction

The testes produce sperm at the rate of about 1,500 per second (125 million per day), and these divide about 380 times before they become mature. Sperm have a lifespan of about 72 days and, as they mature, they move from the testes to the epididymis, the coiled tube at the top of each testis. Over the next two to three weeks, they become capable of moving on their own. They then progress from the epididymis to the vas deferens. During male orgasm, sperm is transported out of the vas deferens, past the seminal vesicles (the glands that contain seminal fluid) and the prostate gland and into the urethra, the tube that connects the bladder to the penis (a valve shuts the bladder off, preventing urine from being released at the same time).

High numbers of sperm are required for a man to be considered fertile, because so few survive the journey from ejaculation into the vagina all the way through to encountering the egg as it makes it way down the Fallopian tube. On average, a man will produce about 5 ml of semen (approximately one teaspoonful), which will contain 100–300 million sperm. In order for a man's sperm count to be considered normal, he needs to have at least twenty million sperm per millilitre of seminal fluid, to produce 2–4 ml of semen, to have at least fifteen per cent of normal-shaped sperm and about 25 per cent with normal motility (able to swim fast and in a straight line).

How sperm are produced
Sperm are made in the testes and take about 72 days to develop. When mature, they move to the epididymis and then to the vas deferens, before being ejaculated during an orgasm.

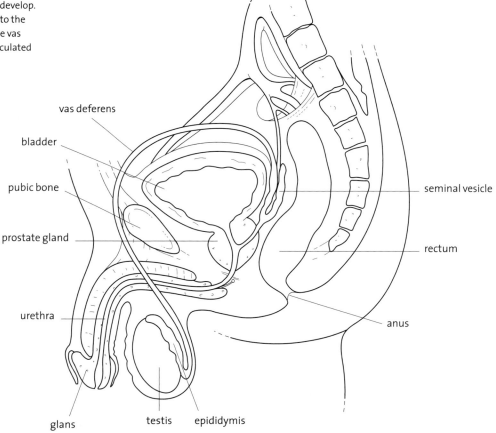

vas deferens

bladder

pubic bone

prostate gland

seminal vesicle

rectum

urethra

anus

glans

testis

epididymis

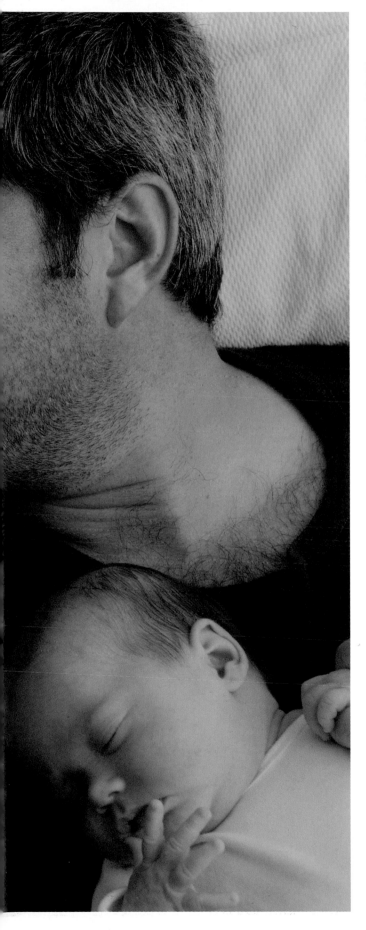

Fertilisation

Several sperm may 'break through' the outer layer (zona) of the egg, but for normal fertilisation only one successfully penetrates into the inner part of the egg, the oocyte. Once the head of the sperm, containing the genetic information, has fertilised the egg, it sheds the tail that has propelled it thus far, leaving it to disintegrate. The newly formed single cell is called a zygote, and within 24–36 hours it has already divided into a two-cell structure and is slowly moving down the Fallopian tube, with the help of muscular contractions and the cilia lining the tube. As it travels, cell division continues to take place, so that by the time it enters the uterus (womb), three or four days after fertilisation, the zygote has become a 16–32 cluster of cells called a morula. When this morula totals about 60 cells (about five or six days after fertilisation) it is known as a blastocyst and there are already two types of cells: an outer layer, which will develop into the placenta, and an inner cell mass, which will develop into the fetus. For the first 48 hours after entering the uterus, the blastocyst floats around before finally implanting itself into a part of the thickened endometrium approximately a week after fertilisation. At this stage, the blastocyst is made up of about 100 cells and it begins to produce the hormone human chorionic gonadotrophin (hCG), which tells the corpus luteum to continue to produce progesterone. This prevents the endometrium from breaking down and menstrual bleeding from taking place.

During the second week after fertilisation, the outer layer of cells, called trophoblast cells, continue to burrow deeper into the uterine lining, while the inner cell mass develops a two-layered disc form, with each layer containing specialist cells: the top layer will become the embryo and amniotic cavity, and the lower layer will become the yolk sac. Furthermore, by the end of that week, the top layer of the disc has developed three distinctive and specialist cell layers, called germ layers, each of which will become different parts of the body. The embryo is the size of a dot, and barely visible to the naked eye.

CONCEPTION

WHAT HAPPENS WHEN TWINS ARE CONCEIVED

There are two types of twins – identical and non-identical – depending on whether they arise from the fertilisation of two separate eggs in one cycle or whether a single fertilised egg subsequently divides.

Dizygotic (DZ) is the term used for non-identical twins, although you will also hear them referred to as dizygous, binovular or fraternal. DZ twins occur when two separate eggs are fertilised by two different sperm and there are two separate zygotes (formed when one egg is fertilised by one sperm) from the very start of the pregnancy. Consequently, DZ twins are genetically no more alike than any set of siblings. About one-third are both girls, one-third boys and one-third boy/girl.

Monozygotic (MZ) twins are identical, and you will also hear the terms monozygous or uniovular. MZ twins arise when a single zygote splits in two at some stage during the first fourteen days after fertilisation. The resulting twins therefore have identical genetic make-up and are of the same sex.

Are my twins identical?

Finding out whether twins are monozygotic (identical) or dizygotic (non-identical) is known as zygosity determination. Reasons why parents want to discover the zygosity of their babies include:

- ▸ to determine the risk of inheriting certain genetic diseases
- ▸ to understand the significance of similar or dissimilar growth and development in their twins
- ▸ to assess the risk of having twins again (there is an increased risk if you have DZ twins)
- ▸ to reinforce their resolve to treat their children as separate individuals particularly if they are MZ
- ▸ to be able to answer other people's most commonly asked question: 'Are your twins identical?'

Twin fertilisation

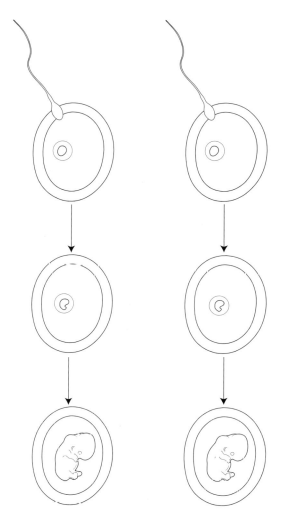

Dizygotic (non-identical) twins occur when two eggs are fertilised by two sperm.

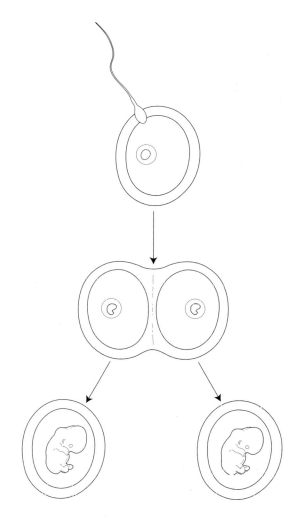

Monozygotic (identical) twins occur when one egg is fertilised by one sperm and subsequently divides.

In a third of cases, it is confirmed at birth that twins are non-identical because they are of different sexes. Similarly, it can be clear from ultrasound examination if they share a placenta and are therefore identical (*see* p. 18). However, if the babies are the same sex but each have their own placenta the only way to determine zygosity is by comparing their genetic make-up. This is an easy and painless procedure to compare their DNA. The most normal way is for a swab to be taken from inside the cheek of each baby. Zygosity determination is not done routinely at birth, but parents can pay to have the test done. Costs vary, as can the reliability of the test, so speak to your doctor for further advice.

DID YOU KNOW…?
Twenty to thirty per cent of monozygotic (identical) twins each have their own placenta (dichorionic).

Chorionicity

Whether their twins are identical or not is important to parents and the children when they are older, but the most significant factor in the management of a twin pregnancy is whether there are one or two placentas. Embryos develop inside an amniotic sac (the amnion), which in turn is surrounded by an outer membrane (the chorion). This outer membrane contributes to the development of the placenta. The term 'chorionicity' in a twin pregnancy refers to the type of placenta, and 'amnionicity' to the number of sacs the embryos are within (*see* diagrams).

It is important to find out the chorionicity of twins in the first trimester of pregnancy, if possible. While all twin pregnancies are treated as higher risk, if your babies share a placenta and fetal circulations they will have a greater risk of complications and health problems and the type of antenatal care you will receive is altered accordingly. Indeed, it is your babies' chorionicity rather than their zygosity (whether they are identical or not) that is most relevant to their welfare during the pregnancy. Chorionicity (and amnionicity) is established by ultrasound scan. The easiest time to do this is between eleven and fourteen weeks (*see* Chapter 3, p. 52).

Dichorionic twins

Dichorionic twins can be either monozygotic (identical) or dizygotic (non-identical). They develop and grow in separate amniotic sacs, which are surrounded by a separate chorion (*see* fig. 1). Dizygotic (DZ) twins are always dichorionic. Sometimes, the placentas of DZ twins fuse (*see* fig. 2), depending on the site of implantation, but this does not alter the fact that all DZ twins are dichorionic and diamniotic (i.e. have two outer membranes and two separate inner sacs). Around one-third of monozygotic twins also have separate (dichorionic) placentas (*see* p. 17). This occurs if the zygote splits within the first three or four days after fertilisation. If it divides after this time, MZ twins will be monochorionic (*see* below).

Monochorionic twins

Monochorionic twins share one chorion, but they may have one or two amnions (*see* figs. 3 and 4). They will always be monozygotic (identical). The type of placenta MZ twins have, and whether they each have their own amnion and/or chorion, depends on the timing of zygote division. If the zygote splits within the first three or four days after fertilisation, MZ twins will be dichorionic and diamniotic, and will have separate placentas (*see* above, and fig. 1). As with DZ twins, the placenta

Types of placenta and amniotic sac

chorion

amnion

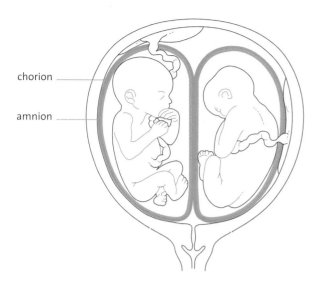

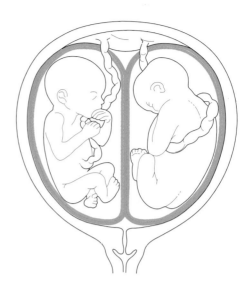

**1. Dichorionic diamniotic
(monozygotic or dizygotic twins)**
The babies each have a placenta, which is clearly separate, as well as their own amniotic sac.

**2. Dichorionic diamniotic
(monozygotic or dizygotic twins)**
There are two placentas and amniotic sacs, but the placentas have fused so that they resemble a single one.

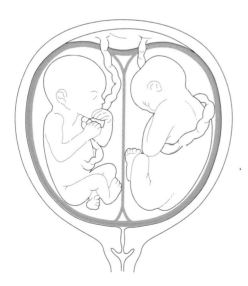

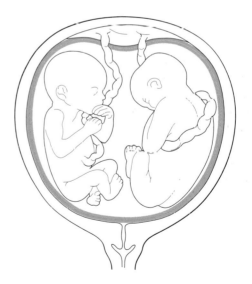

3. Monochorionic diamniotic (monozygotic twins)
These twins share one placenta, but have individual amniotic sacs.

4. Monochorionic monoamniotic (monozygotic twins)
The babies share one placenta as well as a single amniotic sac.

can sometimes fuse (*see* above and fig. 2). If the zygote splits after this date, but before Day 11 after fertilisation, the MZ twins will share the same placenta and blood circulation and be monochorionic (they have the same chorion), but diamniotic (they will each develop inside their own amniotic sac, *see* fig. 3). If the zygote splits towards the end of the two-week period after fertilisation, the MZ twins will share the same placenta and be monochorionic and monoamniotic (they will share the same amniotic sac, *see* fig. 4). This occurs in one to two per cent of twin pregnancies. See also Chapter 4, p. 96 for problems caused by monochorionicity.

> **DID YOU KNOW…?**
> Techniques and outcomes of subfertility treatments are improving all the time, and so, with the acknowledgement that twin pregnancies carry greater risks, practice is now changing to aim for a single pregnancy (e.g only one embryo is transferred in IVF cycles).

Causes of spontaneous twins

The causes of natural conception of twins are not fully understood. A genetic predisposition towards MZ (identical) twins has not yet been identified, and it is not understood why a fertilised ovum sometimes divides in two. The rate of MZ twins worldwide has remained constant over the years, at about 3.5 per 1,000 births. There is no direct cause of DZ (non-identical) twins, but there are many factors that are known to increase the chances of a woman conceiving them. The principal ones are:

- ▶ maternal age: multiple birth rates rise with the age of the mother thought to be due to hormonal changes in the late 30s
- ▶ genetic history: previous non-identical twins on the woman's side of the family
- ▶ race: African races have the highest rate of DZ twins (particularly those from the west coast of Africa), Orientals the least, and Caucasians and Asian Indians lie in between
- ▶ maternal height and weight: the taller and heavier the mother is, the greater the likelihood of her conceiving DZ twins
- ▶ number of previous children: women who have had more than one previous pregnancy are more likely to conceive DZ twins.

The highest rate of twinning through fertility treatment is found in Nigeria, with a rate of 45 per 1,000 births. Parts of Japan are as low as 5.6 per 1,000, whereas England and Wales currently have a rate of approximately 16 per 1,000 births.

Assisted conception

Twin pregnancies that have occurred as a result of the implantation of more than one embryo during in vitro fertilisation (IVF) subfertility treatment are most commonly dichorionic. However, this is not always the case: one embryo may not survive, while the other subsequently splits in two, resulting in identical, MZ (monochorionic) twins. So even if you have had more than one embryo transferred, the chorionicity of the babies still needs to be confirmed (and you may also wish to determine zygosity after birth). For reasons that are not yet fully understood, the chance of embryos dividing after IVF is higher, particularly with blastocyst transfers.

> **CONJOINED TWINS**
> Conjoined twins – that is, babies that are physically joined – arise when the embryo divides after Day 14. Fortunately, these are extremely rare, occurring in between 1 in 50,000 and 1 in 100,000 births. Only about 25 per cent of conjoined twins survive beyond birth, and female twins outnumber males by a ratio of 3:1. The way in which twins are conjoined differs in each case: different parts of the body can be conjoined and the twins can share some organs or none at all. Depending on the situation, surgical separation may be possible, but is usually extremely complex.

2

Looking after yourself

Finding out you are having twins
will bring a flood of emotions, not
only for you but for your partner as well.
Once you know you are pregnant and
have had time to think about the news,
you will probably want to make sure
your lifestyle will help you to keep
well throughout your pregnancy
and give your babies the best chance
of a healthy start in life.

HEARING THE NEWS

Whether planned or not, news of twins usually arouses a range of emotions. If your pregnancy was planned, it will be a source of great excitement for many couples, particularly if you have had difficulty conceiving. If it is a bolt from the blue, you may experience conflicting feelings, from shock through elation to panic about how you will cope.

In either case, there may be some immediate apprehension about the pregnancy and its risks, as well as your ability to care for more than one baby. The practical and financial prospects of having twins can be an immediate and great concern, too, especially if there are more children in the family.

How and when you find out

How early you hear that you are expecting twins often depends on how you conceived. If you conceived naturally and did not have any medical problems early in your pregnancy, you may only find out at your 'dating scan', conducted at between eleven and fourteen weeks (*see* Chapter 3, p. 58). If you have had one or more miscarriages or were in any way concerned about the progress of your pregnancy, you may have had a scan earlier in the first trimester and found out at that stage (*see* Chapter 3, p. 52). Finally, if you conceived using assisted conception, you will usually know that you are pregnant within two weeks of the embryos being transferred, and it is likely that you will have had your first scan two weeks after that. At this stage, if you are expecting twins, you will be able to see two gestational sacs and possibly two fetal poles (the first visible sign of a developing embryo); the heartbeats can be identified by Week 6, sometimes a few days earlier.

How you feel

Women respond to the news that they are expecting more than one baby in a huge variety of ways, depending to a certain extent on how unexpected it is. Similarly, your partner may not react in the same way as you or in a predicted fashion (*see* opposite). It is extremely common to be confused about how you feel about this pregnancy and quite normal to react in conflicting ways, with elation, laughter, relief, shock, numbness, disbelief, tears, anger or worry.

Natural concerns

However much a pregnancy is wanted and however elated you are after the initial news has been given, you may start to feel anxious about what a twin pregnancy entails. Your concerns may centre around:

- the thought of miscarriage
- the risk of something going wrong during your pregnancy/childbirth
- how you will manage financially
- whether you will be able to continue working
- how your living arrangements will be affected
- your ability to cope with more than one baby
- how to care for your existing child(ren) as well as twins
- the loss of control of your previously organised life
- the potential loss of friends
- the effect on your relationship and sex life
- if you are going to be a single parent, how you will face parenthood alone
- the fear of how your body will change during pregnancy
- the realisation that your body/figure after pregnancy may be different
- fear of depression (particularly if you have suffered in the past).

You may feel isolated because you do not know anyone else with young twins and have no one to turn to for advice, but as soon as your pregnancy is confirmed your midwife should give you information that can help you address your concerns, including sources of help. There are various organisations that can help you, including the Twins and Multiple Birth Association (TAMBA) and the Multiple Birth Foundation (MBF). In addition, there are many Twins Clubs run by parents, which can be an invaluable source of information and support. See Useful Resources for further information on these support groups.

You may be anxious about the pregnancy and its risks, especially if it has been very much planned and/or difficult to achieve. This can be especially so if this is not your first pregnancy, largely because you are more aware of what can potentially go wrong, especially when carrying twins. Perhaps you are worried that not being overwhelmingly happy about a twin pregnancy shows you will not be a good parent (whereas, in reality, it is a sign that you care about what sort of parent you will be). You may also find that it is a struggle to relate to the babies that are developing inside you, because it is hard to imagine the reality of what is happening to your body. These feelings may also be a subconscious way of not getting too emotionally attached to the babies in case something goes wrong during the pregnancy. Once again, this is no reflection on your future parenting skills and, usually, by the time the

Depression during pregnancy is thought to affect one woman in ten, yet it is little talked about (unlike postnatal depression, which many women now feel more able to discuss). There is an assumption that women should be thrilled to be pregnant, and while this may be the case for many, it does not apply to all women all of the time. As a result, women often feel ashamed to admit to feeling depressed during pregnancy. The signs of depression are often confused with the physical demands of being pregnant. As a result, the medical profession does not always recognise the symptoms in women they are caring for, and those women remain unaware that they are suffering from depression. Symptoms of antenatal depression vary from one person to another but can include:

▸ lack of interest in the pregnancy/the future
▸ excessive anxiety, stress and/or tearfulness
▸ loss of appetite, or comfort-eating
▸ feeling isolated and lonely
▸ irritability and/or irrational behaviour/thoughts/paranoia
▸ tiredness but inability to sleep (mind over-active)
▸ obsessive-compulsive behaviour (e.g. repeated hand-washing).

The causes of antenatal depression are wide-ranging, and often include worry over some of the issues discussed in this section, leading to ambivalent feelings about the pregnancy. As with postnatal depression (*see* Chapter 7, p. 207), a chemical or hormonal imbalance and a predisposition to depression may also be contributory factors. If a woman has had difficulties conceiving or has previously lost babies – for example, through miscarriage or stillbirth – she is more likely to experience antenatal depression because the pregnancy is so wanted, yet its possible outcomes are greatly feared.

If you think you may be suffering from some of the above symptoms, seek help as soon as possible, and make sure that you are taken seriously by your doctor, midwife and/or obstetrician. You know yourself best, and you will recognise if your symptoms are beyond the common anxieties that women have when they get pregnant. However, it can be helpful if those around you are also aware of the signs. Counselling and support during your pregnancy may be enough to reduce symptoms, but if necessary certain antidepressants can be safely prescribed, which can be very effective. The main thing is to speak up rather than suffer in silence.

first trimester is over and the miscarriage risk has significantly reduced, women are able to feel more relaxed.

Fluctuating moods

As well as experiencing the underlying anxieties outlined above, you may also find that you are short-tempered or tearful in a way that is uncharacteristic. Your body is currently going through many hormonal fluctuations, which are probably responsible in part for these moods. Reassure yourself that in all likelihood this is a temporary situation and it will disappear once you reach the second trimester. Try to ensure you and your partner communicate with each other, so that you each understand how the other is feeling. Your partner will be reassured if they know your uncharacteristic behaviour is temporary and not personally directed at them. And you will find the same applies if they, too, start to behave in an atypical fashion.

Your partner's response

Much of the focus on pregnancy is on you, but your partner, too, may find this time confusing. Hearing that they are to have twins can come as a shock to a partner, whether a welcome one or not, and the range of reactions and feelings they have will be similar to those discussed above for you. In addition, they may start to worry about other issues, such as whether you and babies will be alright or that they will be forgotten by you once the babies are born. These concerns can be exacerbated by not wanting to worry you, so they may find it difficult to share their feelings. Meeting other fathers through Twins Clubs or other support organisations can help.

While some women may find it difficult to relate to the growing fetuses – certainly initially – this is even more common for the partner. This is hardly surprising, given it is not their body that is undergoing enormous physical changes. Until they see a first scan, some partners find it hard to understand the reality of a pregnancy, especially when it is twins. And while many are fascinated by what happens,

others are less keen to know the intimate details of what will happen to your body, especially as some of these can sound quite alarming. So if your partner seems less enthusiastic in learning about every aspect of your pregnancy or in discussing what colour to paint your babies' bedroom, try to avoid feeling dispirited and resentful. This does not indicate a lack of delight at the prospect of having twins, but simply that they are dealing with the situation in a different way and at a different pace from you.

Telling others about your pregnancy

The decision about how soon to tell other people of your pregnancy is a personal one. Many couples tell close family immediately in order to share their elation and receive support, and wait a few more weeks until the pregnancy is established before spreading the news more widely.

Telling family and friends

In the immediate excitement following the discovery that you are pregnant, it is very tempting to tell others your good news. However, many women prefer to wait until they are safely through their first trimester (or after about twelve weeks) before telling even close family, because after this time the risk of having a miscarriage is less. Another reason for delaying is that you may experience a loss of one baby, particularly if one is very much smaller than the other or has an abnormality (*see* Chapter 3, p. 60–1) – it can be best to wait until after fourteen weeks. On the other hand, others may want their immediate family to know that they are pregnant even before they reach the second trimester on the basis that, even if something went wrong, they would prefer them to know rather than have them remain in ignorance. Of course, you may be reading this book having originally told people you were pregnant, only to discover, following the dating scan, that you are in fact expecting more than one baby!

Telling other children

Telling existing children that you are pregnant is often best left until you reach the second trimester, unless there are good reasons not to delay. Small children have little or no sense of time. If you inform them that in six or seven months' time you will be giving them a sibling/siblings (either because you do not yet realise you are carrying more than one baby or because you discover early in the first trimester that you are expecting twins) this is likely to be confusing and impossible for them to grasp. Worse, you may then find that you have to revise the figure up or down once you receive confirmation at the dating scan of how many babies you are actually carrying, and this

can be upsetting for young children. In addition, should anything go wrong with the pregnancy, you will have to deal with their emotions and disappointment as well as your own pain and sadness. The longer you can therefore wait before you tell existing children the better. This will probably mean that you should hold off until you cannot hide the evidence any longer, but you would be surprised at how long you can leave this when children are still small – many do not notice if their mother's tummy starts to fill out.

Telling work

General advice about when to tell your employer and work colleagues is usually 'the later the better', for a variety of reasons. In the same way as for children, if you tell people you are expecting in your first trimester, you may have to revise the information given to your colleagues after the dating scan has identified a twin pregnancy. In addition, although it is illegal to discriminate against a woman because she is pregnant, once your colleagues know that you will be going on maternity leave – and may or may not return – their perception of you invariably changes, if only subconsciously. By delaying informing your workplace, you will also have a better opportunity to work out what could be done to cover for you while you are on maternity leave and what your longer-term plans might be, even though these may change. See also Chapter 8 for information on maternity leave.

In the immediate excitement following the discovery that you are pregnant, it is very tempting to tell others your good news.

Ruth's story

It was my first pregnancy and so I don't have anything to compare it with. Other than very mild morning sickness for the first three months, which limited what I could eat, the most significant change in my diet was a sudden, uncontrollable and insatiable passion for 'white' foods: white baguettes with lashings of butter, pastries, pasta, potatoes, sponge puddings and cheese, to name but a few. I indulged this desire on occasion, but was careful not to put on more than the recommended amount of weight. Aside from having a little of what I fancied, I ate pretty healthily: loads of hearty casseroles, lentils, brown rice, cereal, fresh fruit, baked potatoes and fish, as well as plenty of red meat and leafy greens to guard against anaemia, which is very common among twin mums-to-be. I also drank gallons of water and had a craving for milk (more white food!), so drank a lot of that, too. I really got into cooking and loved the idea of nourishing the little lives I was carrying with good, wholesome food. It paid off in the sense that I went to full term and the boys were decent weights: 3 kg and just over 2.5 kg.

I think that my pregnancy diet was one of the few things that, looking back, I really feel I got right.

ANTENATAL CLASSES

Antenatal classes aim to help you prepare for the birth of your babies, covering what to expect in pregnancy and birth, as well as some early parentcraft skills. It is good to start thinking about whether you would like to attend an antenatal course early in your pregnancy, as popular classes can get booked up quickly.

You are legally entitled to time off from work to attend antenatal classes. Whether you enrol in free, hospital-run classes, in fee-paying ones such as those run by the National Childbirth Trust (NCT) or other private organisations, or in both, is entirely up to you and will depend on the contents and specific approach of the individual classes, as well as their cost, timings and convenience. Whichever type of course you choose, topics will include:

▸ pregnancy and birth choices
▸ what happens in labour
▸ pain relief and breathing techniques
▸ your partner's role in pregnancy and labour
▸ what complications may arise
▸ feeding your newborns
▸ parentcraft techniques (e.g. changing a nappy, bathing a baby)
▸ adjusting to new parenthood.

Try to find a course specifically for multiple births, because information about antenatal care, birth options and what can happen in delivery will be more relevant to your circumstances. Some hospitals have an antenatal class specifically for mothers with twins, but you will need to enquire about what is available locally. There are private classes run by independent midwives and other organisations including TAMBA.

If you are unable to find a class specific to twins or multiple births, you will still find a regular class helpful preparation for pregnancy, birth and parenthood. However, try to enrol in one that provides objective, detailed information on Caesarean sections (about 60 per cent of twin pregnancies are delivered this way – *see* Chapter 5, p. 105 and 126), rather than cursory information on this method of delivery because its main focus

is on vaginal birth. Similarly, information on the different methods of pain relief, including epidurals, should be detailed and balanced. The class leader may be able to add relevant details regarding a twin pregnancy, but if not, ask for more specific information from your midwife or obstetrician.

The likelihood is that you will deliver before 40 weeks, so you should organise and begin antenatal classes early, on the basis that your pregnancy may not go beyond 34–36 weeks. When you enrol, explain that yours is a twin pregnancy and ask to start the course earlier – don't be deterred if you are told this is not necessary. The best classes tend to get booked up quickly, so by the start of your second trimester you should be investigating the various options and deciding which one(s) you would like to attend.

Since nearly all twins are born in hospital (*see* Chapter 3, p. 49), antenatal classes run by the hospital itself give you the opportunity to ask the midwives about any aspect of giving birth there, and there are often obstetricians and other staff present as well. You will also become more familiar with the hospital setting and will be given a tour of the labour ward, which will help you to be more relaxed when you are admitted for the birth.

Antenatal classes are not just designed for pregnant women, but for partners as well. If it is difficult for your partner to attend because of work commitments or because they are caring for your other child(ren), some courses run a specific partners session at some stage during the course. Although antenatal classes include some information on baby care, some organisations also run classes after the birth to help parents during the first few weeks. Even if this is not your first pregnancy, you should still enrol in an antenatal class, and you may be able to find one in your area that is specifically a 'refresher' course. There may be fewer sessions than courses for first-time parents, but they will remind you of breathing techniques and so on.

One of the big advantages of antenatal classes is that it allows you to meet other mothers-to-be. If you work full-time until you give birth, you may not have a network of local friends who are around in the day or who are at a similar life-stage to you. Other new mothers are a great source of support and companionship during the early months after the birth. And it is not unusual for these connections to develop into friendships that last for many years.

EATING WELL IN PREGNANCY

Women's nutritional needs, as well as their tastes and appetites, change during pregnancy. During the first trimester you may suffer from morning sickness, which affects what you feel like eating, and by the third trimester, various digestive side effects of later pregnancy can limit your appetite. Your goal during pregnancy should therefore be to establish a diet that is as healthy and balanced as possible.

There is no evidence that women with twin pregnancies have greater nutritional needs than those expecting singletons. Until the last trimester, there is no need to consume more than the 2,000 calories a day recommended for non-pregnant women. In the third trimester, a woman pregnant with twins will still only need an extra 300–400 calories a day, which is roughly equivalent to a shop-bought muffin or sandwich. The notion of 'eating for three' is simply a myth. It can, at times, be difficult to have an ideal diet, for example, if you are suffering from morning sickness in the early weeks. During pregnancy your body provides all your babies' nutritional needs, so if you are not eating well, it will simply draw on its nutritional reserves. This means that, unless you are undernourished to begin with or have a poor diet throughout the entire pregnancy, the babies will still continue to thrive. However, a good diet is important not just for the babies but for you as well. If your reserves are depleted, not only will you become increasingly tired, but your general health can also suffer, both during pregnancy and afterwards. Try to eat as healthily as you can as often as you can. (As your stomach becomes more compressed, you may find it easier to eat regular, small nutritious snacks rather than larger meals.) Above all, avoid obsessing about food and treat it as a source of pleasure.

WEIGHT GAIN IN PREGNANCY
The weight gained during pregnancy varies from one woman to another, but if you are expecting twins and are of normal weight, you should gain 16–20 kg. The weight gain will be faster in the first trimester than for women expecting singletons, whose weight barely increases during this time. The extra weight you put on during your pregnancy is accounted for firstly by the babies' weight, the amniotic fluid and placenta(s), and secondly by the increased weight of your uterus and breasts, greater blood volume and fat stores, and any water retention.

Nutrition
A healthy diet is one that is varied and nutritious, combining regular amounts of protein, carbohydrates and fat, together with vitamins and minerals. Eating three meals a day from the four main food groups listed below is enough to ensure that you and your babies' nutritional needs will be met.

Bread, cereal, rice, potatoes, pasta
Starchy foods, such as bread, rice and pasta, provide you with energy and should form the main part of your meal. Whole-grain versions (e.g. brown rice, wholemeal pasta, flour) have also retained their vitamin, mineral and fibre content and so are preferable to the refined varieties.

Fruit and vegetables
These contain essential vitamins, minerals and fibre. You should aim to eat at least five portions a day, and sources can be fresh, frozen, tinned or dried. Juicing can be a good way of keeping up your intake when you are suffering from morning sickness.

Meat, fish, eggs, beans, nuts, pulses
Eating twice a day from this food group will provide protein (your protein needs to increase by fifteen to twenty per cent when you are pregnant) and many of these foods also contain iron. However, you should limit oily fish to two portions a week.

Milk and dairy products
Dairy foods are an excellent source of calcium (essential for healthy bones and muscles), as well as vitamins A, B and D. The lower the fat content, the more digestible they are and the greater the proportion of nutrients they contain (these are not present in the fat of milk). Your babies will be deriving their calcium from your existing reserves, so the calcium you take in during your pregnancy ensures that you yourself do not exhaust these, as this could lead to loss of bone mass and osteoporosis in later life. Three portions of milk or other dairy products will meet all your calcium needs.

Vitamins and minerals
The main vitamins, A, B, C, D and E, are all obtained from the food we eat. Similarly, the main minerals, such as iron, zinc, calcium, phosphorus and potassium, are in our normal diet, and in the right combination and proportion required for optimum benefit.

Vitamins and minerals are most effective when they interact with each other through the food we eat. This is because foods contain a complex system of different components. If you are in any doubt about your diet, discuss the issue with your doctor. If you were using a general multivitamin supplement before you got pregnant (rather than one specifically tailored to pregnant women), stop taking it, because it may contain higher doses of certain vitamins, notably A and D, than should be taken during pregnancy. Consuming extra vitamin C (higher than 1000 mg a day) is not advised, because your body will simply eliminate any that is not required. Although iron deficiency can be quite

FOLIC ACID AND VITAMIN D SUPPLEMENTS
Folic acid, which is a B vitamin, helps to prevent neural tube defects such as spina bifida, and although it is present in foods such as pulses and green leafy vegetables, it is the one vitamin that the body absorbs more effectively from supplements and fortified foods than from food itself. Although you should ideally start taking 400 mcg of folic acid per day when you are trying to get pregnant, even if you only start taking it once you know you are pregnant, it will still be of benefit.

Vitamin D is present in only a few foods (e.g. oily fish, fortified margarines, cereals) and is essential for keeping bone maintenance and development. A supplement of 10 mcg per of vitamin D per day helps to keep your bones healthy and provides enough for your babies' first few months of life.

If you are vegetarian or vegan, you should discuss with your doctor how best to keep up your levels of iron, calcium and vitamin B12, and you may well need to take a supplement during your pregnancy and after, especially if you are planning to breastfeed.

This is particularly the case if you are vegan, because vitamin B12 is only found naturally in animal products, such as meat and dairy foods. To maintain your level of iron, eat more fortified cereals, oatmeal, sesame seeds, and dried fruits such as apricots, raisins and prunes. And to ensure your diet contains enough calcium, eat more soya products, nuts, pulses (e.g. chickpeas, lentils, peas, beans), fortified cereals and green leafy vegetables such as broccoli.

If you are vegetarian, as well as the above foods, eat more eggs and dairy products to raise your overall levels of proteins, iron, calcium and vitamin B12.

common in pregnancy, do not take iron supplements unless a blood test has established you are anaemic, because they can cause constipation and stomach upsets.

Hygiene and food safety

Pregnant women are more susceptible to gastroenteritis caused by contaminated food and poor kitchen hygiene, as well as being more likely to suffer from complications caused by these types of infection, such as dehydration. If you follow the basic rules of hygiene below, your chances of being affected are very slim:

▸ Always wash your hands before and after handling food, especially raw poultry/meat.
▸ Defrost and reheat food *thoroughly*. Do not re-heat food more than once.
▸ If heating food in the microwave, ensure that it is hot *everywhere*.
▸ In order to avoid cross-contamination of bacteria, prepare raw meat and fish on a different board from other food and use different knives/utensils during the preparation. Wash your hands between preparing each type of food.
▸ Throw away food past its sell-by date and any suspect-looking food.

▸ Wash all utensils and chopping boards in hot soapy water and rinse thoroughly.

In addition, certain foods should be avoided altogether during pregnancy because they could harm you or your babies. If you are in any doubt, or if you do begin to have any of the symptoms described below, consult your doctor as soon as possible.

Liver and liver products (sausage, pâté)

Liver contains high doses of vitamin A in a form called retinol, and excessive levels of this vitamin may cause fetal abnormalities. Vegetable products (especially fruit and vegetables such as carrots, mangos and apricots) contain high doses of vitamin A in a form called betacarotene and this is safe to eat.

Raw or undercooked eggs and chicken

Eggs and chicken that have not been thoroughly cooked can contain the salmonella bacterium. (Free-range hens can carry the bacteria, but it is more commonly found in battery hens.) Salmonella crosses the placenta and can, in some cases, lead to miscarriage, premature labour and intrauterine death, as well as other neonatal problems. The salmonella bacteria are killed by heat, hence the importance of cooking or reheating these foods fully (for eggs, this means hard-boiled). Dishes that may contain raw eggs include mayonnaise and mousses, so avoid these if in doubt, although, paradoxically, the more mass-produced they are, the less likely they are to contain *fresh* raw eggs – pasteurised egg, egg powder or no egg at all are more common. Symptoms of salmonella will emerge within 12–48 hours of eating the affected food and include vomiting, diarrhoea and fever.

Raw or undercooked meat, unwashed fruit and vegetables

Toxoplasmosis, a fairly common infection to which the majority of the population is immune, is caused by a parasite that is present in raw, undercooked or cured meat. It is also found in cat faeces, and can therefore be caught from fruit and vegetables that have been in contact with contaminated soil hence the importance of thoroughly washing these. Toxoplasmosis infection can be very harmful to the developing fetus (*see* p. 45 for more information).

Unpasteurised or blue cheeses

Rarely, soft, unpasteurised or blue cheeses can contain listeria. This bacterium causes mild flu-like symptoms with nausea and diarrhoea, but it can be potentially fatal for babies. Semi-soft cheeses (e.g. mozzarella), pasteurised processed cheeses, hard cheeses and cream or cottage cheese are safer.

Pâtés and cooked meats

Pâtés and cooked meats can contain listeria (*see* opposite) as well as e-coli, although this is extremely rare. Cooked meats from a reputable source are safe if they are kept in hygienic conditions and for not longer than a few days. E-coli symptoms begin about a week after eating the affected food, and include severe cramps and diarrhoea (with blood). It can lead to kidney failure and ultimately can be fatal for mother and babies.

CARE OF YOUR TEETH IN PREGNANCY

The increase in blood flow and the hormonal changes that occur in pregnancy can cause inflammation of the gums. You may find that they bleed easily whenever you brush your teeth and any swelling can result in food becoming trapped, so you need to pay special attention to your hygiene routine. Visit your dentist regularly during this time to ensure that your teeth and gums remain healthy.

Fish and seafood

While fish is a good source of the fatty acids that are needed in pregnancy, shark, swordfish and marlin should be avoided, and oily fish such as fresh tuna (tinned is fine), salmon and mackerel should be limited to two portions per week, because they contain high levels of mercury, which can affect fetal development. Raw seafood and shellfish should be avoided because of the risk of food poisoning and parasite infections, but thoroughly cooked versions of these foods are fine. It is safe to eat the raw fish used in sushi if the fish has been frozen first (because this will kill any parasites).

Bagged salads

Salads and other prepared chilled foods can harbour salmonella or listeria bacteria, so if possible avoid consuming them or do so only if they are kept in ideal conditions.

EXERCISE

You should try to keep physically active during your pregnancy and do some form of exercise, as this will be beneficial for both you and your babies: it will maintain your fitness levels and can help your physical recovery after the birth.

Physical activity itself cannot cause a miscarriage. However, high levels of certain hormones in pregnancy, notably relaxin, loosen your ligaments, making it easier to damage yourself. Muscles regain their shape after being stretched, but ligaments do not – hence the importance of taking care with weight-bearing exercises. In addition, being pregnant with more than one baby puts a greater strain on the body than being pregnant with a singleton, so what might be possible for a woman carrying one baby might not be suitable for you. Whatever you do, listen to your body, and if in doubt, stop.

Each woman's fitness levels will be different, so it is difficult to generalise about what exercise you should and should not do. If your pregnancy is progressing smoothly and you are used to exercising, you will know your body well enough to know what is right for you (*see* opposite for further information). However, by the end of the first trimester (if not before), you will probably start to reduce the intensity of the exercise or switch to an alternative one, simply because your growing bump will prevent you from continuing.

If you are not used to exercising regularly, do not start up any new sport or activity without first discussing it with your doctor or midwife. They will be able to advise you on a suitable physical activity that you can do during your pregnancy, as well as give you information on specific antenatal exercise classes in your area. You may also be referred to an obstetric physiotherapist, who will be best qualified to help you.

Many women suffer from morning sickness and/or extreme tiredness during the first trimester. As a result, they do not feel like doing any exercise at all. Follow your feelings and only exercise if you feel ready. If yours is a high-risk pregnancy (for example, if you have previously had a miscarriage, have suffered first trimester bleeding, have high blood pressure, or are at risk of premature labour) you may be advised not to exercise at all.

Safe exercise during pregnancy

Sports or physical activities that are beneficial during pregnancy (assuming yours is not high-risk) are ones that do not put undue strain on your joints, your back or your growing uterus. You should avoid:

▶ exercise that involves lying on your back for any length of time, as this can affect blood flow to the placenta(s) – see below
▶ contact sports
▶ sports where you might fall (e.g. skiing, horse riding)
▶ jogging/running or similar activities that involve jumping up and down, as they put pressure on the back, uterus and cervix
▶ scuba diving or, conversely, sports at altitude (more than 2,500 m).

Safe forms of exercise are low-impact, raise the heart rate within safe levels, do not dehydrate you excessively, and improve muscle tone without overstretching ligaments or abdominal muscles.

Start by doing gentle exercise for fifteen minutes, three times a week, building up to 30 minutes only if and when you feel ready. Whatever sport or exercise you do, drink plenty of fluids, do not get overheated or reach a state of exhaustion, and maintain your blood sugar levels to avoid feeling light-headed. Make sure you warm up and cool down thoroughly, and take care not to overstretch and damage your ligaments. If you are in pain or feel dizzy at any stage during physical activity, stop at once.

> **DID YOU KNOW…?**
> From halfway through the second trimester, you should avoid lying on your back for any length of time. This is because a major blood vessel, the vena cava, can become compressed by the weight of the babies, which results in a restricted blood flow to the uterus and placenta(s).

Swimming

Swimming is the best form of exercise during pregnancy. The water supports your expanding uterus and your body as a whole, which is excellent if you have any sort of back pain. You are also less likely to overheat or raise your heart rate excessively. Swimming tones and stretches muscles without placing them under any strain, and improves circulation and the function of your internal organs (especially the kidneys), thus relieving any problems with digestion and constipation. As your bump starts to expand, and especially if you are pregnant during the summer, you will find that being in the water is the only place where you still feel able to move in comfort and where you feel cool.

Walking

Walking provides gentle aerobic exercise – good for your lungs and for increasing blood flow to the placenta – and keeps you mobile. Ensure you are wearing good walking shoes if you are walking outdoors, or use a treadmill at the gym, as these are cushioned and provide better protection for your joints. As your pregnancy progresses, you are likely to find that walking for any length of time becomes more difficult, and may need to wear a harness or belt around your abdomen for extra support.

Recumbent cycling

These stationary bikes are found in gyms and provide a comfortable position when you are pregnant. They are ideal because they do not put pressure on your lower limbs or your abdomen, they tone your legs and buttocks and give you a cardiovascular workout at whatever level suits you.

Weight training

If you are used to doing some weight training, you can continue for a while, working only on your arms and legs – you will know when to stop, and your expanding abdomen will no doubt tell you. However, you *must* use light weights – no more than 2–3 kg – because you risk damaging your softened ligaments if you put too much strain on them.

Yoga and Pilates

These forms of exercise emphasise body awareness and breathing techniques. Pilates consists of slow, controlled movements, and strengthens core abdominal muscles. Yoga decreases stress levels, encourages flexibility and can help relieve backache. Find classes that are specifically for pregnant women, as these tailor the exercises to what is appropriate. A general class will still be of benefit, however, but you must tell the instructor that you are pregnant, as there are some exercises that should not be undertaken.

If your pregnancy is progressing smoothly and you are used to exercising, you will know your body well enough to know what is right for you.

Coping with back pain

Back pain is very common during pregnancy, especially when carrying more than one baby. First, your growing bump causes you to change your posture and arch your back in order to compensate for the weight that you are carrying in front of you. In addition, your ligaments (especially those in your pelvis) become looser in preparation for childbirth. Both changes often cause pain, particularly in the lower back. The exercises below can help to prevent or alleviate symptoms of backache, as they will help to stretch and strengthen the muscles surrounding the pelvis and spine.

Spinal stretch

Sit on your heels, with your feet together and knees slightly apart. Lean forward so that the sides of your bump are lightly supported by your thighs and stretch your arms out along the floor. Have some support for your head if necessary, so that you can rest there for a while and feel your spine lengthening and your lower back stretching out.

Cat humps

Position yourself on all fours, hands and knees shoulder-width apart, with your back flat but relaxed. Arch your back into a cat hump, tightening abdominal and buttock muscles and tucking the pelvis in. Hold for a few seconds then relax to the start position. Repeat five times. This exercise strengthens the muscles that support the lower back and helps to realign the pelvis.

Knee hug

Lie on your back with your knees tucked up towards your chest, either side of your bump. Holding your knees, gently rock from side to side. This exercise is excellent for relieving lower spine tension. Only practise this for a short time in later pregnancy in order to avoid restricting blood flow to the uterus and placenta(s) (*see* p. 36).

Moving with care and protecting your back

In order to protect your back as your uterus expands, you will need to take care in your everyday movements. This will become particularly evident towards the end of the second trimester, when the weight of your abdomen starts to affect the way you stand, walk, sit, bend, carry and lie down. To prevent or reduce symptoms of an overarching back and any back pain, try the following:

▸ Wear a maternity support belt (found in specialist maternity shops, magazines or online). These are worn just below your bump and relieve the pressure on your abdominal ligaments, pelvis and lower back. You can also ask a physiotherapist for advice.

▸ When standing, be as straight as possible with your shoulders back. Imagine a line running from your head, through your shoulders and pelvis and down to the floor. Avoid arching your back. From halfway through the second trimester, limit the amount of time you are standing still, as blood will begin to pool in your legs and you could feel very light-headed.

▸ When sitting down (or driving), place a cushion between the seat and your back to support your lower back and prevent slouching. If you are using a computer, try to have the screen at eye level. Keep both feet flat on the ground to maintain a good posture, but get up at regular intervals to vary your position.

▸ Wear flat or low-heeled shoes (high-heeled shoes will increase your tendency to arch your back and alter your centre of balance).

▸ While in bed or when resting, lie on your side with your knees bent to reduce the pressure on your spine and pelvic ligaments.

▸ When getting up in the morning, swing your legs out of bed and push with your upper arm to avoid pulling yourself up with your back muscles.

▸ If you lift anything (such as shopping bags or toddlers), bend down, keep your back straight and lift them without having to reach out. Use your leg muscles to push you back up.

▸ Have a warm bath (not too hot, to avoid overheating) to soothe aching backs and joints.

EXERCISE

39

 # LIFESTYLE

There are several elements of your life that you may need to think about now that you are pregnant. You will need to get as much rest as possible and minimise stress; you should also be looking at any travel plans you might have between now and the end of your pregnancy, what you might do about work and maternity leave, enrolling for antenatal classes and buying maternity clothes.

Rest and stress

The physical demands of a twin pregnancy mean that it is important to try to stay as rested as possible. During the first trimester, the flood of pregnancy hormones through your body, combined with morning sickness, is likely to leave you feeling tired in a way you have never been before. As you move into your second trimester, you will probably feel more like your old self. Towards the end of that trimester, your expanding uterus and the increasing movement of the babies make sleep more disturbed and difficult, and your levels of tiredness can increase again. It is therefore important to find opportunities throughout your pregnancy to take care of yourself, to rest and to start to delegate some physical tasks.

In addition, look at your lifestyle and try to find ways to simplify your day-to-day activities, eating as nutritiously as possible (see p. 32), and asking others (or paying someone if you can) to take on additional tasks. If you work and commute at peak times using public transport, see if you can change your hours so that you can at least get a seat during a quieter period. Try to find a little time for yourself so that you can unwind in peace and quiet doing something you enjoy. Grab any opportunities to put your feet up and relax.

Travel

If yours is a trouble-free pregnancy, it is safe for you to travel at least until the end of your second trimester and possibly up to 30 weeks. Simple steps will make your journey more comfortable:

- Take plenty of water and snacks to keep up your energy and hydration levels and to avoid having to find (and queue for) suitable food and drink.
- Sit in an aisle seat on a plane, train or coach: you can stretch out a little and it will be easier to make a trip to the toilet.
- Find out where the nearest maternity unit is to where you will be staying, in case you need to seek medical attention. Take your notes with you.

Flying

Most airlines allow pregnant women to fly until the 32nd week (individual airlines vary), but as yours is a twin pregnancy, you should not fly after the 30th week. This is not because flying may cause you to go into premature labour, but simply because you might spontaneously go into labour anyway during the flight. However, despite the airline guidance, you need to consider whether the journey is really necessary, the length of time you will be flying and the nature of the medical facilities at your destination. For example, find out if you and the babies would have the medical help you would need if you were to go into labour or have a late miscarriage either during the flight or at your destination. If you have an increased risk of miscarriage, high blood pressure or a low-lying placenta, have had placental bleeding or a previous premature birth, it is safer to avoid flying altogether, not least to spare you having to seek urgent medical help, should something happen, in a foreign country.

Contrary to popular myth, radiation exposure from flying at high altitude only reaches the upper safety levels if you are an extremely frequent flyer. The notion that reduced cabin pressure and levels of oxygen, especially on long-haul flights, can affect an unborn child does not stand up to scrutiny. The babies are surrounded by amniotic fluid, the amniotic membrane and your uterus, and your body will automatically adapt its circulation and respiratory system so that they will not be affected by any external changes in atmosphere.

If you have to walk a long distance at either airport, consider asking for a mobility vehicle to take you to and from the plane (you will need to contact the airline in advance). In this way, you will also jump the queues at security and passport control, which can be long and exhausting. Avoid airline food and take things that you know are safe to eat while pregnant. Pregnancy increases the risk of deep vein thrombosis, a highly dangerous condition, so walk around the plane at regular intervals and drink plenty of fluids to reduce the risk of blood clots forming in your legs.

Travelling by car, train or coach

Other methods of transport, such as train, car and coach are safe during pregnancy, although you must always wear your seatbelt, however large your abdomen becomes. As your pregnancy advances, you will need to make increasingly frequent stops to stretch your legs and use the toilet, so factor this in when travelling by car, and if you are taking the train or coach, find an aisle seat (*see* list opposite).

Work

As twins are likely to be delivered by or just after 37 weeks, if not before (*see* Chapter 4, p. 92), you should aim to start your maternity leave a few weeks earlier than if you were expecting a singleton. In addition, you may be ready to have a more flexible lifestyle and want to rest more frequently – bear in mind that the physical demands of a twin pregnancy, especially in the third trimester, are greater than those of a singleton pregnancy. Chapters 7 and 8 contains detailed information on the many aspects of working, maternity leave and childcare, but the earlier you can start to think about them and decide what you plan to do, the better. Your plans might change as time goes on, but if you are aware of the various options open to you, as well as what the current legislation is, you will be in a better position to make the right decision. For sources of information about maternity/paternity rights and welfare benefits, see Useful Resources.

Maternity clothes

As your pregnancy progresses, your body will undergo various physical changes that mean you will have to buy specialist maternity outfits. Your clothes will start to feel tight quite early when you are carrying twins, especially if it is not your first pregnancy (your abdominal muscles are never as firm as they were before you were pregnant). You can try to get by for a while by undoing the top button of your trousers or skirt or extending the waistband with a some elastic and a safety pin: loop a length of elastic around the button on the waistband and fasten through the button hole with the pin. You can easily conceal this arrangement by wearing an ordinary, long-length top. You could also invest in a simple, black bump support band to cover the increasing gap between your top and bottom halves, which will also provide a degree of comfort when your bump grows larger. There are many types of support band and elastic waistband kits available online.

There are plenty of cheaper, non-pregnancy clothes that can be worn, at least initially: loose, Empire-line tops, loose-fitting dresses, tunics worn over normal leggings (these will need to be bought larger than your normal size) and jackets or long cardigans (useful for disguising expanding waistlines, especially in work situations). Remember that any clothes you buy now will also serve you for the weeks and months after the birth while you lose the weight you gained in pregnancy (the same applies to the maternity clothes that you will buy).

Maternity bras

The most obvious physical change you will experience in the first few weeks of pregnancy is that your breasts will increase in size. You should therefore invest in some well-fitting maternity bras from as early as the eighth to tenth week. These will see you through the remainder of your pregnancy, as most of the increase in breast size will take place during the first trimester, with only a slight increase at the end of the third trimester in preparation for your milk coming in (*see* Box Chapter 7, p. 157). A shop with a specialist bra fitting service will ensure that you are properly measured and fitted. You may need to wear your bra at night, so it is well worth finding some that are suitably comfortable.

Suggested maternity wear

Ordinary tops will cease to work after a while and your skirts and trousers will no longer stretch round your bump. Maternity tops are longer at the front than at the back to cover your expanding abdomen and maternity trousers and skirts are designed to fit either under your bump or over it. When it comes to the time to invest in special maternity clothes, there are now several affordable ranges available in regular high street shops, as well as from specialist companies (*see* Useful Resources). You will discover that you can manage with a surprisingly limited number of outfits and you can keep costs down still further if you can borrow from other people, particularly if you need something smart for a one-off special occasion (you can hire outfits, too). Bear in mind that, as your pregnancy progresses, you will feel hotter, so you won't need heavy jumpers. You may also find that your shoe size increases, but if you do need to invest in a new pair of shoes, make sure they low-heeled and slip-on for when it becomes too difficult to tie laces – but avoid flat ballet pumps, which offer very little support. The following items will form the basis of a flexible maternity wardrobe:

- a pair of tailored trousers in a practical fabric and colour (because you will be wearing them a lot)
- a pair of jeans or other type of casual trousers
- leggings
- two skirts and/or dresses (dresses may be more comfortable in later pregnancy)
- several tops in colours to co-ordinate with your trousers and skirts, some in a longer length to go over leggings
- one jacket (for smarter occasions or if you work)
- tights (which can also help support your bump and legs)
- underwear
- swimming costume (if planning to go swimming).

THINGS TO AVOID IN PREGNANCY

Some of the dos and don'ts in pregnancy are based on scientific and medical evidence – many of them are not. The information given here is meant to reassure and inform you and, where relevant, to allow you to make up your own mind about how you want to lead your life during your pregnancy.

Caffeine

The advice regarding the safety of caffeine during pregnancy is extremely confusing and contradictory, because studies are regularly being published showing different findings. Some indicate that consuming more than 200 mg a day of caffeine can increase the risk of having small babies or a miscarriage. Other studies looking at this moderate level of intake are inconclusive, but would indicate that if you drink more than six cups of coffee a day, then the miscarriage rate is increased. The reality is that so many women go off coffee and other caffeinated drinks during the first trimester of pregnancy (when the risk of miscarriage is highest) that they rarely need encouragement to reduce their consumption. Caffeine, however, is a diuretic and drains you of fluid – you should be drinking around 1 litre a day of water, fruit juice or herbal tea to stay hydrated. Caffeine may interfere with the absorption of vitamin C and iron, so if possible, aim to limit yourself to a moderate amount or change to decaffeinated varieties.

> ### DID YOU KNOW...?
> 200 mg of caffeine =
> - two cups of instant coffee a day
> - four cups of tea
> - five cans of cola
> - three energy drinks
> - five small bars of chocolate (50 g)

Alcohol

National recommendations indicate that a mild intake of alcohol is not harmful in pregnancy, but the general advice is that it is best to avoid it if possible. Many women drink alcohol before they even realise they are pregnant and then become very worried that they may have irreversibly harmed their babies as a result. Unless you are a very regular heavy drinker, a big night out (or two over a period of a few weeks) is extremely unlikely to have done any damage to your babies. On the other hand, regular, heavy consumption of alcohol is harmful for developing fetuses, can increase the risk of pregnancy complications and the babies having health problems at birth. Fortunately, as with caffeine, it is very common for women to go off alcohol entirely during the first trimester, the time when their babies' organ formation is taking place and when you run a higher risk of miscarriage. Ultimately, however, the decision on whether you drink one or two units of alcohol a week is up to you. If you need help in reducing or stopping your alcohol consumption, see your doctor.

Smoking

Among the barrage of information about healthy lifestyles, there is one certainty: you should refrain from smoking both during and after your pregnancy. The evidence is clear: smoking reduces the supply of oxygen to the placenta and of nutrients to your babies. It therefore increases the risk of miscarriage in the first trimester, of premature delivery and placental abruption in later pregnancy and of fetal growth retardation. If you smoke and are finding it hard to give up, speak to your doctor as soon as possible so that they can help you. If your partner smokes, you and your developing babies can be affected by passive smoking, so they too should try very hard to stop, or should not smoke in your home or around you. Once babies are born, the risk of cot death (SIDS – *see* Chapter 7, p. 181) is increased if one or both parents smoke, even if they do not do so in their babies' presence.

Medication

As a general rule, avoid taking medication while pregnant unless strictly necessary. If you are already taking prescription medication, speak to your doctor as soon as you know you are pregnant. Only they can decide if you should continue with the medication, change it for a more suitable drug or are safe to stop taking it. Never self-medicate or stop taking a prescription drug without seeking medical advice.

Many over-the-counter medications are contraindicated for pregnant women, although this is usually because they have not actually been tested on them. Never take any without speaking to your pharmacist, who will be able to advise you

While you should always check with your doctor that any prescribed medicine is safe to use in pregnancy, here is a general summary of common over-the-counter medication:

► Paracetamol is a safe painkiller. Do not take aspirin, as it has blood-thinning properties, and avoid ibuprofen or codeine.
► Topical steroid creams for skin problems such as eczema should not generally be used unless first discussed with your doctor.
► Cold and flu remedies do not speed your recovery and many contain antihistamines and other substances that are best avoided during pregnancy. Take paracetamol instead.
► Some antihistamines are contraindicated during pregnancy. Ask your doctor or pharmacist to recommend a suitable one.

about any specific harmful effects. If you have taken medication before you realised you were pregnant, try not to worry – in all likelihood it will not have harmed your baby. You can ask your midwife, doctor or specialist if you have any concerns.

Herbal remedies
Certain herbal remedies are contraindicated during pregnancy because they could be harmful to the developing fetus. Do not therefore take any herbal remedies unless you have consulted a herbalist and informed your doctor or midwife about what you are planning to take or have already taken. It is easy to think that because a remedy is natural it is safe. But if it is powerful enough to have some effect, it may be powerful enough to harm your babies.

Environmental hazards
Many women worry that exposure to certain chemicals and environmental hazards, such as radiation from computers, can affect developing babies (particularly during the first trimester when organ formation occurs) or can increase the chances of having a miscarriage. We are surrounded by chemicals in the world we live in, from shampoos to paints and petrol vapours.

Unless you work in an environment in which chemicals and solvents are present in very large quantities – for example, if your job is in a dry cleaners or artist's studio – your babies will not be harmed by small quantities of normal, everyday chemicals.

Hair dyes are another common worry, but these do not affect the fetus because the quantities that might be absorbed are so tiny, and in the case of highlights they are only applied to the hair shaft and not to the scalp. If you are worried about other chemicals at home, such as glues or paint vapours when decorating, ventilate the area as much as possible, or delegate the task to others.

When it comes to radiation exposure (*see* also 'Flying' on p. 41), computers and other machines such as laser printers and microwaves are completely safe: only tiny amounts are emitted from the back of these and other similar machines, and none from the front. Bad posture, prolonged use of the keyboard and staring for long periods of time at a screen are far greater hazards for pregnant (and non-pregnant) women.

Soil and cat litter
Toxoplasmosis is an infection caused by a parasite that is present in cat faeces. This parasite can also be found in soil and cat litter that is contaminated by infected cat faeces, as well as in raw/undercooked/cured meat. Toxoplasmosis is usually virtually symptomless, but can cause mild, flu-like symptoms or longer-term ones similar to glandular fever. Most people are immune because they have already been infected in the past, but if you are not immune and you catch it while pregnant, it can cause miscarriage or stillbirth, as well as birth defects in the fetus. About 2,000 pregnant women per year are infected for the first time by toxoplasmosis; about 800 pass the infection on to their babies and about 80 babies a year are born with serious abnormalities.

To reduce the risk of infection, wear gardening gloves when gardening and rubber gloves when cleaning out cat litter; and wash fruit or vegetables, especially those that you have picked. Symptoms are difficult to detect yourself, so if you are concerned you may have been infected, ask your doctor for a blood test. If infection is subsequently confirmed, antibiotics can reduce the chances of transmission to the fetus. See also p. 34–5 for information about food safety.

Antenatal care

Once you know you are pregnant, you will need to contact your doctor or a midwife to plan your antenatal care as soon as possible. You will come under the care of a team of healthcare professionals, who are there to ensure that your pregnancy is monitored and remains a healthy one. Once it is confirmed that you are having twins, your care will be managed differently usually by specialists in a multiple births team.

BIRTH OPTIONS

Twin pregnancies present risks for both mother and babies. For this reason, once you know you are expecting more than one baby, there will be different factors to take into account concerning where you give birth.

This could be disappointing if you only discovered you were carrying twins at the end of your first trimester and had already made plans for where and how you might deliver on the assumption that you were carrying one baby. But you will soon understand why your pregnancy is likely to be different with twins. The options for your birth will be discussed with you early in your pregnancy (*see* the section on your booking appointment, p. 54), the main consideration being how to make sure you and the babies receive any specialist care you may require, as close as possible to your home.

Risk factors of twin pregnancies
It is important to be aware of the particular circumstances presented by twin pregnancies when considering your birth options. They are often more complex and, overall, carry greater risks of specific complications than singleton pregnancies (both to the mother and the babies).

Risks to the mother
There is an increased risk of pregnancy-induced high blood pressure (hypertension), pre-eclampsia, infection associated with premature rupture of membranes ('breaking of the waters'), bleeding during the pregnancy and deep vein thrombosis (which, in turn, may increase the risks of pulmonary embolism). Specifically:

- the risk of pre-eclampsia is three times higher compared to women expecting singletons
- up to 25 per cent of women suffer from pregnancy-induced hypertension, compared to one to five per cent of those carrying singletons
- twelve per cent develop gestational diabetes, compared to four per cent for singletons

When your twin pregnancy has been confirmed by an ultrasound scan, you will be looked after from that point on by a multidisciplinary team experienced in caring for women with multiple pregnancies.

Midwife

Midwives are not nurses (although some also have a nursing qualification); theirs is a separate profession requiring very specific training in caring for pregnant women and their babies. Midwives will look after a woman throughout her pregnancy, labour and for the first six to eight weeks after the birth (the puerperium). The same team of midwives should monitor you throughout your pregnancy, but you may not see the same one at each antenatal appointment.

Obstetrician

An obstetrician is a doctor specialising in looking after women who are pregnant. If you have a problem-free monochorionic or dichorionic pregnancy (see Chapter 1, p. 18), it would be usual to see a consultant obstetrician about twice during your pregnancy. If you have complications or pre-existing health issues, you are likely to see an obstetrician and/or other subspecialists more frequently. If yours is a complicated monochorionic pregnancy, you may be referred to a specialist fetal medicine unit for another opinion or more detailed monitoring, and this may be at a different hospital from the one where you are booked to deliver the babies. In these cases, the obstetricians and midwives in both hospitals will work closely together to make sure you have continuous care in the best place, depending on your individual circumstances.

Sonographer

A sonographer performs and interprets antenatal ultrasound scans (see p. 52). If you develop complications, or if yours is a monochorionic pregnancy, you are likely to have ultrasound scans at a hospital with a specialist fetal medicine unit, where specialist sonographers are able to investigate further and advise on the best treatment.

▸ miscarriage and early delivery rates are higher
▸ elective and emergency Caesarean rates are higher: over 60 per cent (as opposed to 25 per cent for singletons).

Risks to the babies

Prematurity and low birthweight are the main reasons for increased mortality and long-term disability among twins. The incidences of stillbirth and perinatal death are two to three times higher than for singletons, while the cerebral palsy rate is about six times greater – and higher still for monochorionic (MC) twins. Half of all neonatal deaths in England and Wales are due to prematurity, yet about half of twins are born prematurely and with low birthweight, with about ten per cent of births taking place before 32 weeks. Between 40 and 60 per cent of twins are transferred to neonatal units when they are born. The issue of whether babies share a placenta (and fetal circulations) plays a large part in determining the risk factor in the pregnancy: there is a higher incidence of pregnancy loss with MC twins than with dichorionic twins; MC twins are also more likely to have congenital abnormalities (see p. 60).

It is important, though, to emphasise that even when born prematurely (before 37 weeks), most babies will leave hospital.

The risks to any baby are dependent upon the gestation at birth (the earlier the birth the greater the risk), birthweight (influenced by gestation and growth) and whether there is additional illness in the mother or baby, either existing before or developing after birth. This is why specialist care is needed in twin pregnancies, so that any problems can be identified in order to achieve the best outcomes for both mother and babies.

Hospital birth

Because even uncomplicated, 'low risk' twin pregnancies are still 'high risk' compared to singleton pregnancies, the safest option for twin pregnancies is to give birth in a dedicated obstetric unit within a hospital, where operating theatres and full emergency facilities are available if needed. Depending on where you live, you might have the choice of more than one such hospital, in which case you should spend some time deciding which one is best for twin births. If you do have a choice and if you already had a hospital in mind before you knew you were expecting twins, you may wish to reconsider – indeed, the medical staff may recommend you do so. As all twins are more likely to be born early and may need specialist medical care, you should find out what level of care the hospital's neonatal unit (NNU) is able to provide. However, this needs to be evaluated alongside your antenatal circumstances: you could be attending hospital every two weeks for scans (*see* p. 53), and so ease of access at this stage is important. See Box below for questions you may want to ask about your hospital. For more on neonatal care, *see* Chapter 6, p.140.

Levels of neonatal care

There are three levels of neonatal care, but not every NNU is equipped to offer them all. The level of care needed by premature babies depends on how early you go into labour and the health of your babies at birth. Special care (formerly Level 1) is routinely provided for babies born at 34+0 weeks and more, those of low birthweight (below 2 kg) and those with moderate health problems. For example, a Special Care Baby Unit (SCBU) provides assistance with breathing, monitors the baby's heart rate, treats jaundice and provides tube-feeding. High-dependency care (formerly Level 2) is for babies who need continuous monitoring and includes those born at 28–33+6 weeks and/or with short-term complex care needs (e.g. need help with breathing, intravenous feeding or weigh less than 1 kg). This, as well as all other levels of care, is provided in a Local Neonatal Unit (LNU), although babies needing long-term complex/intensive care are transferred to an NICU (*see* below). Intensive care (formerly Level 3) is for babies born before 28 weeks and those with very complex problems. A neonatal Intensive Care Unit (NICU) provides constant monitoring and (usually) mechanical ventilation.

The most important thing is to be prepared for changes to any plans as your pregnancy progresses. For example, it might be decided later on that it would be best to deliver the babies earlier than was first thought, in which case you would need to be at the hospital with the appropriate level of neonatal care. The midwives and obstetricians will make sure you have all the information you need and will support you throughout the situation – everyone understands that dealing with uncertainty about your delivery is not easy. Remember that what is best for you and your babies should be at the heart of the decisions you and your healthcare professionals make together.

QUESTIONS TO ASK ABOUT YOUR HOSPITAL

Listed below are some of the questions you may want to ask about your hospital. You can also access data on all hospitals and maternity units via the Care Quality Commission's website (*see* Useful Resources).

The birth

▶ What is the hospital's approach to twin births: how are they monitored and delivered?

▶ Is there a specialist multidisciplinary team for multiple births?

▶ What are the recommendations for using epidurals with twin deliveries?

▶ What level of care does the hospital's NNU provide? Where will your babies be transferred to if they need a different level of care?

▶ What is the attitude towards birth plans (*see* Chapter 5, p.103), specifically for twins?

▶ If you think you may use it, what is the policy on non-pharmacological pain relief, such as acupuncture and reflexology?

▶ Will you be able to eat and drink during labour?

▶ Can you wear your own clothes?

▶ Can your partner cut the umbilical cords?

▶ Can anyone else attend the birth (check policy on how many people are allowed in the delivery room)?

Postnatal care

▶ How many beds are there in the postnatal ward?

▶ Are there any amenity rooms (single rooms with en suite facilities, for which you pay a fee)? If so, how are they allocated and how much do they cost?

▶ What is the average length of stay after a vaginal and after a Caesarean birth?

▶ In what ways are mothers of twins helped after the birth?

▶ Do the babies remain with you at all times?

▶ Are partners allowed to stay overnight?

▶ What are the visiting hours and do these apply to partners as well?

▶ Is there a breastfeeding counsellor and any additional support for mothers breastfeeding twins?

Many obstetric units organise tours on a regular basis, and these give you an opportunity to see the delivery suite, as well as to ask questions to the staff, so that you will feel familiar with your surroundings when you come to give birth. Hospital facilities and practices are developing all the time, so even if you used a particular hospital for a previous birth, you may find that things have changed in the meantime.

Bear in mind that if you opt for a private hospital, it is unlikely to be attached to an NHS facility and consequently may not have emergency medical care available on site. If you or your babies (or both) become unwell, you and/or they will need to be transferred to an NHS hospital and this could increase the risks to you or your babies. It will also mean that you may be separated from your babies for a while, until you or they get better. However, the pressure for NNU baby cots is such that it is possible that this could occur even if you are in an NHS facility.

Home births, midwifery units and independent midwives

As there is a greater risk of complications with all twin deliveries, a home birth or one in a midwifery unit is not recommended, even if this is not your first delivery and the previous one was without complications. This is not to limit parental 'choice', but to reduce the risks inherent in a twin pregnancy as much as is possible. In addition, neither of these options would be able to offer epidural pain relief, which may be required to assist the delivery of the second baby (see Chapter 5, p. 112). You could opt for an independent midwife, who may be able to come into the hospital with you for the delivery, but your care may need to be shared with an obstetrician as well – you should, from the start, discuss with her how your delivery will be managed.

DID YOU KNOW...?
The term 'perinatal' refers to the period from Week 24 of pregnancy until 28 days after delivery.

The majority of women expecting twins have good outcomes to their pregnancies and much of this is due to antenatal care, including the advances made in ultrasound scans and other screening tests. The results of these investigations can help you in deciding which delivery option will be the safest for you and your babies.

What is an ultrasound scan?

Your twin pregnancy will be monitored more closely than a singleton pregnancy and you will be offered more frequent ultrasound scans. These aim to check that your babies are developing as they should and to spot as early as possible any health problems that may arise for you or your babies. Ultrasound scanning is a technique used to 'visualise' and assess babies in the womb. It can detect the number of placentas and amniotic sacs, as well as where the placenta is attached. During an ultrasound scan, a water-based gel is applied to your abdomen to allow a probe to move easily over its surface. The probe picks up inaudible, high-frequency sound waves that are emitted when it is passed over a solid object (a baby) surrounded by fluid (the amniotic fluid). These sound waves from the solid object then create an image on a screen. Scanning is painless and in early pregnancy you will need to have a full bladder in order for your babies to be visible. Occasionally (especially before ten weeks gestation) an ultrasound scan may need to be performed transvaginally, where a probe is gently inserted into the vagina. This does not harm your babies, although you may feel a little discomfort from the pressure of the probe.

Establishing the chorionicity of your pregnancy

One of the factors that determine how many antenatal appointments and scans you will receive is the chorionicity of your pregnancy. An explanation of chorionicity (and amnionicity) can be found in Chapter 1. Chorionicity is established by ultrasound scan and is easier to detect during the first trimester, but becomes increasingly difficult after fourteen weeks. The first trimester 'dating scan' is usually the one that determines your twin pregnancy and the sonographer will also try to establish chorionicity at this time (see p. 58). Depending on the position of the babies and where the placenta is implanted into the uterus, it can sometimes be difficult to be sure about your babies' chorionicity. If this is the case, you should be referred to a sonographer who is experienced in scanning twin pregnancies or to a fetal medicine unit as soon as possible.

Establishing whether the pregnancy is monochorionic is important at this early stage, as this type of twin pregnancy has an increased likelihood of developing obstetric problems and is therefore viewed as complex (see Chapter 4, p. 96). Pregnancies that are both monochorionic and monoamniotic are high risk and will be managed by a specialist team based at a fetal medicine centre, or sometimes jointly between a team at a local hospital and a fetal medicine specialist.

Routine assessments

At each antenatal appointment your overall health will be assessed: your blood pressure will be checked, as will your urine for signs of protein and sugar (see p. 63); your hands and legs will also be checked for any signs of swelling, as this could be an early indicator of pre-eclampsia, particularly in the third trimester. You should be offered a screening test for chromosonal abnormalities in the 11–14 Week scan and

AVERAGE DURATION OF PREGNANCY

The average length of pregnancy, called the gestational period, differs according to the number of fetuses being carried in the womb:

Singletons: 40 weeks
Twins: 37 weeks
Triplets: 34 weeks
Quads: 32 weeks

Babies that reach 40 weeks gestation are described as a 'full term'. Those that are born before 37 completed weeks of pregnancy are 'premature'. However, any baby born after 37 weeks but before term is not considered premature, just early – although they may still experience some of the complications of prematurity.

TWINS WITH SEPARATE PLACENTAS (DICHORIONIC)

10 weeks	booking appointment
11–14 weeks	dating scan; screening for risk of chromosomal abnormality: nuchal translucency and serum (blood) test
16 weeks	antenatal appointment
18–20 weeks	fetal anomaly scan (may be on the same day as your antenatal appointment)
20 weeks	antenatal appointment, ultrasound scan and blood test for anaemia (20–24 weeks)
24 weeks	antenatal appointment and ultrasound scan
28 weeks	antenatal appointment, ultrasound scan and blood test for anaemia
32 weeks	antenatal appointment and ultrasound scan
34 weeks	antenatal appointment
36 weeks	antenatal appointment and ultrasound scan
37 weeks	birth offered; if declined, further weekly antenatal appointments and ultrasound scans

TWINS WITH SHARED PLACENTA (MONOCHORIONIC)

10 weeks	booking appointment
11–14 weeks	dating scan; screening for risk of chromosomal abnormality: nuchal translucency and serum (blood) test
16 weeks	antenatal appointment and ultrasound scan
18 weeks	antenatal appointment and ultrasound scan
18–20 weeks	fetal anomaly scan (may be on the same day as one of your antenatal appointments)
20 weeks	antenatal appointment, ultrasound scan and blood test for anaemia (20–24 weeks)
22 weeks	antenatal appointment and ultrasound scan
24 weeks	antenatal appointment and ultrasound scan
28 weeks	antenatal appointment, ultrasound scan and blood test for anaemia
32 weeks	antenatal appointment and ultrasound scan
34 weeks	antenatal appointment and ultrasound scan
36 weeks	birth offered; if declined, further weekly antenatal appointments and ultrasound scans

the 18–20 Week scan is to check specifically for abnormalities. Two of the ultrasound scans you are offered check specifically for abnormalities in the babies. Neither is obligatory, but if you agree to them, an obstetrician or midwife should explain to you, in advance of each one, how and why they are carried out and what might happen when you get the results. Screening for abnormalities is more complex with two babies, so counselling and discussion with your healthcare professionals – both before and after the test is undertaken – is very important (*see* p. 55).

The exact number of antenatal appointments and scans you eventually receive will depend on your personal circumstances, but the chart above shows the general practice for twin pregnancies.

Your twin pregnancy will be monitored more closely than a singleton pregnancy and you will be offered more frequent ultrasound scans.

The booking appointment

The first visit to the midwife after your pregnancy is confirmed is known as the 'booking appointment'. It is likely to be the longest of your routine antenatal appointments and may be the first opportunity you have had to talk in detail about your pregnancy, whether or not you already know that you are expecting twins.

Your booking visit may last for up to two hours, during which time you will be given a special record book to take home, in which all the notes from your appointments will be made. From now on you should always bring it with you when you visit the midwife or obstetrician. The midwife you see will take a detailed medical history and you may be asked about your and the babies' father's ethnic origins. Make a note in advance of the date of your last menstrual period (LMP) because she will use the information to calculate your estimated date of delivery (EDD), based on an average 40 week gestation for all babies. However, the majority of twins are born by 37 weeks (*see* Chapter 4, p. 92 for more information). If you have had treatment for subfertility it is best to tell the midwife and show her the results of the scans you may have had already.

The midwife will measure your height, weight and blood pressure. She will examine your hands, legs and abdomen and ask you to provide a urine sample, which will be tested for signs of protein and sugar (the sample may also be sent for culture to check for infection). You will be offered a blood test at this visit or be asked to return for one in the near future. This will determine your blood group and rhesus factor, and will check for anaemia, rubella immunity and haemoglobinopathies (genetic blood disorders), as well as screening for other diseases such as syphilis, hepatitis B and HIV.

In addition to carrying out these tests, your midwife will discuss other issues: for example, what to expect during your pregnancy, whether you have any worries, any history of anxiety or depression, and any other health information. If you have had medical problems in the past, for example, previous terminations or pregnancy losses, gynaecological/abdominal operations or sexually transmitted diseases (STDs), it is important that you mention these, as these may affect the management of your current pregnancy. Try to be as honest as you can during this discussion. The midwife is there to help you, not judge you. If you do not want your partner to know about any particular issues, or do not want them included in your medical notes, then specify this to the midwife. If you have had subfertility treatment using donated eggs or sperm it is advisable to tell the midwife and obstetricians, as this will be significant for genetic screening tests or diagnosis of genetic conditions you may need to undergo, should any

DID YOU KNOW…?
Your antenatal notes date your pregnancy using weeks and days. The first figure refers to the week of gestation, and the second figure, preceded by '+' refers to the number of days after the beginning of that week. For example, if your notes show 13+6, this means thirteen weeks and six days.

concerns arise in your pregnancy. In addition, depending on your situation, you may want to enquire whether you can have access to the following: a mental health professional, specialising in antenatal and perinatal health problems; a woman's health physiotherapist, specialising in pregnancy, to help you with any physical problems you may experience; a dietician, to ensure that you are eating adequately.

Your booking visit is also an opportunity to discuss the birth, although if you do not yet know that you are expecting twins, you may have to revise your plans at a later date (*see* Chapter 2 for how and when you find out, p. 24). However, it is a good time to talk through all the options with the midwife, who will be able to give you information about the hospitals that are local to you, what facilities and practices each has, and so on (*see* Box on p. 50 for questions to consider). You are not obliged to make any firm decisions at this point and issues can be raised at any of your subsequent antenatal appointments.

Care after subfertility treatment

If you have had subfertility treatment, you will know very early on that you are carrying more than one baby, usually at around six or seven weeks after an ultrasound scan confirms that you are pregnant. If your treatment was done through an NHS hospital, you may be referred to their antenatal clinic, either directly or by your doctor. (Remember that the places where you will go for your antenatal appointments and delivery are likely to be different from where you received your subfertility treatment.) However, you are not obliged to attend that hospital, and you can ask to be referred elsewhere if you wish. If your treatment was performed privately, you will need to contact your doctor or midwife to organise your antenatal care. You may also choose to have your antenatal care privately. In all these cases, your healthcare professionals will know as soon as it is confirmed that you are carrying twins and will be experienced in how to care for your specific needs.

Deciding whether to have scans and tests

The use of antenatal scans and tests to determine fetal abnormalities (*see* p. 58 and 61) means that all parents are faced with some important decisions in pregnancy, made more complex for you because you are expecting more than one baby. Before you proceed, you should be given specific information about what the results may mean for each baby and what decisions you may have to make afterwards. Take the time you need to decide whether you want to go ahead with the test, even if it means coming back at a later time.

Issues to consider

Although it is offered to all pregnant women, screening and testing for abnormalities is optional and before agreeing to go ahead you should consider the following:

- Screening simply gives a probability of the babies being affected; the only way of knowing if a baby is affected is to have a diagnostic test, which carries a risk of miscarriage.
- There is an increased chance of receiving a 'false positive' result with twin pregnancies. This is where the baby/babies appear to have a higher risk of being affected, whereas in reality they are not.
- Not all abnormalities can be detected by ultrasound scans or invasive tests and no test is 100 per cent accurate, so just because nothing is detected does not mean that your babies have no abnormalities.
- You should consider what you will actually do with the information after you have been given the result.

It is difficult to know in advance exactly what risk figure you would consider to be too high. It is also important to realise that the risk that has been calculated for you indicates the likelihood of your having an affected baby *at term* (pregnancies affected by fetal abnormalities may miscarry before they reach 40 weeks gestation).

If the probability of your having an affected baby is deemed by your healthcare professionals to be high (*see* p. 58 for figures), you will be offered a diagnostic test. You could:

- decline the test, and hope that the babies will be fine
- decide to have the test, bearing in mind the potential risks, because you prefer to know for certain if there is an abnormality or not.

Some couples choose not to have screening tests because they know that they would not wish to undergo an invasive test or a termination of the pregnancy should the circumstances arise, nor do they want to spend the rest of the pregnancy worrying about their risk result.

If you decide to have a diagnostic invasive test, you should bear in mind that, with a two per cent chance of a miscarriage, you may be at greater risk of losing the pregnancy than of carrying one or two babies with an abnormality, although if the test is carried out in a fetal medicine unit, the risk is likely to be at the lower rather than the higher end of the scale. Only you can decide if you prefer knowing, even if, in so doing, you risk miscarrying your pregnancy.

What to do when you know for sure

If the results of your test indicate with almost total certainty that one or both babies does have an abnormality, there are three options available to you, all of which will be discussed in detail with your specialist obstetrician and others in the medical team caring for you. You may:

- continue with the pregnancy, knowing that you can now inform and prepare yourselves in advance for the challenges you will face once the baby/babies are delivered
- opt, depending on your specific situation and if this is medically possible, for a selective termination of the affected fetus (*see* Box, p. 65)
- choose to terminate the pregnancy.

Some abnormalities are more serious than others. Your healthcare professionals will need to explain as fully as possible the nature of the abnormality, and what the implications are for you and for the affected baby/babies. These include whether an affected fetus is likely to die at or soon after birth, or could survive into early or later childhood, or adulthood. They will also discuss what the child's likely level of disability and/or suffering will be. Bear in mind that this can be difficult to determine accurately and that they can only give you an indication of the range of problems and challenges that you and an affected child will encounter.

The medical profession still cannot offer cast-iron guarantees of what will happen, but can only give information based on existing knowledge of the condition and of your situation. Ultimately, only you and your partner can decide which option you will choose, based on your particular circumstances, the medical condition involved and your personal belief system. For more on the issues surrounding screening and diagnostic tests, consult the NHS Fetal Anomaly Screening Programme (FASP) website (*see* Useful Resources).

Trine's story

My second trimester had its ups and downs. I felt less nauseous after twelve weeks and started to feel the babies move at around seventeen or eighteen weeks – it was a bit like a flutter and was so exciting. Having told some people at twelve weeks I was pregnant, after a straightforward anomaly scan at twenty weeks I felt more confident and told the whole world. I loved telling people it was twins – you get the funniest reactions. We were sailing along until a routine scan at 24 weeks, when I was diagnosed with polyhydramnios (too much amniotic fluid). This can lead to premature labour but, more worryingly, it can be a sign of serious birth defects (including chromosomal abnormalities or problems with the central nervous system). I was whisked off to be seen by extra doctors and booked in for further tests, which was all very scary. What was later explained to me was that the fluid levels were flagged as extra high because the standard measurements are based on singleton pregnancies. So mine weren't actually that bad, given I was expecting twins, but a regular scan doesn't make allowances for that. I was closely monitored with fortnightly scans and eventually the fluid levels corrected themselves. It was a frightening time, though, and it taught me not to take anything for granted.

The dating scan

Your first ultrasound scan after your booking appointment is likely to be the 'dating scan' and, ideally, should be carried out between 11+0 and 13+6 weeks. This may be the first time you discover that you are expecting twins. The sonographer will identify the number of placentas and look at the membrane thickness. From this examination the chorionicity of the pregnancy can be defined with 98–9 per cent certainty.

Both babies will also be assessed and the crown–rump length measured (referred to as CRL in your notes), most commonly when they are between 45 mm and 84 mm in length from the top of the head to the base of the spine; the head circumference (HC), the distance around the baby's head, is also noted (but usually after fourteen weeks). See also Box on p. 61 for further information about fetal measurements. The largest CRL measurement allows an exact calculation to be made of the babies' gestational age, so that their growth during pregnancy can be monitored. If you would like a picture of your babies, you can ask for a copy of the image at this and any subsequent scan, although there may be a small charge for this.

If the dating scan is done during the time frame indicated above, the nuchal translucency can be measured (if you give consent), which forms part of the screening for Down's syndrome risk.

Screening for chromosomal abnormalities

The test usually suggested for twin pregnancies to assess the risk of one or both of the babies having a chromosomal abnormality is the 'combined test'. It is the most sensitive method of screening. Some hospitals only screen for the most common chromosomal abnormality, Down's syndrome (Trisomy 21), whereas others also include other rarer types. For more information on chromosomal abnormalities, *see* Box on p. 60.

The first part of the test is a scan, performed between 11+0 and 13+6 weeks, to measure nuchal translucency (NT); this involves taking a measurement of the fluid at the back of each baby's neck and forms part of the calculation of risk for Down's syndrome. The other part involves a blood (serum) sample, taken between 10+0 and 13+6 weeks, which measures the levels of two hormones, human chorionic gonadotrophin (hCG) and pregnancy-associated plasma protein (PAPP-A); if you are carrying a baby or babies affected by a chromosomal abnormality, you may have abnormal levels of these hormones in your blood. The NT measurement, combined with the hormone levels and other factors (including maternal age), then enable a calculation to be made to indicate whether the babies have an increased risk of having Down's syndrome or other chromosomal abnormalities.

The result of the combined test is given in the form of '1 in...', for example, '1 in 1500', and the higher the second number, the lower the likelihood of a chromosomal abnormality. It is important to remember that this is a *screening* test; it does not *diagnose* – you are simply given a probability of the babies being affected. It is worth considering this probability figure in different ways: 1 in 100 is equivalent to one per cent; 1 in 20 is five per cent; 1 in 5 is twenty per cent, and so on. For monochorionic twins the risk is, effectively, *per pregnancy*: either both babies will be affected or neither will, since they are monozygotic and therefore have the same chromosomes and genes. (Very rarely – in less than 0.1 per cent of cases – monochorionic twins have different chromosomal make-up.) For dichorionic twins, the risk is given *per baby*.

Screening after fourteen weeks

It is not recommended that a blood test alone is used for twins. However, if you have missed your first trimester NT scan (i.e. you are more than fourteen weeks pregnant), you should be offered second trimester serum screening. This blood test measures four hormones released by the placenta and hence

it is called the 'quadruple test'. It has a lower detection
rate (because it does not include the NT element of risk
assessment) and cannot determine the risk for each baby,
only per pregnancy.

What happens next

The majority of women who undergo screening for
chromosomal abnormalities will receive a low risk
result (*see* Did you know? above). Remember that
low risk does not mean *no* risk: there is still a chance,
however small, that your baby/babies could be
affected. No further action will be taken after a
low risk result unless you specifically request it.
If the result indicates a high risk of having an
affected baby at term (based on a 40-week
gestation), you will be offered a diagnostic test,
either amniocentesis (usually between fifteen
and 21 weeks) or chorionic villus sampling
(usually between eleven and fourteen weeks).
In this case, you should be given information
and offered counselling by a healthcare
professional who has specialist expertise
in twin pregnancies, or you could be referred
to a fetal medicine specialist.

Congenital abnormalities

A congenital abnormality is an abnormality that a baby is born with. It can be an error in the number or structure of chromosomes (a chromosomal abnormality) or a problem with one or more genes (a genetic abnormality), caused by environmental or other factors. These result in structural differences in the way babies are formed. Most abnormalities are discordant, irrespective of chorionicity. This means that it is much more likely that one baby will be affected and the other not, regardless of whether or not they share a placenta.

The 40,000 genes that constitute our genetic make-up are arranged in pairs along the two strands of chromosomes present in the nucleus of each cell in our body. Monochorionic twins have a higher risk of congenital heart problems and other physical malformations than dichorionic twins, due to the division of the single-cell zygote after fertilisation (*see* Chapter 1, p. 17 and 18); these abnormalities may also occur as a result of an unequal share of blood through the placenta as the embryos develop. Congenital abnormalities occur in about ten per cent of monochorionic twins and usually affect both twins or, very rarely, just one of them.

Chromosomal abnormalities

Chromosomal abnormalities occur either when there is only one copy of a particular chromosome (the other half of the pair is missing) or when there are three copies instead of a pair. For example, Down's syndrome (*see* below) is caused by having three copies of chromosome 21, which is why it is referred to as Trisomy 21. It is well established that maternal age is linked to an increased risk of a baby being affected by a chromosomal abnormality, as is increased paternal age (although to a much lesser extent). As there are two babies, there is also a greater likelihood of chromosomal abnormalities in twin pregnancies.

There are more than 300 known chromosomal abnormalities, many of which are incompatible with life and result either in the pregnancy miscarrying or (more rarely) in the baby surviving for only a short time after birth. Some, however, result in developmental or behavioural problems with no structural malformations. Down's (Trisomy 21), Edward's (Trisomy 18), Patau's (Trisomy 13) and Turner (45, X/Monosomy X) syndromes make up 98 per cent of all chromosomal abnormalities and, of these, Down's is the most common.

Genetic abnormalities

Environmental factors can damage genes, particularly during the first trimester when major organ formation is taking place. For example, certain drugs (recreational or medicinal) can cross the placenta and affect the developing embryo. Similarly, a lack of folic acid is known to affect the development of the central nervous system and could lead to the baby developing a neural tube defect, such as spina bifida.

Genetic abnormalities can also be caused by one or more faulty genes. Genes are either dominant or recessive. If a gene is dominant, only one copy is required (from one of the parents) for that gene's characteristics to be dominant in the child. If the gene is recessive, a copy from *each* parent is required for the characteristic to be dominant. Dominant and recessive genes affect all our physical and mental characteristics, from whether we have blue or brown eyes (the gene for blue eyes is recessive, the one for brown eyes is dominant) to whether we are more susceptible to certain diseases.

Some genetically inherited diseases are carried by a dominant gene (e.g. Huntingdon's disease). Others, such as cystic fibrosis, are carried on a recessive gene, so each parent has to have a copy of that gene for the condition to be passed on, although it will not be passed on in every case. Some diseases are sex-specific: haemophilia, for example, is caused by a recessive gene on the female X chromosome but it only develops in men. This is because in a woman, her other X chromosome will be normal and therefore dominant, whereas in a man the other chromosome will be Y, and the defective X haemophilia-bearing chromosome will overcome its effect.

It is much more likely that only one baby will be affected by an abnormality and the other not, regardless of whether or not they share a placenta.

The fetal anomaly scan will record four key measurements to check that your babies are the right size for their gestation. These measurements, which will be checked on all future scans, will be recorded in your maternity notes as abbreviations:

BPD Biparietal diameter   The distance between the side bones of the baby's head
HC Head circumference   The distance around the baby's head at the widest point
AC Abdominal circumference   The distance around the baby's abdomen at the widest point
FL Femoral length   The length of the thigh bone
NAD No abnormality detected   Refers to other physical structures, such as the heart, brain spine, etc

The fetal anomaly scan

This ultrasound scan principally looks for any structural abnormalities (also called congenital abnormalities – *see* Box, p. 60), in the developing fetuses and will be offered between 18+0 and 20+6 weeks. As with all scans, sometimes the babies' positions can make it difficult to measure and check every feature, so you may have to walk around a little or come back later when the babies might have moved. This scan also looks at the placenta(s), the umbilical cords and the number of amniotic sacs, and checks that the babies are the right size for their gestational age. The main features that are assessed for each baby are:

▸ femoral length, abdominal circumference, head circumference and biparietal diameter (*see* Box above) – these are also measured at every growth scan
▸ the fetal heart, including the four heart chambers and the large blood vessels
▸ the structure of the lungs, stomach, intestines, liver, kidney and bladder
▸ the structure of the brain, skull and spine (each vertebra is counted, to check for spina bifida)
▸ hands and feet
▸ the structure of the mouth and nose (to diagnose cleft lip)
▸ the position of the placenta; if it is low-lying – which occurs in one in three pregnancies at this stage – its position will be monitored at future scans (only one per cent are low-lying placenta at the time of birth)
▸ the position of the umbilical cord
▸ the volume of amniotic fluid in each sac
▸ the sex of your babies – although it is not always clear and mistakes do occur (if you do not wish to know, let the sonographer know in advance).

If any abnormalities or anything unusual is detected, your healthcare professionals will discuss with you what this means and what options are open to you.

DID YOU KNOW...?

Many parents pay for four-dimensional ultrasound scans in order to get more frequent and visually detailed images of their babies. However, these do not offer any more *medical* information than is given in your routine ultrasound scans.

Growth scans

These ultrasound scans check that the pregnancy is progressing as it should. This includes:

- measuring the size of the babies (at two-week intervals)
- estimating the amount of amniotic fluid (liquor) in the sac(s)
- calculating the blood flow through the umbilical cord or fetal blood vessels (known as a Doppler scan), if there is abnormality in growth or liquor volume
- monitoring for twin-to-twin transfusion syndrome (TTTS) from 16–24 weeks in monochorionic pregnancies
- monitoring for intra-uterine growth restriction (IUGR) from twenty weeks.

If there is a greater than 25 per cent difference in estimated weight between the babies or something unusual in any of the other measurements, you will be referred to a specialist fetal medicine unit for further investigation. Each scan will last approximately half an hour. For information on TTTS and IUGR, see Chapter 4, p. 96–7.

Glucose tolerance test

Your urine is tested at each antenatal appointment for the presence of sugar. It is common for pregnant women to have raised levels of sugar at one of the antenatal visits during the second or third trimester, but if it is still raised at the following visit, you will be asked to have a glucose tolerance test (GTT) in order to establish whether you are developing gestational diabetes (suffered by twelve per cent of women expecting twins). This involves fasting for a certain period of time (often overnight). You are then given a glucose drink and your blood is tested two hours later to see how your body has coped with the sugar.

Gestational diabetes can affect the growth of your babies and increase your risk of developing later pregnancy and labour complications. The condition can often be managed by diet alone and it disappears after you give birth, but 50 per cent of women who have gestational diabetes will go on to develop type 2 diabetes or high blood pressure in later years.

Blood tests for anaemia

There are several different types of anaemia (a reduced number of red blood cells), but the most common form is caused by iron deficiency. Anaemia is a frequent side effect of pregnancy, but is more common among women expecting twins; other changes in the body also cause a 'dilution' of haemoglobin. Blood tests at 20–24 weeks and again at 28 weeks will identify if you need to take an iron supplement.

DIAGNOSTIC TESTS

There are two tests that women may be offered if a congenital abnormality is suspected. As they are invasive tests, meaning that they require entry into the body, the procedures themselves carry some risk, so the tests will only be offered to you if they are felt to be strictly necessary. They are the only way of diagnosing and therefore confirming an abnormality, as opposed to screening for it.

Amniocentesis

This is the most common diagnostic test and can be performed after fifteen weeks. It is used to test for a range of structural abnormalities, and will be offered if your screening test for chromosomal abnormalities indicates a high risk.

It can also be used to detect genetic diseases such as cystic fibrosis and sickle cell anaemia, if there is an indication that your babies could be affected. Amniocentesis carries a risk of miscarriage, which is slightly greater with multiple pregnancies than with singletons. For example, in dichorionic pregnancies (where two separate puncture sites are required) the miscarriage rate is approximately two per cent. Only fetal medicine specialists who have the experience and expertise should carry out these invasive procedures. The operator must have scanned each baby in detail prior to the procedure and have mapped their positions, so that the correct one is identified (*see* Box, p. 58). This is crucial if an abnormality is detected.

Using ultrasound as a guide, a thin needle is inserted through the abdominal and uterine wall (anaesthetic gel is sometimes applied to your abdomen to numb the area first). The needle aspirates (sucks up) a small amount of amniotic fluid, which will contain some of the baby's cells. These are then cultured in a laboratory where they divide and multiply, enabling a genetic or chromosomal analysis to be done. Most chromosomal abnormalities (though not all) can be identified or excluded within four days.

Amniocentesis A very fine needle is inserted through the abdominal and uterine wall, using ultrasound as a guide, in order to remove a small amount of amniotic fluid. In dichorionic pregnancies, this procedure is performed for each baby, as they have separate amniotic sacs.

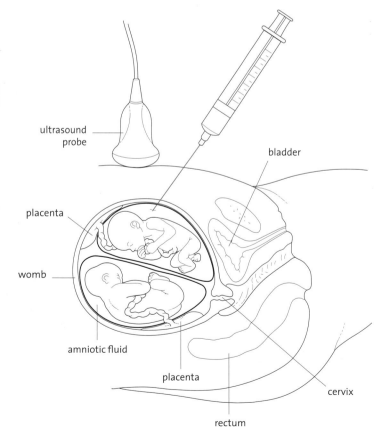

ultrasound probe

bladder

placenta

womb

amniotic fluid

placenta

cervix

rectum

Chorionic villus sampling

Chorionic villus sampling (CVS) is used to test for common chromosomal abnormalities, such as Down's, Edward's, Patau's and Turner (45, X) syndromes, and certain genetic diseases. This procedure is similar to that of amniocentesis (although occasionally the needle is inserted via the cervix), but can be performed earlier, at between eleven and fourteen weeks and involves taking a small number of cells from the placenta. Again, results are available in four days. The techniques needed for CVS in twins is specialised and should be performed in a centre with the appropriate expertise. The localisation of the twins and their placenta(s) is once again important; separate needles are usually placed into the placenta of dichorionic twins to avoid cross- contamination. The miscarriage rate is the same as with amniocentesis.

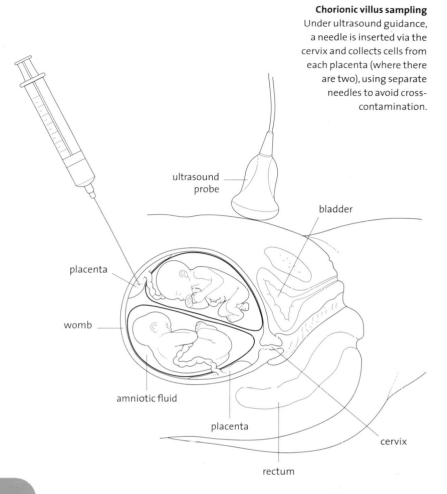

Chorionic villus sampling
Under ultrasound guidance, a needle is inserted via the cervix and collects cells from each placenta (where there are two), using separate needles to avoid cross-contamination.

ultrasound probe

bladder

placenta

womb

amniotic fluid

placenta

cervix

rectum

SELECTIVE TERMINATION

When a fetus is affected by a serious abnormality, or the poor health of one fetus is putting the other (healthy) twin at risk, parents are now given the option of terminating one fetus, a procedure known as 'selective termination'. This is a distressing decision for anyone to have to make, and your specialist obstetrician will discuss in detail with you what the procedure involves and all the issues surrounding it. There is a small risk of miscarriage, and there may be further complications if your twins are monochorionic, in which case other options may have to be considered. The termination is done at a specialist fetal medicine centre and does not usually affect the surviving twin.

Under ultrasound guidance, a drug is injected into the affected fetus, causing the heart to stop. The fetus then shrinks in size significantly over the next few weeks, although it is still there at birth. You should discuss with your healthcare professionals whether or not you want to see what remains of your baby – ask for a photograph to be taken if you are not sure.

It is extremely upsetting to have to carry a dead baby and a sense of guilt and loss after the birth are common. These feelings can be similar to those who have experienced a miscarriage or stillbirth (*see* p. 98–9 for more). However, because this procedure is quite rare, you may find that others have less understanding of what you have been through and therefore you may experience difficulties in finding the appropriate help. Contact the Multiple Birth Foundation and Antenatal Results and Choices for further advice and support (*see* Useful Resources).

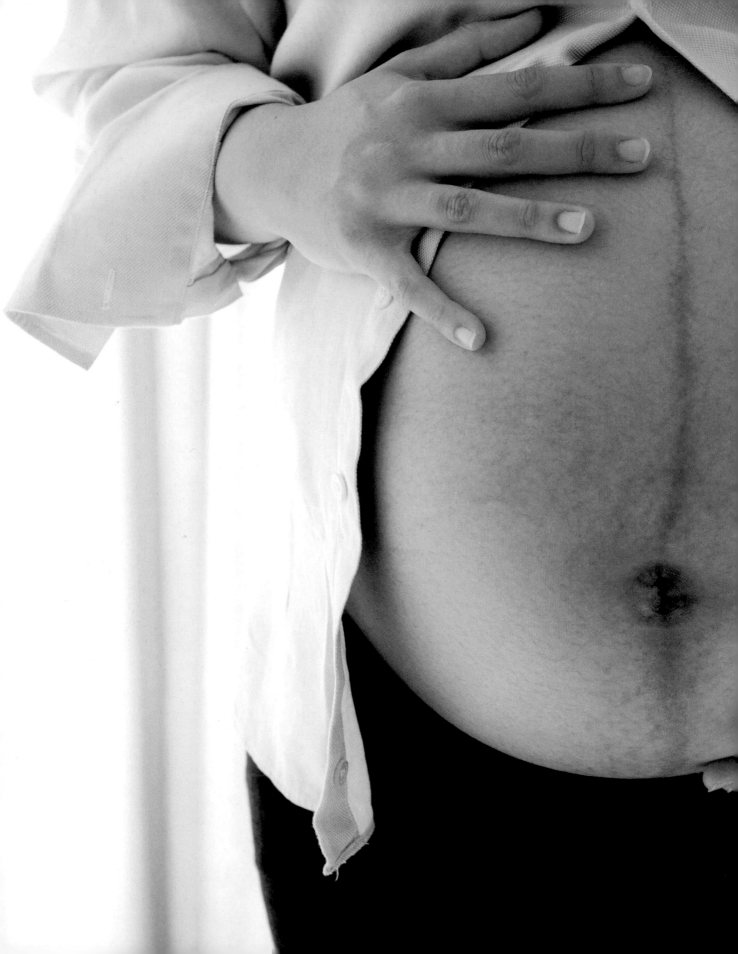

4

The three trimesters

The length of a pregnancy, called the gestational period, is divided into three parts or trimesters, each of approximately three months. During this time, your body undergoes many complex changes and your babies develop in fascinating ways, some of which are common to all pregnancies, while others are specific to twins.

First trimester: timeline of key events

BABIES

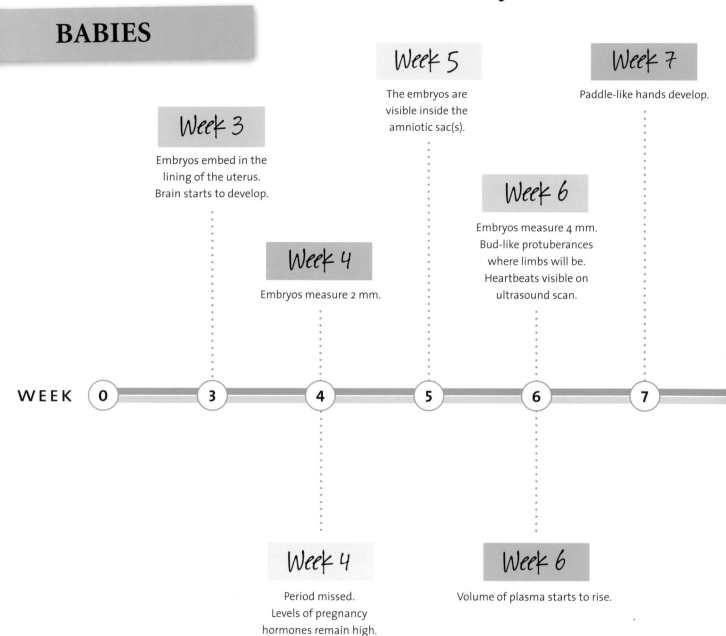

Week 3

Embryos embed in the lining of the uterus. Brain starts to develop.

Week 5

The embryos are visible inside the amniotic sac(s).

Week 7

Paddle-like hands develop.

Week 4

Embryos measure 2 mm.

Week 6

Embryos measure 4 mm. Bud-like protuberances where limbs will be. Heartbeats visible on ultrasound scan.

WEEK 0   3   4   5   6   7

Week 4

Period missed. Levels of pregnancy hormones remain high. Uterus begins to expand.

Week 6

Volume of plasma starts to rise.

MOTHER

Week 8
Shoulders and elbows start to develop. Eyes have some pigment.

Week 10
All major organs and umbilical cord formed. Heart has four chambers and beats at approximately 180 beats per minute. Babies measure 30 mm crown to rump. Tongue and 32 tooth buds in place.

Week 12
Fingers separate. Tiny nails visible. Bones harden.

Week 9
Brain is four times the size it was in Week 6.

Week 11
Ovaries/testes fully formed. Head comprises one-third of crown to rump length.

Week 13
Heart beats at 160 beats per minute. Babies measure 80 mm and weigh five times more than in Week 10. Placenta fully functioning.

8 9 10 11 12 13

Week 9
Breasts heavier, larger and tender. Nipples and surrounding areola darken.

Week 12
Volume of red blood cells rises slowly throughout trimester. Increase in blood supply to all major organs.

Week 8
First symptoms of pregnancy, including mood swings, tiredness and morning sickness. Blood supply to uterus has doubled.

Week 10
Blood supply to kidneys increases by 30 per cent (over the trimester).

Week 13
25 per cent of blood flow is directed to the uterus to support growing babies and placenta(s), five times more than when not pregnant.

Your pregnancy's gestation is traditionally calculated from the first day of your last menstrual period (LMP), which is termed Day 1. If you have had IVF, the start of the pregnancy will be calculated from the date of embryo transfer. If you are pregnant by the time your next period is due 28 days later (the average length of a cycle), you will be referred to as four weeks pregnant. The first trimester is considered to finish at the end of the thirteenth week.

Your babies: Weeks 0–5

Fertilisation and how twins are conceived is described in detail in Chapter 1, along with a full explanation of zygosity (i.e. whether or not your twins are identical), chorionicity (what type of placenta has formed) and amnionicity (the number of inner sacs). If your twins are dizygotic (and therefore the result of two fertilised eggs), each will implant in the endometrium (the lining of the uterus) approximately six days after fertilisation. If your twins are monozygotic, the early embryo may already have split into two by the time it enters the uterus, leading to dichorionic diamniotic twins (two placentas and two sacs); this is the case for 20–30 per cent of monozygotic twins. The egg may split later, between the fourth and eleventh day, in which case the resulting twins will be monochorionic and diamniotic (one placenta and two sacs). And if they split between the eleventh and fourteenth day (which is rare), they will be both monochorionic and monoamniotic (one placenta and one sac). Whatever type of monozygotic twins are present, cell division and development of the early embryos continues during the first trimester at the same speed as if they were dizygotic twins or a singleton (although one twin is often slightly larger than the other) and the timing of when they embed in the endometrium also remains the same. This is why it is possible to date your pregnancy very accurately on the basis of measurements taken at your first ultrasound 'dating' scan (*see* Chapter 3, p. 58).

Just before the embryos embed in the endometrium, the cells have already specialised into three different layers, called germ layers, and these will grow into the various body parts of each baby:

- ‣ the outer layer (ectoderm) will develop into the hair, skin, nails, nervous system and brain
- ‣ the middle layer (mesoderm) will form the heart, blood vessels, skeleton and cartilage
- ‣ the inner layer (endoderm) will form the digestive and respiratory systems (bladder, bowels and lungs).

> **DID YOU KNOW…?**
> Increasingly, gestational age is calculated from crown–rump length of the (larger) baby, measured by ultrasound scan in the first trimester. This is more accurate than LMP dates, and so the due date you will have initially been given may be adjusted later on.

Once the embryos have implanted in the endometrium, the outer layer of cells, called trophoblast cells, burrow deeper into the lining and will eventually become the placenta, while the inner cells continue to divide to form what will become the baby. By Week 4, even before most women know they are pregnant, the embryos measure 2 mm each – about the size of a pinhead. One week later, they are just visible on an ultrasound scan, and the spinal cord can be seen as a row of dark cells, known as a fetal pole. These cells fold in on themselves lengthwise to become the neural tube, at the top of which are two large lobes that will form the brain. The building blocks for the babies' main organs are already in place and although the heartbeats cannot be detected until the end of Week 5 or the start of Week 6, blood is already flowing through a primitive heart structure.

By the end of Week 5, the embryos can be seen inside a fluid-filled bubble called the amniotic sac. (Very rarely, twins share one sac – *see* Chapter 1, p. 20). This is covered by an outer layer or sac called the chorion. The outer layer of the chorion becomes the early placenta and burrows into the endometrium using little finger-like projections called chorionic villi. Once the placenta is fully developed, these villi will enable the exchange of blood, oxygen and other nutrients to take place between your circulation and each baby, thus providing their vital support system.

Obesity is calculated to mean a Body Mass Index (BMI) of over 30 (a healthy range is a BMI of 18.5–24.9). To find out your BMI, divide your pre-pregnancy weight in kilograms by your height in metres squared. Obesity is known to give rise to a wide range of pregnancy complications, not only for the woman but for her babies as well. These include:

▸ diabetes (both gestational and pre-existing)
▸ pre-eclampsia
▸ gestational hypertension (affecting up to one in four women carrying twins)
▸ late miscarriage (pre-24 weeks), stillbirth or premature birth
▸ slower labour
▸ difficulties in administering regional anaesthesia (e.g. epidurals)

▸ greater likelihood of Caesarean section
▸ post-partum haemorrhage
▸ post-Caesarean wound infection
▸ growth problems for the babies
▸ higher rate of congenital abnormality in babies
▸ increased percentage of neonatal deaths
▸ maternal death.

You are likely to be monitored more closely if your BMI is higher than it should be, and your birth options may be reduced as a result of any complications you have developed or are likely to experience during labour (e.g. it can be harder to monitor the babies). These options will be discussed with you as your pregnancy progresses. You should be given advice about what to eat by your midwife or you may be referred to a dietician.

Your body: Weeks 0–5

Some women say that they 'feel pregnant' from the moment they conceive, but for many – even those carrying twins – the symptoms of pregnancy do not usually begin until Week 6. During this initial six-week period, however, your body will already have started to change. Your uterus has begun to expand from its non-pregnant size (which is roughly the size of a large plum), although others will not notice any change in your abdomen until Weeks 14–16. The proportion of plasma (the watery element of the blood) is higher and the amount of blood that flows to your uterus is increasing. The levels of the three main pregnancy hormones, oestrogen, progesterone and human chorionic gonadotrophin (see Box, p. 72), remain raised. These are responsible for the many changes in your body that help to maintain the pregnancy until the placenta is sufficiently developed and can take over towards the end of the first trimester.

Detection of a twin pregnancy

Even if you know you are pregnant at around four weeks (or slightly before, if you had a blood test following fertility treatment), the earliest you can detect a twin pregnancy is in Week 5, using ultrasound scanning. At this point, there will be two separate gestational sacs (unless your twins are monoamniotic) and, perhaps, two fetal poles; the heartbeats of the babies will be detectable by Week 6, if they were not already. Scanning may be done via your abdomen or transvaginally (see Chapter 3, p. 52), but an early scan such as this is not routinely offered to pregnant women unless there are specific reasons for doing so.

During this initial six-week period, your body will have already started to change. Your uterus has begun to expand, although others will not notice any change in your abdomen until Weeks 14–16.

Your babies: Weeks 6–10

During this period, the weight of the embryos quadruples and they increase in length from 4 mm to 30 mm from crown to rump, although it is quite usual for one baby to be slightly larger than the other (measurements given here apply to the larger twin). External and internal changes are happening so fast that by the start of Week 10, all the basic major organ formation has taken place.

By Week 6, the embryos can be seen: they have a comma-shaped appearance, with bud-like protuberances where the four limbs will be. By the start of Week 7, small paddle-like hands appear, with primitive shoulders and elbows starting to develop a week later. The babies' heartbeats can be clearly identified by an ultrasound scan at this time, although they are so fast that they are more like a flutter.

The head grows faster than the rest of the body to make room for the fast-developing brain. The head is bent over the body to start with, before a neck gradually forms, and a central nervous system and backbone develop so that the head and body straighten out a little. Primitive facial bones and features start to form during these weeks. The eyes, nose and mouth are visible on an ultrasound scan, and by Week 8 the eyes have some pigment, although they remain closed behind lids for many more weeks. Ears and the inner ear canals start to form, the mouth contains a tiny tongue with rudimentary taste buds by Week 10, and tooth buds for future teeth are in place in the developing jawbone.

Between Weeks 6 and 10, internal changes are as fast as external ones. By Week 9, the brain has quadrupled in size from Week 6, and the spinal cord and central nervous system are evolving fast. By Week 10, the heart has the four chambers and valves that enable it to pump blood around the baby's circulatory system. It beats at 180 beats per minute, slower than in Week 7, but twice as fast as an adult heart. The digestive system is also developing quickly, with the intestines forming loops that protrude through the abdominal wall. The developing babies are less susceptible to potential damage from external factors (such as drugs or infections) beyond Week 10, and it is also very rare for congenital abnormalities to develop after this time.

The babies' support system is also developing fast: the chorionic villi (the finger-like protuberances on the outer surface of the chorion) are becoming more concentrated in one area of the uterus and this is gradually transforming

THE ROLE OF THE THREE MAIN PREGNANCY HORMONES

The three principal hormones that maintain a pregnancy have very specific functions.

Oestrogen

Increasing levels of oestrogen cause the endometrium to thicken and become receptive to a pregnancy. This allows the embryos to embed safely and to receive the nutrients they require to continue to develop. Oestrogen also stimulates the growth of milk glands in the breast, causing the breasts to become tender (as they often do before the start of your period). This tenderness usually disappears by the end of the first trimester.

Human chorionic gonadotrophin

Unlike oestrogen and progesterone, human chorionic gonadotrophin occurs only during pregnancy and it is the one measured, either in your urine or in your blood, to give you a positive pregnancy result. The hCG level in your blood is likely to be higher than it would be for a singleton pregnancy, although this is not in itself a reliable indicator of twins. In addition to supporting implantation of the embryos, hCG stimulates the thyroid gland (situated at the front of the neck) into producing the hormone thyroxine, which speeds up your metabolism. This is necessary in order to cope with the increase in blood volume and organ size during pregnancy.

Progesterone

The hormone progesterone softens ligaments in preparation for labour, dilates blood vessels and thickens cervical mucus, preventing bacteria from entering the uterus. The dilation of blood vessels is essential, because it allows the greater blood volume to be pumped to all organs of the body without raising your blood pressure to dangerous levels. Much of this extra supply is needed to enable new blood vessels to form in the developing placenta(s).

into the placenta. The villi are developing more and more blood vessels; these burrow into the uterine wall so that they can access your circulation and, as the placenta, will be able to support the pregnancy.

Your body: Weeks 6–10

In this period, your breasts start to look larger and feel heavier; the nipples and the surrounding areola begin to darken; and the little pimple-like protuberances on them, called Montgomery's tubercles, become more prominent. By Week 8, the blood supply to your uterus has doubled. This is also the time when most women begin to notice the less welcome side effects of pregnancy, and some may be worsened by the increased hormonal surge required to maintain a twin pregnancy during the first trimester. The following symptoms are among those that arise most frequently during the first trimester, and usually between Weeks 6 and 10. However, it is important to stress that the degree to which you experience these does not have a bearing on how well established your pregnancy is and in fact, you may not experience some or any of these at all.

Mood swings

Changes in mood are very common in early pregnancy due to hormonal changes and the wide range of feelings you are likely to have about becoming a parent, particularly a mother of twins. For a detailed discussion on your emotions in early pregnancy, see Chapter 2, p. 24–5.

Extreme tiredness

Although not all women experience it, fatigue occurs quite frequently during the first trimester and may begin without warning. One day you are a normal, active woman, then suddenly you completely lack energy and may even need to have a nap by the time you get home from work. This overwhelming tiredness is probably linked to the pregnancy hormones that are now flooding through you. In all likelihood, you will regain your normal energy levels by the end of this trimester, but in the meantime you should listen to your body and rest whenever you can.

Changing tastes

Some women report a metallic taste in their mouth and a heightened sense of smell as early symptoms of pregnancy. In addition, it is common to develop aversions for certain foods, tastes and smells, and – conversely – to have cravings for others. Again, these differences are thought to be the result of hormonal changes in the body. The most common foods, tastes and smells that you might no longer be able to tolerate are coffee, tea, alcohol, fish, red meat, certain fruit and vegetables, cigarette smoke; this intolerance can be exacerbated if you are also suffering from morning sickness (see p.75). Foods that you may start either to crave or at least to tolerate are: starchy, bland foods, salty or pickled foods (e.g. Marmite, pickled onions), peppermint and ginger (e.g. in teas). Occasionally, women develop a craving for a non-food item such as coal or tar, a condition known as pica. While this is rare, you should have it investigated, as it may be a sign of deficiency in certain nutrients, such as iron or zinc.

This is also the time when most women begin to notice the less welcome side effects of pregnancy, and some may be worsened by the increased hormonal surge required to maintain a twin pregnancy during the first trimester.

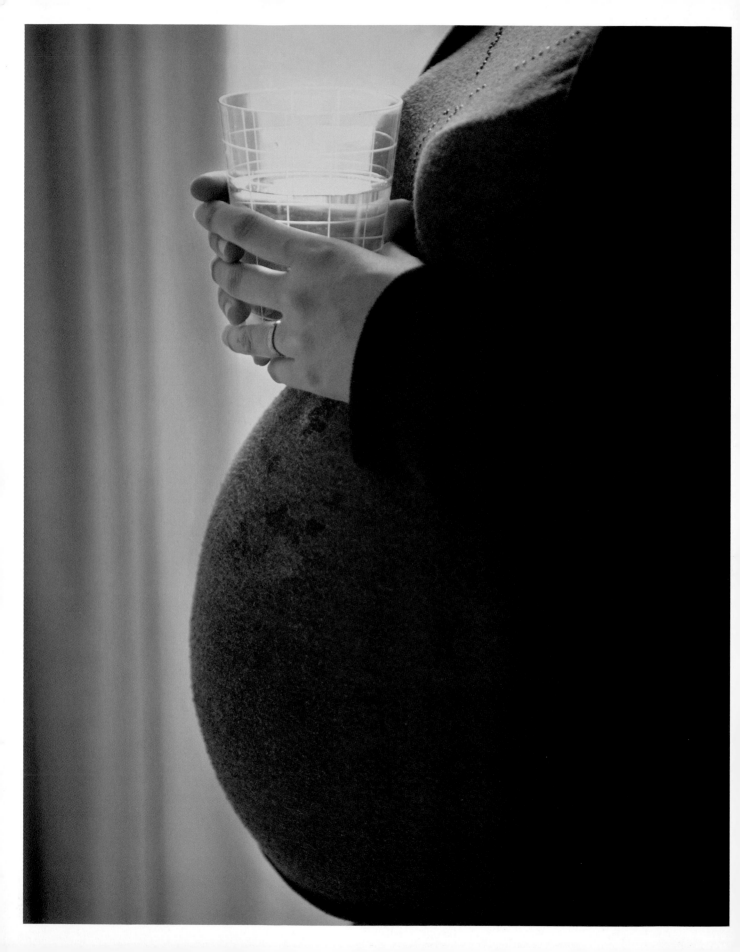

Morning sickness

Morning sickness is a somewhat misleading term that applies to both nausea and vomiting. It affects about three-quarters of pregnant women, particularly during the first trimester, although it is more common in twin pregnancies. Symptoms usually begin by about Week 8 and disappear by the end of Week 14, though some women suffer from it for longer or even throughout their entire pregnancy. There is no 'normal' pattern of morning sickness: some women suffer from nausea but are never actually sick; some suffer symptoms all day, others at the start of the day (especially when they first get up) or later in the day. Again, it is not a sign of the overall health of your pregnancy: some women do not experience morning sickness at all, yet go on to deliver perfectly healthy babies.

Surprisingly, perhaps, it is not known what causes morning sickness, nor why some women suffer from it more than others. Many believe that hormones (notably hCG and progesterone) play a part, but there is still no proof. Others believe that it occurs in response to low blood sugar levels (e.g. first thing in the morning before you have eaten) or to tiredness (e.g. in the early evening). There are some common tips to alleviate the worst of the symptoms:

▸ Avoid rich, fatty or spicy foods, as well as acidic foods such as fruit juices.
▸ Opt for easy-to-digest bland, starchy foods, such as plain pasta, biscuits, toast, crackers, plain cereals (fortified with vitamins and minerals) with skimmed milk (which is the most digestible and still full of calcium and protein).
▸ Eat little and often, and try to drink plenty of fluids.
▸ Drink ginger or peppermint teas as a digestive; other bland herbal teas (e.g. chamomile) can also help keep up your fluid intake.
▸ Wear acupressure wristbands or take ginger capsules (available in pharmacies) to help reduce symptoms of nausea.

HYPEREMESIS GRAVIDARUM
Persistent vomiting in pregnancy is called hyperemesis gravidarum. This condition affects a small percentage of women who are unable to keep down any food or liquids. Like morning sickness, it is more common in twin pregnancies. If you are persistently sick for more than just a few days, you will soon become weak and dehydrated, so you should consult your doctor or midwife without delay.

DID YOU KNOW…?
Many hospitals have a dedicated Early Pregnancy Unit, staffed by doctors, midwives and sonographers, specifically to deal with any problems in pregnancy up to thirteen weeks.

Seek advice from your midwife before taking any oral treatments for nausea and sickness. You may be one of the few who are vomiting so badly that you are unable to keep down any food and liquids. This is not harmful for the babies if it only lasts for a few days, because they will simply draw on your own nutritional reserves. If the problem persists beyond that, consult your doctor as you may be suffering from a condition called hyperemesis gravidarum (see Box below).

Sore breasts
Raised oestrogen and progesterone levels can cause your breasts to feel very heavy and extremely tender to the touch. Having a good support bra can help, as can wearing a sleep bra at night (see Chapter 2, p. 43).

Frequent urination
The need to pass urine more frequently is caused by two factors. First, your uterus is starting to increase in size and so is pressing on the bladder; second, the kidneys are now receiving 30 per cent more blood flow and filtering more fluid, and are therefore producing more urine.

Urinary tract infection (UTI)
The higher level of progesterone present during pregnancy relaxes the muscle in the urinary tract. This means that bacteria (usually from the bowel) can enter the urethra more easily and cause an infection in the bladder. All pregnant women have a urine test at each antenatal visit, which is checked for infection. If you develop a stinging or burning sensation when passing urine, consult a doctor or midwife as soon as possible. If a UTI is detected, it can then be treated with antibiotics. In the meantime – and, indeed, routinely during your pregnancy – drink as much fluid as you can in order to keep flushing the bacteria out of your system. If left untreated, UTIs spread up into the kidneys, which could cause permanent damage.

Pelvic aches and pains

Mild to moderate aches and pains in the pelvic region are common during the first trimester, because all the ligaments and muscles are starting to loosen and expand in preparation for the birth. While uncomfortable, they are nothing to worry about, as long as they are temporary. However, if you are at all concerned, or if the pain is acute and/or permanent, consult your doctor immediately. For more on pelvic pain, backache and sciatica, see p. 85 and 86.

Bleeding

Bleeding in the first trimester should always be taken seriously, although it does not necessarily indicate that you are miscarrying your pregnancy. It can range from a little light spotting to heavier bleeding, including the passing of blood clots, and the blood can also range in colour from brownish to pink to bright red. You should get it checked out by a doctor as soon as possible. Contact your doctor if you are not yet booked in with your hospital. You may be offered, or can request, an ultrasound scan (this will be done transvaginally), as this may be able to clarify where the bleeding is coming from in order to ascertain whether or not the pregnancy is affected (*see* p. 98–99 for information on miscarriage). Bleeding is often unexplained, in many cases it stops after a short while or is intermittent throughout the first trimester.

Your babies: Weeks 11–13

All the major organs and body systems are now formed and these continue to grow and mature at great speed during the next few weeks.

The body straightens out, although at Week 11 the head still makes up one-third of the crown–rump length. The limbs continue to grow, fingers and toes are starting to separate out and nails form, although the upper limbs develop at a faster pace than the lower ones, which will only catch up some weeks later. Calcium is being deposited on the entire skeleton, so that bones are becoming harder. This process, called ossification, is on-going and, indeed, continues into early adolescence. Facial features are more pronounced and recognisable, and the internal sexual organs – the ovaries for girls and testes for boys – are now fully formed, although the penis and clitoris are not yet distinguishable. By the end of Week 13, the intestines are enclosed behind the abdominal wall and the stomach is connected to the mouth and intestines. Average length is now 80 mm from crown to rump, the heart beats at 160 beats per minute and each baby weighs approximately five times more than at the start of Week 10.

Although the umbilical cords are in place (*see* right), the babies are still receiving most of their nourishment from the yolk sac(s), situated in the space between the amnion and the chorion. Each baby floats in about 30 ml of amniotic fluid (unless it is a monochorionic monoamniotic pregnancy), although this will increase in volume as the pregnancy progresses. The fluid is sterile and protects the babies throughout pregnancy. The placenta(s) is fully functioning by Week 13 and is attached to the uterine wall by the chorionic villi, which continue to multiply and embed in the endometrium. Specialised villi are able to access maternal blood vessels in order to provide the babies with oxygen and nutrients and to anchor the placenta(s). Each baby is attached to an umbilical cord, which consists of three intertwined blood vessels: one is a large vein that carries oxygen-rich blood and nutrients from the maternal circulatory system via the placenta to the baby, while the other two are smaller arteries that transport the baby's waste products back, again via the placenta, to the mother's circulatory system. The mother's and the babies' circulations remain completely separate, so that once the placenta is fully functioning, the babies are protected from any harmful substances, such as infections, that may be present in the mother's blood.

Your body: Weeks 11–13

Women often notice their abdomen expanding at this point (although this can vary), as the uterus rises up above the pelvic rim. This is earlier than those carrying singletons, who usually do not start to 'show' until the end of the first trimester. By the end of the first trimester, at least 25 per cent of the blood being pumped around your body – your cardiac output – is directed to the uterus, because blood vessels are constantly being formed and the placenta(s) is developing. While your heart does not beat much faster during pregnancy, the amount of blood pumped through the heart at each beat increases significantly. The reason your heart can cope with this is that the pregnancy hormones, especially progesterone, have relaxed your entire circulatory system, including the muscles of the heart, enabling your blood pressure to remain at a safe level. You may also notice other symptoms:

► You have a permanently stuffy nose and occasional nosebleeds, as a result of additional mucus production and dilated blood vessels.
► Blue veins become visible on your breasts, because of increased blood volume and your dilated circulatory system.
► You don't need to urinate as frequently, as your uterus has started to move up into the abdominal cavity, reducing the pressure on your bladder.
► You sometimes feel light-headed or dizzy.

BLOOD VOLUME IN TWIN PREGNANCY

Your blood volume will increase by around 75 per cent, from around 5 litres at the start to a little under 9 litres by the end. The volume of plasma (the watery fluid) increases quickly from the moment you become pregnant to the end of the first trimester, while the oxygen-carrying red blood cells also increase, though at a slower rate. This ensures that your blood does not become too dilute, which would cause you to become anaemic. The increase in plasma volume then increases more slowly from the start of the second trimester through to the end of your pregnancy, while the production of red blood cells speeds up.

Dealing with dizziness

Dizziness or light-headedness can be caused either by low blood sugar (especially if you are finding it difficult to eat properly) or by changes in your circulation. Try to stay hydrated and eat plenty of carbohydrates, and avoid standing or sitting for long periods of time, as this can result in insufficient blood reaching your brain. If you feel faint, squat or lie down to allow the blood to circulate properly once more.

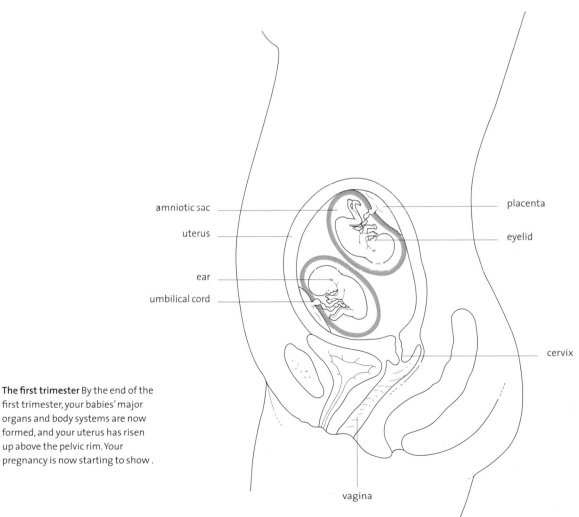

amniotic sac

uterus

ear

umbilical cord

placenta

eyelid

cervix

vagina

The first trimester By the end of the first trimester, your babies' major organs and body systems are now formed, and your uterus has risen up above the pelvic rim. Your pregnancy is now starting to show .

Alex's story

My identical (monochorionic diamniotic) twin boys, Joshua and Harry, were born at 35+2 weeks by emergency Caesarean section, weighing 2.3 kg and 2.1 kg.

Finding out we were having twins was a huge shock. I was only just getting my head around being pregnant when we were then told that we would be having two babies. I won't ever forget my husband's face: he automatically went into 'worry mode' – how were we going to afford everything, what about the increased risk of complications, and so on. I just couldn't stop smiling. Although it was exciting, there were times during the pregnancy that were scary. Early on, I had a bleed and the lack of control over the situation made it so difficult. Luckily, it didn't cause any serious problems.

I remember feeling very overwhelmed at times and when we attended an antenatal day run by a Twins Club, I walked in, burst into tears and left. After ten minutes I went back in and all was fine. In fact, we found the day really useful. It is helpful attending an antenatal class specifically for multiples, because many things about your pregnancy are different. It can be frustrating when you attend a regular class and they constantly say how something won't apply to you, but then don't give information to help you.

You are told early on that, because you are having twins, there are increased complications in pregnancy and birth, which can be scary to hear as a parent. Having said that, I had a good experience – so, better than many of my friends who were having one baby – so, even though there is an increased risk of complications, it doesn't necessarily mean they will happen. I always knew I would have a Caesarean section, so it wasn't a surprise when I did. However, I did have it as an emergency Caesarean section. My waters broke at home after I had spent the day Christmas shopping. I went to hospital straight away ... The boys were born a second apart! It all happened so quickly: one minute you are waddling down a corridor to the theatre with a massive bump, the next, these little things are being given to you – it's surreal, but amazing.

Second trimester: timeline of key events

Week 15
Fingernails more clearly visible.

Week 17
Taste buds form on the tongue. Eyebrows and eyelashes growing. At start of week measure 13 cm from crown to rump and weigh five times more than in Week 13.

Week 14
Eyes now positioned at front of face; eyelids still closed but eyes sensitive to light.

Week 16
Scrotum and rudimentary penis visible in males. In females, uterus is fully formed, vagina has begun to hollow out and ovaries contain three million eggs.

Week 20
Facial muscles are developed, so that babies' grimacing is visible by ultrasound scan.

WEEK (14) (15) (16) (17) (18) (20)

Week 15
Volume of red blood cells increases to keep up with higher water content of blood earlier in pregnancy.

Week 18
During this trimester, you gain around 500 g per week, or 6–6.5 kg in total. Between Weeks 18 and 22, start to feel babies moving.

Week 17
Filtering capacity of kidneys 60 per cent higher than normal. Uterus reaches navel by end of week.

Week 20
Heart is pumping 7 litres of blood per minute round the body, up from 5 litres.

MOTHER

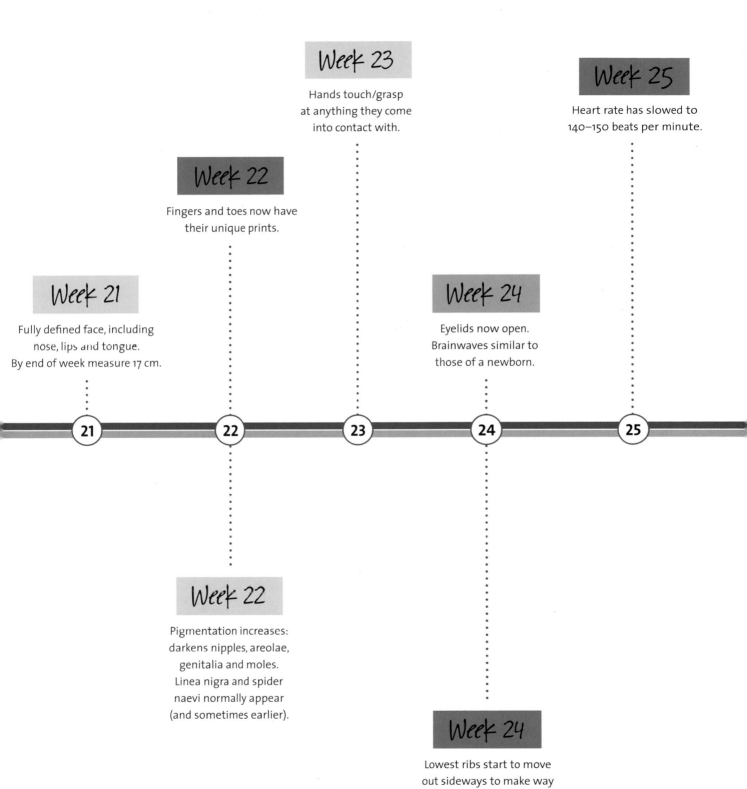

Week 23

Hands touch/grasp at anything they come into contact with.

Week 25

Heart rate has slowed to 140–150 beats per minute.

Week 22

Fingers and toes now have their unique prints.

Week 21

Fully defined face, including nose, lips and tongue. By end of week measure 17 cm.

Week 24

Eyelids now open. Brainwaves similar to those of a newborn.

21 22 23 24 25

Week 22

Pigmentation increases: darkens nipples, areolae, genitalia and moles. Linea nigra and spider naevi normally appear (and sometimes earlier).

Week 24

Lowest ribs start to move out sideways to make way for expanding uterus.

The second trimester covers the period from the beginning of Week 14 to the end of Week 25. The placenta(s) is now fully supporting the pregnancy, and the babies will be growing so fast during this trimester that you will soon feel their movement. Initially, this is a 'fluttering' sensation, but as the babies increase in size and strength, the movements will become firmer and more defined.

Your babies: Weeks 14–17

The legs are now growing at a faster pace than the arms, so by Week 16, the limbs are more in proportion with the rest of the body. The arms are long enough for the hands to meet in front of the body and, because of continuing neurological development, the babies gain an increasingly wide range of movements, including being able to stretch out their limbs, clench and unclench their hands, and even suck their thumb if it happens to come near their mouth. These movements are not conscious, however, but are purely reflex actions. By the start of Week 17, the babies measure 13 cm from crown to rump, and weigh five times more than in Week 13. External male genitalia, the scrotum and penis, are visible although not fully developed; in females the uterus is fully formed and the ovaries contain three million eggs, and the vagina has started to hollow out.

The facial features continue to develop, with the eyes now on the front of the head. Although the fully formed eyelids remain closed for many more weeks, the retina at the back of the eye is sensitive to outside bright light. By Week 16, the external ears are fully formed and can pick up external noise, and the facial muscles are sufficiently developed that, by the end of Week 17, the babies can be seen on an ultrasound scan appearing to grimace. The downy hair on the head begins to thicken and contains some pigment by the start of Week 17, fine eyebrows and lashes are starting to grow and taste buds are forming on the tongue. The digestive system is in place and the kidneys and stomach are starting to function, allowing the babies to swallow small amounts of amniotic fluid. This is excreted back into the pool as urine, which is then eliminated via the umbilical cord and placenta before passing into the mother's bloodstream.

The placenta continues to develop and filters many harmful substances that may be in the mother's blood. The amniotic fluid is increasing in volume and by the end of this period each baby will float in around 200 ml. This acts as a cushion against the outside world and enables the babies to practise their increasingly complex muscular development.

Your body: Weeks 14–17

This is the time when some of the unpleasant side effects of pregnancy – notably extreme tiredness and morning sickness – subside for most women. You may rediscover a level of energy and an appetite that you last experienced before you became pregnant. Your growing abdomen will become noticeable to others, and you may look up to six weeks more pregnant from now until the end of pregnancy than a woman carrying a singleton.

The volume of red blood cells increases sharply in the early part of the second trimester to catch up with the greater volume of plasma that occurred in the first trimester (this prevents you from becoming severely anaemic). Your kidneys are filtering an additional 500 ml of blood every minute (60 per cent higher than normal), and the additional blood flow to your skin, mucus membranes and organs means that you start to feel hotter than normal and to sweat more. Your uterus reaches your navel by the end of Week 17, whereas for a woman pregnant with a singleton this would not happen for another three weeks. You gain weight fast during this trimester because both babies are growing rapidly and the quantities of amniotic fluid are also increasing.

Your babies: Weeks 18–21

By Week 18 the babies' movements, though not conscious, are more co-ordinated and deliberate. The membranes between them (assuming they do not share the same amniotic sac) are clearly visible on an ultrasound scan by Week 20. Although they are very thin they are highly elastic and resistant, so when a baby kicks or stretches out, it will not be damaged. Much of the basic physical development is complete, although the brain continues to develop until birth, and the lungs, digestive, immune and central nervous systems still need to mature. The facial features are now fully defined. By the end of Week 21, each baby on average measures 17 cm in crown to rump length.

Ossification of the bones continues as calcium is deposited on the skeletal structure. As the central nervous system develops, the babies' movements become increasingly varied

and precise. As the babies grow, the head is more in proportion with the rest of the body, although it still makes up one-third of the total length. The lungs are not yet functioning (oxygen and nutrients are obtained via the umbilical cord and placenta) but they are filled with amniotic fluid, which is essential to their development.

The body is covered in thin downy hair called lanugo, which acts as an insulating layer until the babies have developed enough body fat to keep warm. Lanugo remains until around Week 36 (babies born prematurely are often still covered with it). It also helps the thick white coating, vernix caseosa, to remain on the babies' bodies during gestation. This waxy substance is secreted from the sebaceous glands during this trimester and coats the body so that the skin does not become waterlogged. Gradually, from Week 18, the babies will start to develop a very small, thin layer of fat under the skin, so that the red blood vessels, which until now had been very visible, will gradually become less so, and the skin will change from being translucent to reddish in appearance. Small amounts of insulating brown fat are also deposited around key areas, such as the nape of the neck and the kidneys.

The volume of amniotic fluid has increased by Week 20 to around 350 ml per baby is maintained at a constant temperature of 37.5°C, which is slightly higher than the mother's body temperature.

Your body: Weeks 18–21

You will start to feel your babies moving. At first, you may mistake the sensation for that of slight wind or unexplained flutterings in your abdomen, but within a few days, the movements will become more apparent and unmistakably those of your developing babies. Women with twins do not feel their babies moving any earlier than those pregnant with singletons; first-time mothers tend to feel their babies move a little later than those who have been pregnant before.

Many changes to your skin occur during the second trimester, most of which disappear after the birth. Fine lines may appear on your face, neck and chest. These are called 'spider naevi' and are the result of extra blood being pumped round your body. Pigmentation to your skin increases, and this is most noticeable in your nipples, areolae, moles and genitalia, which have all become darker. You may also notice a dark line running down your abdomen. Known as the 'linea nigra', this marks the place where the left and right abdominal muscles meet and, as they begin to separate to make way for your expanding uterus, the line will become more pronounced in appearance. Some women also notice patches of skin, often on their face, which are a different colour from their normal skin tone. These are called chloasma. In fair-skinned women,

the patches will be darker, and the reverse will be the case in darker-skinned women. The blue veins on your breasts, the result of the changes to your circulation, are more noticeable. Your hair is also glossy and thicker, because you lose less hair than you normally would (although you will lose the hair you should have lost during pregnancy once you have given birth). Your heart is pumping 7 litres of blood per minute, an increase in 2 litres from your pre-pregnancy state. The increase in blood flow and hormones, and the fact that you feel hotter than usual, mean that you will probably feel and look 'glowing' during the second trimester.

By the time you are twenty weeks pregnant, you may look as if your pregnancy is more advanced. Support tights will become essential, and you may need to wear a support belt around your abdomen for greater comfort. As the trimester progresses, you are likely to experience some of the later pregnancy side effects. They are extremely common (although that does not make them any less unpleasant) and are rarely a sign of something serious, although you should always discuss them with your doctor or midwife.

> ### DID YOU KNOW…?
> By Week 20, the amount of blood being pumped through your heart every minute has increased by 40 per cent.

Placenta praevia

It may be found from one of your ultrasound scans that your placenta (or one of them, if you have two separate placentas) is currently lying in the lower part of the uterus and is near or across the opening to the cervix. This is termed placenta praevia. The condition is more common with twin pregnancies because the placenta(s) covers more of the uterine wall than in a singleton pregnancy. You are also at greater risk of placenta praevia if you have scarring from previous uterine surgery (e.g. from a previous Caesarean section) or have fibroids (see p. 95).

If placenta praevia has been identified, your obstetrician will monitor the situation as your pregnancy progresses. Although it is seen in about one-third of pregnancies at this stage of gestation, only a small percentage of women still have a low-lying placenta by the time they give birth, because in the intervening weeks, the uterus has expanded and the placenta is now situated higher up. If your placenta is still blocking (or partially covering) the cervix nearer delivery, you will need to give birth by Caesarean section. See also p. 94 for bleeding caused by placenta praevia.

Abdominal and pelvic pain

As the uterus grows ever higher into your abdominal cavity, your ribs will begin to move sideways to make enough room; in addition, your abdominal and pelvic muscles and ligaments continue to stretch and loosen. The generalised aches and pains these movements cause continue through this part of the pregnancy, though often with greater frequency than during the first trimester. However, if you have persistent abdominal pain, you should be checked by your midwife.

If your pain is ongoing and more severe, you may be suffering from Pelvic Girdle Pain, also known as Symphysis Pubis Dysfunction. Pregnancy can affect the symphysis pubis joint at the front of the pelvis, as well as the sacroiliac joints in your lower back, causing throbbing or more intense pain in the pelvic region. Specific symptoms include:

▸ tenderness or pain in the pubic area
▸ lower back pain
▸ difficulty in walking, climbing stairs and turning over in bed
▸ a 'waddling' gait
▸ pain in the buttock and down one leg (similar to sciatica)
▸ feeling that a hip is 'out of place'.

While there is no cure for this painful condition, symptoms can be improved by physiotherapy and a specially designed exercise programme to help realign the pelvis and improve its stability (ask your doctor or midwife for a referral). Wearing a pregnancy support belt can also be of benefit. You should aim to keep mobile, but try to rest frequently. Avoid lifting heavy bags or pushing large objects (e.g. supermarket trolleys), climb stairs one at a time and, when getting dressed, put your tights, trousers and so on over your feet while sitting, before standing to pull them up.

Varicose veins

Bulging leg veins, or varicose veins, are extremely common during pregnancy as a result of the changes in your circulation and hormones, although a family history of varicose veins is a factor in whether or when you might develop them. Although they are not necessarily painful, varicose veins can be unsightly. Wear support tights and try to avoid standing or sitting still for long periods of time (pooling blood in your legs is a contributing cause). When sitting down, raise your legs up on to a support in front of you. Varicose veins usually improve after the birth, or disappear altogether, but in some women, the veins remain dilated and may need treatment at a later date.

Haemorrhoids

Haemorrhoids are, in effect, varicose veins in the anal and/or vulval area, and are often referred to as 'piles'. They are extremely common and can begin at any time during a pregnancy, caused by the pressure of the babies' weight in the pelvic area. Constipation can also contribute to these veins becoming dilated, so try to stay active, to eat a diet with sufficient fibre and to drink plenty of fluids to encourage regular bowel motions. Haemorrhoids can cause throbbing or itchiness in the affected area, but over-the-counter creams or ointments can relieve these symptoms.

Leg cramps

Many women find that they are woken during the night by leg cramps. It is not known why these occur, but they are not a sign of anything serious. Simply try to stretch out the affected leg and flex the foot so that it is at a right angle to your calf. If necessary, massage the area until the problem goes away.

Stretch marks

Stretch marks are caused by the collagen under the skin tearing as it expands. They can appear on your breasts, abdomen, thighs and buttocks and initially are reddish in colour. With time, however, they fade to a silvery white colour that is less noticeable. It is still not really known why some women get stretch marks and others do not. There is a strong genetic element that determines whether they appear and how extensively, but being pregnant with twins also makes their appearance more likely. The gradual loss of elasticity in skin as we age probably means that older mothers are more affected than younger ones. Creams and oils that allegedly prevent stretch marks are unlikely to work, simply because they cannot penetrate effectively into the layers of collagen deep beneath your skin.

Your babies: Weeks 22-25

There starts to be a little less space for the babies to move around in, but they are increasingly active, stretching out their limbs and grasping anything that comes within their reach, such as the umbilical cord or their other hand. Fingernails and fingerprints (see Box below) are fully formed, the eyelids have opened, and, although the babies have no conscious thoughts at this stage, their brainwaves are similar to those of a newborn baby born at 40 weeks of gestation. The brain continues to develop, however, while the heart rate has slowed down and, by the end of this trimester, it will beat at 140–150 beats per minute. Small amounts of fat continue to be deposited beneath the skin.

The weight gain of twins progressively slows down relative to a singleton's, so that at the end of this trimester, there is still very little difference in weight between a singleton baby and twins. The volume of amniotic fluid has reached approximately 500 ml per amniotic sac.

FINGERPRINTS IN MONOZYGOTIC TWINS

Monozygotic twins are, by definition, virtually genetically identical (they have the same DNA), but each twin will have their own unique set of fingerprints. This is partly because DNA does not make a perfect copy of itself each time it divides – in replicating from a single cell to the vast number of cells required to create a human being, there will be tiny mutations along the way. More significantly, fingerprints are not solely a genetic characteristic: the developmental environment in the uterus is a factor, too. For example, the position of each fetus in the uterus, the amount of blood and nutrients received by each (which depends on the length and diameter of the umbilical cords) and the rate of growth of the fingers in the first trimester all play a part in creating the final shape of the fingerprints. So, although the fingerprints of monozygotic twins will be more alike than those of unrelated people, with similar whorls, ridges and loops, it is still possible to spot differences.

Your body: Weeks 22-25

You will notice your babies moving every day, although you may not be able to tell which is which, nor which body part you can feel. You may also notice that the babies are quieter at certain times of the day and more active at others, or move if you are in a certain position. Over time you may notice some sort of pattern to the movements, though do not worry if this is not apparent because each pregnancy is different and it can be hard to notice what each individual baby is doing. If you feel no movements over a 24-hour period, or if the pattern of movements feels abnormal, contact your hospital at once.

Back pain and sciatica

Back pain may become more of a problem at this stage. It may also change from being generalised lower backache to a more specific pain in one area of your back. The weight of the babies can compress the sciatic nerve, which runs from the spinal cord down through the back of the leg, leading to a painful condition called sciatica. Symptoms of sciatica include a sharp pain in the lower back, buttocks and/or one or both legs; you may also experience tingling or numbness in these areas.

You should always discuss your symptoms with your doctor so that your particular problem can be correctly diagnosed. Specific exercises, such as stretching and pelvic tilts, can alleviate backache or prevent it from becoming worse and you should take as much care as possible to protect your back when moving around (see Chapter 2 p. 39 for suitable exercises and advice on back care and posture). A warm bath can also relieve generalised lower back pain. Some osteopaths are experienced in dealing with pregnancy-related back pain, so you could ask your doctor if they could recommend a good practitioner (who must be registered on the national register – see Useful Resources). A skilled osteopath never does any manipulation of the spine on a pregnant woman, but will relieve symptoms using massage.

Heart palpitations

The hormonal changes that occur during pregnancy frequently cause palpitations. These are heartbeats that are irregular and therefore more noticeable, and which feel like a fluttering or pounding in your chest. Palpitations can occur at any time in the pregnancy and, while they may be alarming, they are unlikely to be a sign that anything is wrong with your heart and will disappear after the birth. However, if these temporary disturbances of rhythm are also accompanied by chest pain, breathlessness or dizziness, then you should see your doctor or midwife to rule out anything more serious.

Digestive problems

While difficulties with digestion can begin at any stage in pregnancy, they usually start during the second trimester. The pregnancy hormones, notably progesterone, that are responsible for relaxing your muscles also leave your digestive system working more sluggishly. This means that food stays in your stomach for longer, giving you indigestion and a feeling of heaviness. This can cause constipation and bloating. The sphincter at the top of your stomach is also more relaxed, so gastric juices can escape back up into your oesophagus, resulting in heartburn. Indigestion and heartburn are especially acute towards the latter stages of pregnancy, when your uterus is compressing all your internal organs and considerably reducing your stomach capacity. There are various ways in which you can reduce problems with digestion. For indigestion and heartburn:

▸ eat little and often
▸ avoid fatty, spicy, rich or acidic foods
▸ eat bland, starchy, easy-to-digest foods
▸ drink semi-skimmed or skimmed milk before or in between meals to neutralise stomach acid

▸ when lying down, raise your head up with an extra pillow to prevent acid juices flowing back up into the oesophagus
▸ avoid lying down/sleeping for two hours after a meal.

If your heartburn is affecting you badly, your doctor can prescribe antacid medication that is safe to take during pregnancy. There are also some simple remedies for constipation:

▸ increase your intake of high-fibre foods, such as fruit and vegetables, certain cereals, brown rice and wholegrain bread
▸ try to keep exercising or moving around (swimming is excellent in later pregnancy as it puts no pressure on your abdomen or lower limbs)
▸ drink 2 litres of fluid a day – water and herbal teas are best (avoid diuretic drinks, such as coffee, tea or colas).

Again, if your constipation makes you uncomfortable, ask your midwife to suggest or prescribe suitable laxatives.

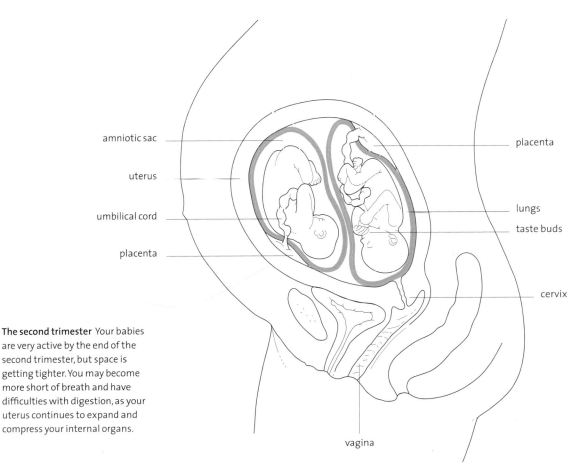

amniotic sac

uterus

umbilical cord

placenta

placenta

lungs

taste buds

cervix

vagina

The second trimester Your babies are very active by the end of the second trimester, but space is getting tighter. You may become more short of breath and have difficulties with digestion, as your uterus continues to expand and compress your internal organs.

Third trimester: timeline of key events

Week 27

Resting or active periods more noticeable, though those of one baby may not coincide with the other's.

Week 29

Lungs maturing continuously: bronchioles in place, alveoli forming fast, production of surfactant starts.

Week 31

Scalp hair fuller. Lanugo starts to thin out.

Week 28

Skin creases on hands appear. Eyes can blink.

Week 30

Crown to rump length 28 cm. Testes descend in male babies.

WEEK 26 27 28 29 30 31

Week 26

Blood pressure starts to rise very gradually until last four weeks of gestation. Belly button may invert. Braxton Hicks contractions may start.

Week 30

Colostrum may start to leak from breasts.

MOTHER

Week 34
Lungs mature enough for many babies born now to breathe unaided. Face less wrinkly. More fat on body.

Week 36
Heart beats at 110–150 beats per minute. Most vernix caseosa disappears. Have developed ability to suck. Head of presenting baby starts to descend into pelvic cavity (especially in first pregnancies).

Week 33
Organs are mature, except lungs.

Week 35
Crown to rump length 32 cm. Volume of amniotic fluid peaks.

Week 37
Babies move less because space is very tight. Lanugo has virtually disappeared.

32 **33** **34** **35** **36** **37**

Week 34
Breathlessness at its maximum.

Week 36
Once first baby's head is engaged, breathing and digestion may ease a little. Blood flow to uterus ten times that of when not pregnant.

Week 32
Sleeping now more difficult. Need to urinate frequently.

Week 37
If babies not delivered, Braxton Hicks 'practice' contractions are common.

Reaching the third trimester feels like a significant milestone in your pregnancy, the final leg of your journey. This is especially so with twin pregnancies, which are generally delivered by 37–8 weeks if labour has not begun spontaneously before then.

Your babies: *Weeks 26–29*

From Week 26 the weight gain of a twin pregnancy will begin to differ from that of a singleton. This is because a woman's body is able to support twins in the same way as a single baby only up until this stage. The difference becomes increasingly marked as the third trimester progresses and from Week 28 the growth rate of twins gets progressively slower compared to that of singletons. Twins also start to lack space in the uterus and this can also restrict their growth. See p. 97 for more information on intra-uterine growth restriction (IUGR).

The babies are nonetheless developing continuously. The skin contains more pigments, and the hair is thickening and growing. Babies now respond to external sounds and, for example, will wake or move when they hear outside noise or music. They have more distinct resting and active periods, too, although one baby's pattern will not necessarily be the same as the other's. By Week 28 the hands have skin creases and the eyes can blink.

The lungs are maturing throughout this time. By Week 29, bronchioles are in place, alveoli are forming, and the lungs start to produce a substance called surfactant, which provides elasticity and allows them to expand and contract when oxygen is breathed in and out. The quantities of surfactant that are initially produced are not sufficient for babies who are born at this stage to breathe unaided, but the amount will gradually increase over the next few weeks as the lungs continue to mature. The lungs continue their development throughout the childhood years, which is why respiratory problems such as asthma often improve significantly or disappear altogether by the time children are in their teens.

Your body: *Weeks 26–29*

As your abdomen grows you will need to urinate more frequently and may find that when you laugh, sneeze or cough, you leak a small amount of urine. This is called 'stress incontinence' and is caused by the pressure on the bladder, which in turn stretches and puts pressure on the pelvic floor muscles. Regular pelvic floor exercises (*see* Chapter 7, p. 203) will help to strengthen and protect these muscles. Urinary infections are common in the third trimester, although you do not always have obvious symptoms. However, if you do develop any pain or a stinging sensation when passing urine, or if there is any blood in it, consult your doctor, as you may need to take antibiotics to treat the infection. Back problems may be increasing, as may the discomfort in the ribcage that you might have experienced in the previous trimester. Anaemia is also common during the third trimester (*see* p. 94), which is why your blood will be tested at 28 weeks.

Braxton Hicks contractions

You may start to feel occasional tightenings in your abdominal area. These are known as Braxton Hicks contractions and are thought to be part of the body's preparation for the birth. The uterine muscles transiently tighten, causing your abdomen to feel hard to the touch. These 'practice' contractions are very irregular and usually painless, if occasionally a little uncomfortable. They tend to be fairly frequent in twin pregnancies and will increase as your due date approaches – by the end of your pregnancy, you may experience several episodes a day. There is no particular pattern to the contractions, unlike those during labour, which occur at regular intervals, however far they may be spaced out. If you start to experience more than four Braxton Hicks contractions an hour, however, you should call your midwife or the hospital to check whether this is an early sign of labour.

Fluid retention and carpal tunnel syndrome

Your body is retaining fluid as a natural part of the physical processes that take place during pregnancy. As a result, your hands, feet or ankles may start to swell up – your midwife will check them at every antenatal appointment to ensure that any puffiness is within the normal limits. Any sudden or significant swelling, however, should be checked promptly by your doctor or obstetrician, as this can be an early sign that you are developing pre-eclampsia (*see* p. 95).

Additional fluid caused by water retention can compress the nerves and ligaments in the wrists, causing symptoms of tingliness or even numbness in the fingers or hands. This is called 'carpal tunnel syndrome' and it will disappear at birth when fluid retention ceases. In the meantime, if symptoms are very bad, your doctor can prescribe a splint for you to wear around your wrists.

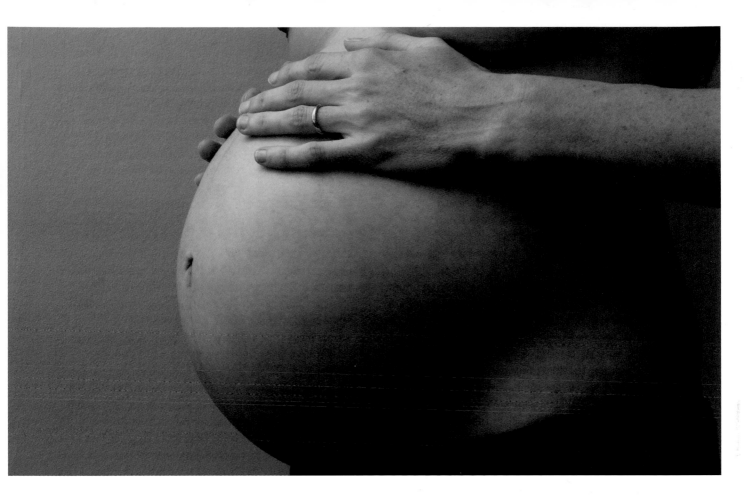

Thrush

From time to time, many women experience the vaginal fungal infection known as thrush, and it is extremely common in pregnancy due to the decreased acidity of the vaginal fluids. Symptoms include itchiness in the vaginal area and a vaginal discharge that changes from its normal clear, mucus-like appearance to a thicker, whiter, curd-like one. Episodes of thrush can be avoided or reduced by limiting your intake of sugary or yeast-based foods, by wearing cotton underwear and by avoiding tight trousers or nylon tights, which prevent air from circulating in the area. You can buy over-the-counter creams and pessaries, which together will treat the fungal infection, but remember also to keep the vaginal area as clean as possible and to wipe yourself from front to back. If at any stage, your discharge develops a strong smell, a greenish/ yellow colour and/or the vaginal area becomes red and sore, consult your doctor as you may have developed another type of vaginal infection. These can cause premature labour, so it is important you are treated promptly.

Protruding belly button

Women often find that their belly button turns outwards during the third trimester, and is sometimes even visible through clothes. This is only a temporary situation, and after the birth, your belly button will revert back to its normal, pre-pregnancy state. However, if you have a pierced belly button, remove any rings or jewellery so that they do not get caught on clothing.

Your Babies: Weeks 30–33

By week 30, the testes descend. There is less space inside the uterus, so although your babies' movements remain regular, they are less strong than during the second trimester. Nonetheless, if the movements change and you are concerned, you should alert the hospital at once.

The babies are gradually putting down layers of fat beneath the skin and gaining weight. Lanugo, the very fine downy hair that covers their body, is still there, but by the time the babies reach their final month, it has started to thin out. The hair on the scalp, however is fuller. At Week 30, the crown to rump length is 28 cm. The organs, with the exception of the lungs, are now fully functioning. By the end of Week 33, however, the lungs have matured sufficiently that many babies born at this stage are able to breathe unaided, or require only a few days' ventilation (*see* Chapter 6, p. 138 and 141).

Your body: Weeks 30–33

Your continually expanding uterus is pushing up your diaphragm, causing a reduction in your lung capacity. This may make you feel breathless, so try not to over-exert yourself at this time. In addition, you may find that you are not sleeping so well, as your growing abdomen makes it more difficult to find a comfortable position. Lying on your back is no longer recommended, because the weight of the uterus can compress the major veins transporting blood back to your heart (*see* Chapter 2, p. 36). Lying on your side is the best option, and many women find that placing a pillow or a folded spare duvet under their abdomen and between their legs makes this position more comfortable.

Colostrum, the nutrient-rich liquid that precedes breast milk, may start to leak from your breasts. Your blood volume reaches its maximum by this stage of pregnancy. It is now just under 9 litres, approximately 75 per cent more than in your pre-pregnancy state. Not surprisingly, your blood pressure rises a little during the third trimester to accommodate this final increase. However, any sudden rise will be investigated and monitored by your healthcare professionals in case it is a sign of hypertension or of pre-eclampsia (*see* p. 95).

Skin rashes

Skin problems often occur during the later stages of pregnancy. You will tend to sweat more as you get larger and hotter, and this can cause rashes, particularly in any folds or where clothing rubs against your skin. Rashes can also occur if the skin becomes too dry and flaky, another common side effect of pregnancy. In both cases, avoid using perfumed soaps, gels and creams, and use fragrance-free, emollient products. Keep your skin clean and dry, and exposed to fresh air where possible, so that any sweat can evaporate. Consult your doctor if the rash becomes uncomfortable. If, however, your itching suddenly becomes severe (at any time in the pregnancy), see your doctor without delay, as you may have obstetric cholestasis (*see* p. 94).

Sex

Even in late pregnancy, sex is still perfectly safe for the majority of women, and will not trigger labour. However, if you have a history of premature delivery, threatened premature labour or later pregnancy bleeding, or if you have placenta praevia (*see* p. 94), you should avoid penetrative sex.

Your bump will be so large that some of your usual positions may no longer be possible, so you will have to find new ones. It is common for a couple's sex life to change at this stage: you might be tired and feel uncomfortable when lying down, and your partner may be concerned about hurting either you or the babies. Try to reassure each other that this is not a lack of desire for the other person, but is simply a reflection of other emotions, feelings and physical situations. And as well as communicating verbally, try to stay connected physically with the help of plenty of kissing, touching, caressing or cuddling, so that you maintain a closeness and bond even if you are not having sexual intercourse.

Your babies: Weeks 34–37

Although weight gain continues until birth, twins born at 37 weeks will, on average, weigh 2.5 kg, about 800 g less than a singleton born at 40 weeks. This is partly due to the extra time that singletons usually have to grow, and partly to the lack of space in the uterus and the dwindling ability of the placenta(s) to nourish more than one baby. The heart beats at 110–150 beats per minute.

At Week 35, the babies measure 32 cm crown to rump, there is more fat on the body and, as a result, the face has become less crinkly. Space is now so restricted that the babies are unlikely to change positions from now on. One twin will be lower down than the other inside the uterine cavity, and this baby is referred to as the 'presenting twin' (this is not necessarily 'Twin A/1' as described in your antenatal notes). See Chapter 5, p. 107 for more details on presentation. Lanugo is less visible now, as is the vernix caseosa. Should the babies be born now, they will in all likelihood be able to breathe unaided, and those born after Week 36 will have the ability to suck.

The volume of amniotic fluid peaks at Week 35 and then starts to decline slowly until the birth. The placenta(s) will be providing the maximum amount of nutrition, oxygen and support to your babies by Week 35. After that time, its ability to support the pregnancy slowly starts to reduce, so that from Week 38 it is working much less effectively, increasing the risk of fetal death. This is why a twin pregnancy is rarely allowed to continue after 38+0 weeks.

Your body: Weeks 34–37

The blood flow to your uterus is now ten times that of its non-pregnant state. If you have been experiencing Braxton Hicks contractions, they are likely to be much more frequent now. If they are occurring more than four times per hour, or are becoming uncomfortable, you should contact your hospital to see if you are going into labour.

If one of the babies is positioned with its head down, the head may start to descend into your pelvic cavity in readiness for labour – this means the head is becoming 'engaged' (*see* Box right). Engagement creates space higher up in your abdominal cavity, and so you may notice that your breathing and digestion become slightly easier as a result.

ENGAGEMENT

The descent of a baby's head into the pelvic cavity is called 'engagement' and usually happens from around Week 36 in first pregnancies. It occurs later – and sometimes not at all – in subsequent pregnancies because the muscles of the uterus are looser than they once were, which means they exert less downward pressure on the baby. There are various levels of engagement, which are determined by abdominal palpation, and these will be noted in your medical notes as follows:

- ▸ High/Fr (free): not engaged
- ▸ NE/Neng: more than half the baby's head is above the pubic bone
- ▸ E/Eng: less than half of the head is above the pubic bone (i.e. the head is engaged).

Not engaged More than half the presenting baby's head is above the pelvis brim, so it is 'not engaged'.

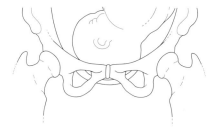

Engaged When more than half the presenting baby's head has descended into the pelvic cavity, the baby is 'engaged'.

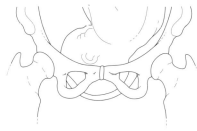

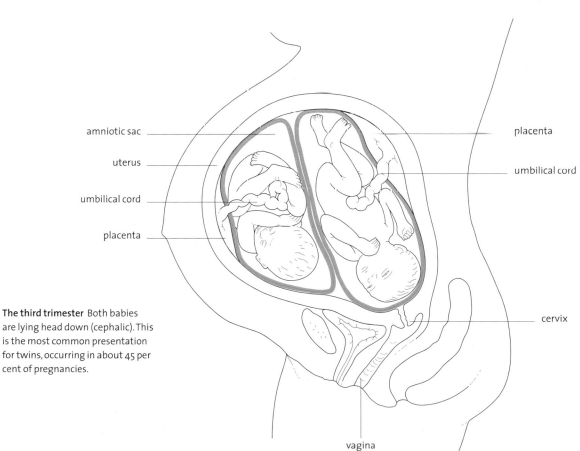

amniotic sac

uterus

umbilical cord

placenta

placenta

umbilical cord

cervix

The third trimester Both babies are lying head down (cephalic). This is the most common presentation for twins, occurring in about 45 per cent of pregnancies.

vagina

HEALTH COMPLICATIONS

Many women expecting twins have a healthy pregnancy. However, as twin pregnancies are considered high risk, you will need to be aware of the possible complications, and you and your growing babies will be monitored carefully throughout.

For mothers

Ectopic pregnancy

When an embryo implants outside the uterus it is known as an ectopic pregnancy. It is most likely to be detected between Weeks 6 and 10, although it is very rare (affecting one per cent of pregnancies) and may even happen before you know you are pregnant. It can cause a range of symptoms, with varying degrees of intensity:

- ▶ vaginal bleeding
- ▶ diarrhoea, feeling faint, pain on passing stools
- ▶ shoulder-tip pain, a referred pain caused by blood leaking into the abdomen
- ▶ pain on one side of the lower abdomen, either developing sharply or slowly getting worse.

You should always see your doctor if you have any of these symptoms, so that it can be properly diagnosed and treated. Treatment can be in the form of medication to stop the egg growing or surgery to remove it. If abdominal pain is severe, it may be caused by a ruptured Fallopian tube (the site of implantation), resulting in sudden and heavy internal bleeding. This is life-threatening and you should call an ambulance immediately, as emergency surgery is needed.

Anaemia

Anaemia occurs when the plasma (the fluid element of your blood) increases beyond its normal proportions to the red blood cell count. Red blood cells carry oxygen and other nutrients (including iron). Therefore, if your blood is too dilute, fewer cells (and nutrients) will be present. Anaemia is common in women expecting twins and it is important that it is detected, as it can lead to complications in the pregnancy, depending on the severity. You should be tested for anaemia once during your second trimester (at 20–24 weeks) and again in your third (at 28 weeks).

Symptoms of anaemia include extreme tiredness, lethargy and pallor, as well as dizziness or light-headedness. These can often be mistaken for normal symptoms of later pregnancy, hence the need for formal testing. If anaemia is diagnosed, you will be prescribed iron supplements, usually in pill form, but if your anaemia is severe, injections may be required. Try also to eat iron-rich and folic acid-rich foods (see Chapter 2, p. 33). A small number of women do not respond to iron and folic acid replacement, and so will require specialist investigation and treatment. Anaemia is rarely harmful to the babies (other than in extreme cases), as they will continue to draw on your reserves.

Placenta praevia

About twenty per cent of bleeding before delivery is caused by placenta praevia. The bleeding is painless and varies in severity, but you should call the labour ward at once so that they can advise you what to do. Although this type of bleeding does not immediately affect your babies, they may need to be delivered promptly by Caesarean section.

Placental abruption

This occurs when part (or, in extreme cases, all) of the placenta comes away from the uterine wall. Depending on the severity of the abruption, the amount of bleeding can vary. It can be accompanied (though is not always) by acute pain in a specific area of the uterus, or by a more generalised pain in the abdominal area. This very serious condition is more common in women who have high blood pressure or who smoke, but it can also happen to those who have no obvious risk. You must be admitted to hospital as an emergency (do not attempt to drive yourself: call an ambulance), after which doctors will assess the severity of the condition. Sometimes the bleeding subsides on its own after a period of complete bed rest. On other occasions, a decision is made to deliver the babies at once by Caesarean section.

Obstetric cholestasis

While itchy skin is a common side effect of pregnancy (see p. 92), severe itching, especially on the hands and feet, may be a sign of obstetric cholestasis, a rare liver condition that is potentially very serious for you and your babies. If it is diagnosed promptly and they are delivered in time, the babies will not be affected. After the birth, the condition will resolve itself without complications or the need for further treatment.

Incompetent cervix

The cervix normally remains tightly closed until labour is due to begin. However, in some women the cervix is abnormally weak and starts to open earlier in the pregnancy, leading to miscarriage or premature birth. This condition is known as an incompetent cervix and usually happens in the second trimester when the pressure exerted by the babies on the cervix becomes greater. If you have lost several previous pregnancies in the second trimester, an incompetent cervix may be suspected. The evaluation, investigation and treatment of such cases in a twin pregnancy involves very specialist management and will be discussed with you.

Fibroids

Benign uterine growths, or fibroids, are very common, especially among older women. Hormones present during pregnancy can cause them to increase in size, reducing the space in the uterus for the babies to grow. This can sometimes lead to intra-uterine growth restriction (*see* p. 97) or causes the babies to find a less than ideal position (or 'lie' – *see* Chapter 5, p. 107) in the womb. Alternatively, fibroids sometimes outgrow their blood supply and begin to degenerate, and this can trigger premature labour. If fibroids are diagnosed, your healthcare professionals will monitor them as your pregnancy progresses.

Gestational hypertension

Blood pressure that rises for the first time after the twentieth week of pregnancy to more than 140/90 is known as gestational hypertension. Left undiagnosed, it can result in serious problems in the pregnancy and increase your lifelong cardiovascular risk. Once hypertension has been detected, your blood pressure will be measured more regularly and your urine tested for protein (a sign of pre-eclampsia – *see* below) at each visit. Depending on the severity of your condition, you may be given drugs to lower your blood pressure and a blood test to monitor for pre-eclampsia and detect any other problems. If your blood pressure is very high, you may be admitted to hospital for more continuous monitoring and observation.

Pre-eclampsia

Hypertension combined with other signs and symptoms is an indication of pre-eclampsia. These symptoms include:

▸ sudden swelling of the face, hands/fingers, feet/legs (as opposed to the gradual, more generalised puffiness)
▸ vomiting
▸ severe stomach pain
▸ unexplained headaches and blurred or disturbed vision
▸ protein in the urine.

The risks of pre-eclampsia are serious and, for the mother, include increased incidence of a stroke, damage to kidneys and liver, severe placental bleeding, blood-clotting difficulties and development of eclampsia (*see* below). For the babies, it can result in poor growth in the womb, premature birth and stillbirth. Pre-eclampsia is more common in multiple pregnancies (affecting around one in three), first pregnancies, women whose previous pregnancy was more than ten years ago, women over the age of 35, or those who are overweight, have diabetes or pre-existing high blood pressure.

There is no specific treatment that can be given for pre-eclampsia other than delivering the babies, although women at risk may be offered a low dose of aspirin (75 mg per day). If your case is mild, you may be allowed to continue your pregnancy for a little while longer. You and your babies will be closely monitored in the meantime. However, if the situation is more serious, your babies will be delivered by Caesarean section. Once the babies are born, your blood pressure will return to its pre-pregnancy level.

Eclampsia

If left untreated, pre-eclampsia may develop into eclampsia. As a result of high blood pressure, blood vessels go into spasm, leading to brain seizure. The outcome can be fatal for both the mother and her babies. Emergency treatment is required to save the mother's life, and immediate delivery of the babies takes place via Caesarean section. Fortunately, midwives and doctors are very aware of any signs of pre-eclampsia, and so eclampsia itself is now rare.

Gestational diabetes

The onset of diabetes in pregnancy is known as gestational diabetes, and usually begins during the second trimester. With type I or type II diabetes (*see* p. 96), the pancreas does not produce enough insulin to metabolise the glucose (sugar) in the blood. With gestational diabetes, the placenta produces hormones that neutralise insulin, with the result that your blood sugar levels start to rise.

Gestational diabetes is more likely to occur if a woman is obese (*see* p. 71), over the age of 30, or has had the condition in a previous pregnancy. Overall, around twelve per cent of women carrying multiples develop gestational diabetes. The health risks for you and your babies include:

▸ high blood pressure and pre-eclampsia
▸ miscarriage, stillbirth and fetal abnormalities
▸ problems with the babies' growth
▸ excessive amniotic fluid around the babies (polyhydramnios –*see* p. 97).

Although the sugar levels in your urine are tested regularly, other signs that you may be developing gestational diabetes include abnormal levels of thirst and the need to urinate even more frequently than you were experiencing earlier in your pregnancy. If the level of sugar in your urine is raised, you will be advised to reduce your intake of sugary foods, to eat a healthy diet and to take gentle exercise. If it is still high the next time your urine is tested, you will be asked to do a glucose tolerance test to see how well you are able to metabolise sugar. If, after this, you are diagnosed with gestational diabetes, a dietician, midwife and specialist doctors will ensure that you are given the right advice and medical care to maximise the chances of a successful outcome for your pregnancy. Your babies' development will also be monitored closely using ultrasound scans to ensure they are growing at the right rate. Fortunately, with correct dietary control of blood sugar levels, a woman with diabetes or gestational diabetes is often able to carry her babies to 37 weeks with no adverse effect, although daily insulin injections may sometimes be necessary. Gestational diabetes disappears as soon as the babies are delivered, although you have a 50 per cent chance of developing diabetes yourself in subsequent years.

Pre-existing diabetes

If you suffered from diabetes (type I or type II) before you were pregnant, you will be monitored closely throughout your pregnancy and may need specialist medical help. As the pregnancy reaches an advanced stage and sugar levels become more difficult to control, it is often considered safer for your health and that of your babies to have an elective (planned) Caesarean delivery.

For babies

Monochorionic twin pregnancies

Twin pregnancies in which the babies share a placenta are known as monochorionic (*see* Chapter 1, p. 18 for further information). Monochorionic (MC) pregnancies are known to present higher risks than dichorionic ones. The greatest risk is the loss of a baby before 24 weeks gestation, most often caused by Twin-to-Twin Transfusion Syndrome (*see* right). There are also potentially serious problems for the surviving twin if one baby dies during the second or third trimester. Labour and birth carry greater risks with MC pregnancies, and you are more likely to be advised to have a Caesarean section (*see* Chapter 5, p. 106).

For the one per cent of MC pregancies that are also monoamniotic, the risk of complications is higher because the babies share the same amniotic sac as well as the same placenta. In addition to the risks discussed for MC pregnancies,

there is a high likelihood of the umbilical cords becoming entangled at some stage during the pregnancy, which may lead to fetal death.

Twin-to-twin Transfusion Syndrome (TTTS)

Monochorionic pregnancies are sometimes subject to problems caused by the blood vessels linking the two fetuses within the placenta. Since the babies share the placenta and circulatory systems, this can lead to an unbalanced blood flow between the two. The result is that one twin (the donor) receives insufficient amounts of blood from the placenta, develops low amniotic fluid levels (oligohydramnios, *see* opposite) and suffers from growth restriction; the other twin (the recipient) develops an excessive amount of amniotic fluid (polyhydramnios) and develops increased pressure within the heart, causing 'overload' of its circulatory system. Spontaneous premature labour can occur as a result of the increased volume of amniotic fluid and, depending on gestation and the severity of the condition, shifts in blood pressure and flow to the brain may lead to neurological problems in one or both twins. Miscarriage and stillbirth are also common if TTTS is unrecognised and untreated. TTTS arises in around fifteen per cent of monochorionic diamniotic pregnancies and accounts for around one in six of all perinatal deaths (deaths occurring just before or soon after birth).

If yours is a monochorionic pregnancy, you will be monitored for TTTS using ultrasound scanning at least every two weeks from sixteen weeks until 24 weeks gestation, after which it is rare for the condition to begin. The first sign that you may be developing TTTS is usually a discrepancy in the amniotic fluid volume contained in each amniotic sac, noted on the ultrasound scan. If your doctors suspect TTTS might be the cause, you will be referred to a specialist fetal medicine unit for treatment and monitoring on a weekly basis.

Treatment for the condition is complex, so will be carried out only in severe cases and by a highly skilled team based in a centre specialising in invasive fetal medicine. It often involves laser ablation (precision cutting or burning with an intense

DID YOU KNOW...?

If yours is a monochorionic pregnancy, consult your midwife or doctor immediately if you notice a sudden increase in the size of your abdomen. This is due to a change in the amount of amniotic fluid and is a symptom of TTTS.

beam of light) of the relevant placental blood vessels, directed by a fetoscope inserted through the mother's abdomen. There is a risk that the treatment will be unsuccessful, that one or both twins may not survive, or that they develop serious abnormalities in their heart and/or nervous system. However, in the majority of cases there is a successful outcome in both or one of the babies.

Uncomplicated monochorionic twins may be delivered at 36 weeks to avoid the risk of acute changes in blood pressure and blood flow between the babies. The options will be carefully explained to you in terms of the risks and benefits to your babies' health, so that you are able to make the decision that you feel is right for them.

Intra-Uterine Growth Restriction

Intra-uterine growth restriction (IUGR) is where a baby's growth in the womb slows from its normal rate or, in rarer cases, stops altogether. (It therefore becomes smaller than expected for its gestational age, or SGA – see Chapter 6, Box on p.139.) This condition affects around ten per cent of pregnancies, and is as common in monochorionic pregnancies as in dichorionic ones. IUGR can arise as a result of a variety of factors, including smoking and excessive alcohol intake by the mother (reducing good placental development and blood supply to the babies). However, it most frequently occurs because of increasing placental insufficiency as the pregnancy progresses, resulting in the baby/babies receiving poor levels of oxygen and nutrients. IUGR usually affects one baby only and may be accompanied by low amniotic fluid volume (oligohydramnios – see right) for the smaller baby. Decisions in the management of the pregnancy have to be made on an individual basis and may be complex, particularly in cases of monochorionic twins. As this baby is more likely to experience distress during labour, a Caesarean section is often advisable.

Regular ultrasound scanning from twenty weeks onwards will check for any signs of IUGR, and will enable your doctors to estimate the weight of each baby. If there is a difference of 25 per cent or more in the size and estimated weight of each baby, you will be referred to a fetal medicine unit for further assessment and management of your pregnancy. If IUGR is diagnosed, you will be scanned more regularly and your babies' progress carefully monitored (this may require referral to a fetal medicine unit). It may be that, at some stage in your pregnancy, your doctors decide that it is better to deliver them sooner rather than later, because the benefits of an early birth outweigh those of continuing to stay in the womb. All options will be carefully considered and discussed with you before any decision is made. Babies with IUGR are more likely to suffer from health complications after birth. Most, however, catch up quickly in terms of growth, unless they are suffering from another underlying condition, are premature or are extremely small for dates.

Polyhydramnios and oligohydramnios

Polyhydramnios is an excess of amniotic fluid surrounding one or both babies, and is diagnosed during routine ultrasound scans. This condition can arise for a variety of reasons:

▶ In a monochorionic pregnancy, the presence of TTTS results in a larger amount of amniotic fluid for one baby.
▶ Poorly controlled diabetes/gestational diabetes in the mother causes the baby/babies to produce large amounts of urine.
▶ A congenital abnormality prevents the baby/babies from swallowing or absorbing the fluid.

Sometimes there is no obvious cause of polyhydramnios, but if the problem is severe, it can lead to premature labour, so fluid may need to be drained from the amniotic sac in order to relieve the pressure on the uterus.

Oligohydramnios is the term for an insufficient amount of amniotic fluid surrounding a baby. It can be a sign of IUGR, or, if polyhydramnios is present for the other baby, an indication of TTTS in monochorionic pregnancies. You are likely to be referred to a specialist fetal medicine unit for further investigation and assessment. Frequent monitoring of fetal growth and amniotic fluid can indicate the best time to deliver the babies.

Miscarriage and stillbirth

In the UK, a miscarriage is defined as the loss of a pregnancy before 24 weeks. You will also hear or read the term 'abortion' when referring to this kind of loss. Miscarriage happens most frequently in the first trimester – 75 per cent occur before twelve weeks. This is termed 'early' miscarriage. The loss of a pregnancy between thirteen and 24 weeks is called a 'late' miscarriage. A baby who has died in the womb after 24 weeks is known as an 'intra-uterine death' and recorded as a 'stillbirth'.

Whatever your particular situation, miscarriage and stillbirth are immensely distressing, but there are organisations that can help you come to terms with your loss (see Useful Resources). In addition, you may find reading about bereavement in Chapter 6, p. 150 helpful.

Although miscarriage is the most common complication of pregnancy, the exact number per year is unknown. This is because the miscarriage happened so early that the woman did not realise that she was pregnant, and so it is not recorded in any data. Nevertheless, it is thought that fifteen to twenty per cent of pregnancies end in miscarriage, mostly before twelve weeks of gestation. There are many causes of miscarriage and stillbirth, some pertaining to the underlying health of the mother, others due to abnormalities in the baby/babies. Multiple pregnancies have a higher risk, and greater maternal age is also a factor; stillbirths are more common in males and among babies that are small for gestational age (see Chapter 6, Box on p. 139). However, many miscarriages and stillbirths remain unexplained and more research is still needed before the reasons can be fully understood.

Early miscarriage of pregnancy

About two-thirds of early miscarriages occur because the babies had a chromosomal defect that was incompatible with life. This type of miscarriage is more likely to be a 'one-off' (unless you and your partner are carriers of a particular genetic abnormality), and most women go on to have successful subsequent pregnancies. See Chapter 3, p. 60 for more on congenital abnormalities.

Miscarriages in the first few weeks of pregnancy resemble a late, slightly heavier period. Towards the end of the first trimester, the bleeding that occurs during a miscarriage may be accompanied by abdominal pain or cramping. Occasionally, women have no symptoms at all and only discover at their first ultrasound scan that their babies have died. This is known as a 'missed' or 'delayed' miscarriage.

If you have any bleeding or cramping, you will be referred to your nearest Early Pregnancy Unit for assessment. An ultrasound is often used to confirm whether a miscarriage is taking place. It can also reveal whether your miscarriage is 'complete', meaning that your uterus has expelled all the pregnancy tissues. If it shows that the babies have died but a miscarriage has not yet begun, or that the miscarriage is 'incomplete' (i.e. some tissues have remained), then you will be advised on the best course of treatment. It is important that all tissues from the pregnancy are removed in order to avoid infection and haemorrhage. In many cases, bleeding will begin naturally in time, but you may be offered tablets or pessaries to open the cervix and start the process. If the tissues have not been completely expelled after three weeks of bleeding (occurring in fifteen per cent of cases), they may need to be removed surgically under general anaesthesia.

Late miscarriage of pregnancy

Miscarriage after twelve weeks is relatively rare. Miscarriages at this time are more likely to be caused by blood disorders, a structural problem with the umbilical cord, placenta, uterus or cervix, or can be the result of an infection or severe food poisoning, such as salmonella or listeria (see Chapter 2, p. 34).

The physical symptoms of late miscarriage can be the same as those of early miscarriage (see above) or, if your pregnancy is more advanced, you may experience a rupture of membranes (waters breaking) and contractions similar to going into labour. As with early miscarriage, there may be no symptoms at all and you may discover that both of your babies have died only at your next ultrasound scan. This will come as a great shock and may be hard to comprehend. Your obstetrician will discuss with you what the next course of action should be, and may advise induction of birth.

Because the date of legal viability is 24 weeks, the death of babies before this time will not be registered and no death certificate will be issued. Many parents find it very upsetting that this late loss of their babies is referred to as a miscarriage. Losing babies before they could survive on their own does not make it any less painful, nor does it make the existence of those babies any less real for parents. For further information on ways to remember your babies, see Chapter 6, p. 151.

Stillbirth

When a baby dies in the womb after 24 weeks it is termed 'intra-uterine death' and recorded as a 'stillbirth'. Around one in 200 births are affected, and twins are at greater risk, particularly those that are both monochorionic and monoamniotic. Recognised causes of stillbirth are congenital abnormalities, problems with the placenta or poor health in the mother, but many are still unexplained and it remains impossible to predict which *seemingly* healthy babies will be stillborn. The cause of death may still be unclear at birth, even after a post-mortem has been performed (for which your written consent is needed).

Labour usually begins spontaneously within two weeks of the babies' deaths, although many women are extremely distressed by carrying dead babies and opt to be induced earlier. Think about whether you want to spend some time alone with your babies after the birth, and whether you want to hold them, take photographs and have keepsakes such as footprints or the blankets they were wrapped in after birth.

Stillbirths in Great Britain (but not Northern Ireland) must be registered and there will also need to be a funeral. Your hospital should be able to help you with these arrangements (*see* Chapter 6, Box on page 151.).

The loss of one baby

It is thought that at least ten per cent of pregnancies that begin with two embryos result in the birth of only one baby. The loss of one of the embryos is most likely to occur before eight weeks of pregnancy. When one baby dies during the first trimester, the remaining tissues are often completely reabsorbed, causing one of the twins to 'disappear'. This is known as 'vanishing twin syndrome'. On many occasions, this will happen before a twin pregnancy was even detected, but the increased use of early ultrasound scans (particularly in assisted conceptions) means that the phenomenom is now more widely observed. First trimester loss of one twin can be symptomless, or it may follow the pattern of a miscarriage, resulting in some bleeding, with or without lower abdominal pain or cramping (which is associated with the increased risk of loss of the other baby).

The loss of a baby after the first trimester occurs in approximately two to five per cent of dichorionic pregnancies. It poses a relatively low risk to the health of the other, even if the twins are monozygotic. However, for all monochorionic twins the risk of the other baby dying is very high because of the shared circulation through the placenta. If the baby does survive there is also a high chance that there may be damage to the brain and other organs and close specialist follow up and monitoring will be required. With dichorionic twins, the aim will be to allow the pregnancy to continue so that the surviving twin can grow and mature so that it has the best chance of being born healthy. You should be aware that, at delivery, the remains of the dead baby are likely to be present (although it may have been reabsorbed into the placenta, depending on the stage at which the loss occurred). This may take the form of a compressed, parchment-like body called 'fetus papyraceous'. You should discuss with your partner and your healthcare professionals whether you wish to see this or not, although no final decision on this needs to be made until the actual delivery.

It can be very distressing to continue the pregnancy with the dead fetus alongside the healthy one, and parents naturally feel torn between mourning the baby they have lost and cherishing the survival of the other. These feelings often resurface at birth and support should be made available to you at the hospital, both during your pregnancy and afterwards, including bereavement counselling from a midwife, nurse or trained counsellor.

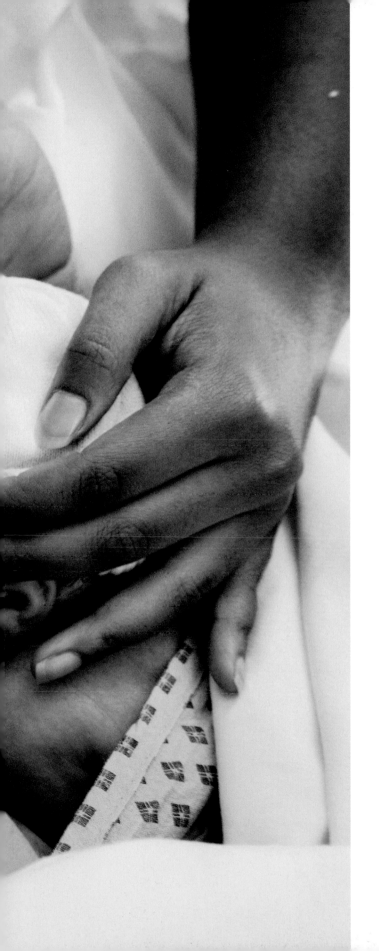

5

The birth

You will soon be welcoming your
babies into the world! You are probably
thinking a lot about the birth itself
and the preparations you need to make
for it – not least about what happens
if you go into labour prematurely.
If it has not been discussed already,
a decision needs to be made towards
the end of your pregnancy about
the timing of the birth and whether
to plan for a vaginal delivery or
a scheduled Caesarean section.

GETTING READY FOR THE BIRTH

Preparing for the arrival of your babies during the last few weeks of pregnancy is exciting, although it can sometimes feel as if time is passing slowly. Given that many twins are born early, you should aim to have everything ready for the birth in good time say by 32 weeks, so that you are well prepared.

Packing your bag

Given the nature of twin births, it is highly likely that you will be giving birth in hospital (*see* Chapter 3, p. 49). You will need to take personal items with you, as well as things for the babies. Make sure you have a bag packed well in advance, so that you are ready to go at any moment. This also takes away the worry of forgetting something essential on the day. Even if you have a Caesarean section planned (*see* p. 106), you will still need a bag, as you may go into labour spontaneously before the scheduled date of delivery. It makes sense to have three bags, or a larger bag divided up into three sections:

▸ **First bag/section**: everything you need for labour (modified if you are having an elective Caesarean)
▸ **Second bag/section**: everything you need post-birth
▸ **Third bag/section**: everything you need for the babies.

Check with your hospital to see if there is anything in particular that they do not supply – some no longer provide infant formula unless there is a medical need – as well as whether there are any specific items that are not allowed (e.g. mobile phones). Remember, though, that even if you do forget something essential, there will probably be time for someone to bring it in after you have been admitted to hospital. You are likely to have your own list of personal essentials, but you might consider the those listed below.

YOUR HOSPITAL BAG

First bag – for labour
▸ old nightdress or T-shirt (it is likely to get soiled)
▸ warm socks
▸ towel and flannel (also good for cooling you down)
▸ lip salve, moisturiser/face spray (hospitals are often very hot)
▸ extra pillows (hospitals invariably only provide one)
▸ TENS machine, alternative pain relief (if using)
▸ battery-operated music system or MP3 player
▸ light reading (e.g. magazines)
▸ massage oil (if desired)
▸ water, fruit juice or isotonic drinks (cartons with straws are easier to use), easily digestible snacks.

Second bag – post-birth
▸ nightwear, front-opening for breastfeeding (should open easily to below bra level for ease of movement)
▸ dressing gown, slippers
▸ thick sanitary pads to absorb heavy bleeding after birth (*see* Chapter 7, p. 200 for more about lochia)

▸ disposable knickers in case of leakage (high-waisted to avoid, in the event of a Caesarean, the elastic rubbing against the incision line once the dressing is removed)
▸ maternity bra, breast pads (if breastfeeding)
▸ toiletries, including nipple cream if breastfeeding
▸ ear plugs and eye mask for occasional rest or sleep
▸ mobile phone and charger (if allowed) and/or change for hospital phone
▸ snacks for the first 24 hours (you may feel hungry outside of hospital mealtimes)
▸ loose, comfortable maternity clothes for going home.

Third bag – for the babies
▸ 1 pack of disposable nappies, premature size (will fit up to about 3 kg)
▸ 2 muslin cloths per baby
▸ 2 vests and babygros per baby (ensure easy to take on and off – *see* Chapter 7, p. 170)
▸ bottles, teats, infant formula (if using and not supplied by the hospital).

Things to do

There are a several other things that can be organised in advance of the birth in order to give you peace of mind. Store all relevant telephone numbers in your mobile phone as well as your partner's, and put a list somewhere visible at home. These should include: the labour ward; doula or other birth partners; friends/family/existing childcare; a taxi company.

Ensure your hospital notes and, if you have one, your birth plan (see below) are with you at all times, rather than stored in your hospital bag. Find out where the hospital entrance is, especially for night-time admissions, as this may be different from the main daytime entrance. If you plan to arrive by car, make sure you know where you can park at all times, and store sufficient amounts of change in the car (out of sight).

Stock up your freezer as much as possible. Be pragmatic: ready meals or pre-cooked food that require minimal preparation are best. If applicable, finalise any childcare arrangements and ensure all concerned know what to do and are available when they say they will be. A back-up plan may be advisable. Where possible, young children's routines should remain the same so that there is continuity in their lives.

Making a birth plan

Many women choose to draw up a 'wish list', called a birth plan, for labour and birth, even when it involves an elective (planned) Caesarean section. Birth plans are not compulsory or even necessary – plenty of women give birth without one – but they can be useful both for you and your healthcare professionals in making the birth as close as possible to what you would like.

You should discuss with your midwife and obstetrician what your hopes are for labour, to find out if any of these are not possible, either because of the circumstances of your own pregnancy or because of hospital policy (see Chapter 3, p. 50). Be guided by the experience of the obstetrician and midwives and their medical knowledge of your particular situation. Their ultimate concern is your welfare and that of your babies.

A birth plan can help you feel more relaxed and in control of the situation when you go into hospital. Conversely, if the situation is such that your birth plan cannot be followed, you may feel that control is taken from you, leading to later feelings of depression or guilt. So, when writing a birth plan it is advisable to remember a few key things:

▸ The aim is to deliver your babies safely, and for you and them to be in the best health possible.
▸ Remain flexible: given the additional risks in twin pregnancies, you may not be able to have the type of labour and delivery you hoped for.
▸ Labour is not an exam: you don't 'fail' if it doesn't go according to plan.
▸ The manner in which you give birth does not determine what sort of mother you will be.

If you would like to make a birth plan, read as much as you can beforehand, especially about Caesarean sections, given that over 50 per cent of twin births are by this method (and almost certainly if your pregnancy is monochorionic). Talking to other mothers is useful too, as they may have helpful tips from their own experience. However, bear in mind that twins are likely to be monitored closely or even continuously, which may limit your options. Elements you could consider for your birth plan include:

▸ outlining who your birth partner(s) is and what they will be doing to support you (see p. 104)
▸ what you like to be called
▸ what atmosphere you want in the room (e.g. quiet; music playing; low lighting)
▸ pain relief preferences (an epidural is commonly advised – see p. 112)
▸ preferences for cutting the cords (partner or midwife), delivery of the placenta(s), vitamin K injections.

Discuss your birth plan with your partner in advance of the birth, so that they can help you make some decisions and know what it contains. Try to keep it to a brief series of bullet points – a longer and complicated list reduces your chances of sticking to it and will be difficult for staff to follow.

Choosing a birth partner

Birth partners have a vital role to play in labour. They are there to support and encourage you, not just emotionally and physically, but also in practical ways. In order to do so, they should:

- be as informed as possible regarding both labour and Caesarean sections
- be aware of possible complications, because their role will be to keep a calm head, should any problem arise
- be assertive: they may need to seek help for you if something is happening and you need medical attention, information or reassurance
- be sensitive to your needs and listen to what you are saying you want
- not be offended if your moods change from one moment to the next (this is very common)
- avoid eating and drinking too obviously in front of you, complaining about tiredness, headaches or other minor ailments
- try to keep their sense of humour!

For many women, their birth partner – the person they want to accompany them during childbirth – will be the father of the babies or a female relative. Increasingly, however, women are opting for the services of a doula. Doulas can offer invaluable support to a woman before, during and after childbirth (*see* Chapter 7, p. 215 for post-birth information). In labour, doulas do not advise or get involved medically but, because they are experienced in childbirth and usually have had training in their role, they can provide helpful suggestions and encouragement for breathing, labouring positions and relaxation methods. This can give women and their partners much-needed confidence and reassurance in what can be an unfamiliar and sometimes daunting situation (*see* Useful Resources for how to find a doula local to you).

YOUR DELIVERY OPTIONS

At the beginning of the third trimester, you will have a discussion with your healthcare professionals regarding your choices about the birth. As your due date approaches, you will need to decide together as to the best time to deliver your babies and which will be the safest method.

Approximately 50–60 per cent of women carrying twins deliver spontaneously before 37 weeks. If you have not gone into labour as you approach the end of the third trimester, the timing of the birth will need to be discussed with you. All women expecting twins are offered the opportunity to have their babies at 37 weeks (36 weeks for monochorionic twins, after steroids have been administered to help the babies' lung function). This is because the placenta works less efficiently after this time, which means the babies will no longer be receiving enough oxygen and nutrients. If a monochorionic (MC) pregnancy is complicated in any way, it is likely that delivery will be advised at 34–36 weeks. Delivery may also be advised earlier than 37 weeks if:

► the health of your babies in the womb is found to be deteriorating
► your membranes rupture ('waters break' – see p. 116) but you do not spontaneously go into labour within 24 hours
► you are suffering from pre-eclampsia or diabetes.

If you prefer to continue with the pregnancy for longer or want to wait for labour to begin naturally, you will need further close monitoring until delivery because of the increased risks of babies dying in the womb after 38 weeks.

Once the timing of the delivery has been decided, you will need to discuss the most appropriate method of giving birth: vaginal labour or Caesarean section. This is decided medically on standard principles based upon the presentation of the first twin (see p. 107). There may, however, be other issues, such as your overall health and that of the babies, which will determine which method may be preferable. For example, in babies with an estimated fetal weight that is either small (less than 1,500 g) or large (more than 4,000 g), the merits of attempted vaginal birth versus Caesarean section will be discussed with you. A Caesarean section

may also be advised for MC pregnancies with complications. Those that are also monoamniotic are almost always delivered by Caesarean section at 32–34 weeks to reduce the risk caused by cord entanglement.

Vaginal delivery

Vaginal deliveries take place in over 40 per cent of twin births and can be induced medically if spontaneous labour has not occurred (see p. 124). Delivering vaginally is not advisable for all twin pregnancies, and so you and your doctors will consider your particular situation in detail and assess the risks and benefits of each method of delivery for you. Depending on individual circumstances and hospital policy, a vaginal delivery would be considered if:

► both babies are in a cephalic presentation
► the presenting baby is cephalic, the second baby is breech, and both babies are of a good and similar size (over 1,500 g each) and dichorionic
► in some monochorionic pregnancies, both babies are cephalic.

Because of the potential for and increased risks of unexpected complications during labour, your obstetrician will often discuss epidural anaesthesia with you (see p. 112). This is not just to provide relief from the pain of contractions but so there is anaesthesia already in place if an assisted delivery (see p. 122–3) or a Caesarean section is required. This is also why all twins should be delivered by midwives and obstetricians used to managing and monitoring such pregnancies, and in a delivery suite with immediate access to epidural and general anaesthesia and operating theatres.

Caesarean section

A Caesarean section is an operation to deliver a baby. Due to advances in medical practice, a Caesarean section (also termed a 'Caesar', 'C-section' or CS) is now a widely used procedure. It can either be 'elective', meaning that it is planned in advance, or it can be termed an 'emergency', meaning that something has happened during the course of labour that makes this the safest method of delivery. The term 'emergency' sounds alarming, but it is used to denote a medically unscheduled procedure – it does not necessarily signify an immediately life-threatening situation (although this might, of course, be the case).

The decision to perform a Caesarean is made on an individual basis. All operations carry a small risk, and this will need to be fully discussed with you, including the reasons for the recommendation and any other options you might have, so that your informed consent can be obtained. An emergency Caesarean usually takes place within approximately 30 minutes of the decision.

Your medical circumstances

You may have certain medical conditions, which either existed before the pregnancy or have developed as a result, that make vaginal birth a high-risk option:

▸ high blood pressure, pre-eclampsia, diabetes or problems controlling blood sugar levels
▸ a heart problem or serious disability
▸ low-lying placenta(s) or placenta praevia (*see* Chapter 4 p. 94)
▸ some causes of third trimester vaginal bleeding
▸ you have had a previous Caesarean section
▸ your pregnancy is monochorionic.

Your babies' circumstances

There are many reasons why a Caesarean section may be the safest method of delivery for your babies. The chorionicity of your pregnancy and presentation of your babies, as well as any conditions detected by ultrasound scan, are significant factors:

▸ the presenting baby is breech (especially high risk in a monochorionic pregnancy, more so if this is a first labour)
▸ one or both of the babies has an underlying health problem or fetal abnormality
▸ one or both of the babies weighs under 1,500 g, and is either not growing well or has intra-uterine growth restriction (IUGR)
▸ the pregnancy is monochorionic and the babies have developed twin-to-twin transfusion syndrome (TTTS)
▸ the babies are showing signs of fetal distress
▸ the pregnancy is monochorionic and monoamniotic.

For more on IUGR, TTTS and the complications presented by monochorionic pregnancies, see Chapter 4, p. 96–7.

VAGINAL BIRTH AFTER A CAESAREAN SECTION

In the past, if you had previously given birth by Caesarean section, all subsequent deliveries would be by this method. This was largely because the incision made in your abdomen was vertical, which meant that there was a significant risk of uterine rupture caused by contractions in a subsequent labour. Now that a horizontal incision in the lower part of the abdomen is used, that risk is very much reduced. A subsequent vaginal birth after a Caesarean section (VBAC) is therefore considered possible in certain circumstances (e.g. if both twins are cephalic), as long as there are no contraindications either for the woman or for her baby/babies. The risks and benefits of a VBAC will therefore be discussed by you and your doctors in relation to your own situation and will affect the decision you eventually take.

Emergency Caesarean section

The reasons why a Caesarean section may be performed as a matter of emergency include:

▸ insufficient progress in labour (e.g. your contractions have slowed down/become weaker, your cervix is not dilating, you are getting too tired to push)
▸ fetal distress during labour (e.g. heart rate dips, meconium detected in amniotic fluid – *see* p. 118)
▸ the placenta starts to separate from the uterus
▸ the presentation of one/both babies changes during labour
▸ labour has begun prematurely and the babies' health means that this could put them at risk
▸ a prolapsed cord of one of the babies during delivery (usually because of breech presentation), which could cut off oxygen supply to the descending baby.

HOW YOUR BABIES ARE POSITIONED

One of the elements in the decision about which will be the best method of delivery is the position – or 'presentation' – of the babies in the womb during the third trimester.

Presentation will have been recorded at each of your antenatal appointments and is confirmed by scanning (establishing this by abdominal palpation alone is difficult in a twin pregnancy). Babies can be positioned longitudinally (vertical), horizontally (transverse) or diagonally (oblique) and this is termed the 'lie'. In a longitudinal lie, each baby's presentation is determined by the part of its body that is closest to the pelvis: it can either be vertical head down (cephalic) or vertical bottom first (breech). Hence, with twins, there are seven variations of presentation and lie – see diagrams on p.108–9.

DID YOU KNOW...?
The baby that is closest to the vaginal canal is called the 'presenting twin'. This is not necessarily 'Twin 1' or 'Twin A', as referred to in your antenatal notes – see Box, p.54.

The method of delivery chosen depends on the presentation of the first twin and the various options will be discussed with you. The breech presentation increases the risk of complications in a vaginal birth. The largest part of the body, the baby's head, comes last, and there is a chance that it could be difficult to deliver. Furthermore, the umbilical cord can prolapse, meaning that it slips out from underneath the body of the descending baby and emerges from the vagina. Exposure to air then causes the cord to constrict, thus depriving the baby of oxygen. It can also be intermittently compressed by the passage of the baby's body as it descends through the vaginal canal, which also restricts the oxygen supply during the delivery.

If both twins are cephalic, then vaginal delivery has a high chance of a safe outcome. If the first twin is cephalic and the second non-cephalic (i.e. breech or transverse/oblique), then the second twin can be delivered either as a vaginal breech, by trying to turn the baby to a cephalic presentation

(less likely) or by Caesarean section. If it is the presenting twin that is breech and complications arise during labour, the consequences for both babies, and for the mother, could be very serious. So if the first or both babies are presenting in a non-cephalic way, then a Caesarean section will be offered.

Although it is important to assess each baby's presentation throughout pregnancy, this can change right up to and during labour itself, especially for the second twin, which is why a decision on what sort of delivery to have can only ever be made with the information available at the time.

The method of delivery chosen depends on the presentation of the first twin and the various options will be discussed with you.

The seven possible presentations

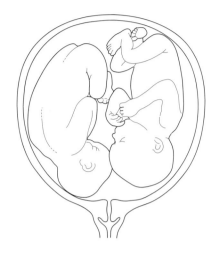

Cephalic–cephalic Both babies are head down. This is the most common presentation, occurring in about 45 per cent of twin pregnancies. Vaginal delivery of the babies stands a high chance of success.

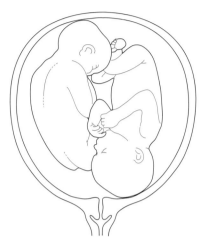

Cephalic–breech The presenting twin is head down and the other is bottom first and this accounts for about 25 per cent of presentations. Vaginal delivery of the first twin may be followed by an assisted or Caesarean delivery of the second.

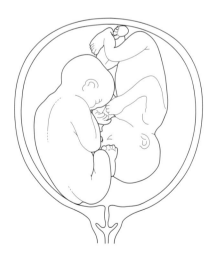

Breech–cephalic The presenting twin is bottom first and the other is head down. About ten per cent of pregnancies present this way. In the majority of cases, you will be offered delivery by Caesarean section.

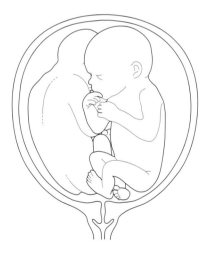

Breech–breech Both babies are bottom down. This presentation accounts for about nine per cent of twin pregnancies. In the majority of cases, you will be offered delivery by Caesarean section.

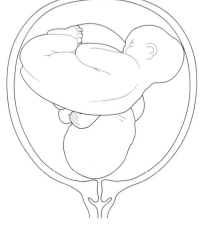

Breech–transverse or oblique The presenting twin is bottom down and the other is lying horizontally (as shown) or diagonally across the uterus. In the majority of cases, you will be offered delivery by Caesarean section. The oblique lie is often transient and becomes longitudinal in labour.

Cephalic–transverse or oblique The presenting twin is head down, with the other lying either horizontally (as shown) or diagonally across the uterus. A vaginal delivery will be discussed with you, and will depend on a range of factors (e.g. whether you have had a previous vaginal delivery, the size of the twins).

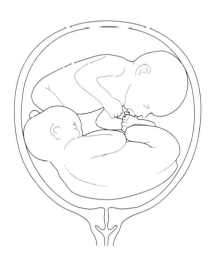

Transverse–transverse Both babies are lying horizontally across the uterus. Variants of the three transverse and oblique presentations account for around eleven per cent of twin pregnancies. In the majority of cases, you will be offered delivery by Caesarean section.

Victoria's story

One of the most daunting aspects of having twins is wondering what your delivery will be like. At approximately twenty weeks I discovered that I was going to be having boy/girl twins. Following a scan at roughly 33 weeks, I was told that the girl was head down and the boy was lying across me, above her with his head pointing to my left. Further scans revealed that the babies' positions had not changed and probably wouldn't from now on. I knew that, ideally, for a vaginal delivery the babies should both be head down. The midwife said that I could definitely try to deliver the girl vaginally but, because of the position of the boy, they could not confirm what would happen. It was explained to me that, following the delivery of the girl, the midwife would try and turn the boy to face head down, but that this didn't always work. I began to realise that there was a possibility that I could be given an emergency Caesarean section following a vaginal birth. This prospect was daunting and frightening. With the advice and encouragement of my midwife and my husband, I decided that the best thing for me to do was to schedule an elective Caesarean at 38 weeks and hope that I would be able to keep the babies in until then. I was very lucky, as I reached the date and had a very straightforward Caesarean delivery.

PAIN RELIEF DURING LABOUR

Modern medicine has allowed women to choose what, if any, pain relief they need during childbirth. This can range from non-medical methods such as massage or breathing techniques through to medical anaesthesia.

Until they have experienced it for themselves, nobody can know how they will cope with labour. The most helpful thing you can do is to find out as much as you can about what can happen in a twin birth and what pain relief is suitable for different situations, to remain open-minded and realistic about what you opt for, and to listen to the advice of your healthcare professionals. Avoid feeling pressurised or overly influenced by others (especially those who have not given birth to twins) – remember, you have nothing to prove and need suffer no 'loss of face' if you do have pain relief. The reality is that pain can be exhausting and creates physical tension that can slow down labour and make you too tired to push effectively. It can also leave you with bad memories of what should be possibly the most extraordinary experience of your life: giving birth to your babies. The two principal forms of medical pain relief used in childbirth are:

▶ regional anaesthetics (e.g. epidurals), which numb the lower part of your body
▶ analgesics (e.g. gas and air), which relieve the general feeling of pain.

There are also non-drug-assisted forms of pain relief, such as TENS machines, breathing techniques and massage.

Regional and local anaesthesia
A drug that numbs sensation in a large area of the body is called a regional anaesthetic; a local anaesthetic numbs a small area only. In order to prevent pain in the abdominal area during labour, an anaesthetic is administered via epidural, spinal block or pudendal block. In the first two cases, you will be unable to move your legs or stand up, and so you will deliver your babies lying on a bed. None of these methods of pain relief affects the babies.

Epidural
An epidural is a drug injected into the epidural space in your spinal column via a very thin catheter. This numbs the nerve fibres so that they are no longer able to send signals back to your brain that you are in pain. Epidurals are usually recommended for women carrying twins for several reasons:

▶ If the labour is induced (as is routinely offered for twin pregnancies that advance to 37 weeks and beyond), contractions are likely to be more intense.
▶ If an assisted delivery is required for the second twin, anaesthesia is already in place.
▶ If an emergency Caesarean needs to be performed because of unforeseen complications during the birth, then the epidural can simply be topped up as necessary.

An epidural is only carried out by an experienced anaesthetist. In order for the drug to be administered, you will be asked to sit on the bed or operating table, leaning slightly forward, or to lie on your left side. The area on your back where the anaesthetic will be inserted is cleaned with antiseptic solution and numbed with a small injection, so that you will not feel any pain as the hollow needle containing the catheter goes in. You will need to keep very still at this point, but if you have a contraction, the anaesthetist will stop what they are doing until it is over. The epidural starts to work almost immediately, and you will feel a cold feeling of numbness working its way gradually down from your abdomen. After a short while, the anaesthetist will check that it has taken effect. You should not be able to feel any contractions nor move your legs. Because your blood pressure can drop, you will be given fluids via a drip. A catheter is inserted to drain off urine, as you will not be able to sense whether your bladder is full (nor walk to the toilet).

An epidural can slow labour down, but it allows for a faster assisted delivery should it be necessary, which is particularly important if the second twin is in distress. It takes around 30 minutes to set up and a further 30 minutes to be completely effective – bear this in mind if have decided not to have one at the start of your labour, but find you need one for immediate pain relief later on; it is also possible that the anaesthetist may be engaged elsewhere and is not able to attend to you straight away. If labour is progressing very quickly or you have arrived at the hospital already quite advanced, it may be not be possible to administer an epidural, in which case other pain relief options may be offered.

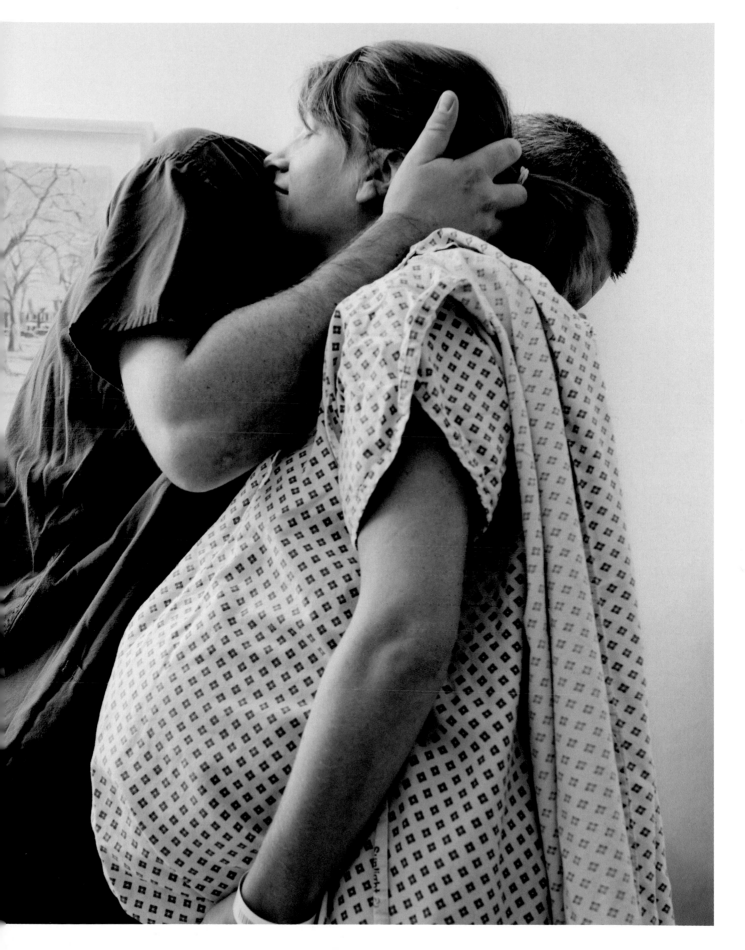

Is there a risk of spinal damage, paralysis or other serious problem?

The latest research shows that epidurals are extremely safe. A recent study looked at all groups of patients given epidural anaesthesia, which included not only women in labour but also children and elderly patients (who often have epidurals for operations because general anaesthesia is too risky for them). When a death or injury occurred (which was rarely), this was a result of the patient's underlying condition, rather than mistakes by the anaesthetist, and in most cases, the patient was elderly.

Many women are worried about moving during a contraction while the needle is being inserted into the epidural space, but anaesthetists will always stop and wait for the contraction to subside before continuing. It is extremely rare for the catheter to move inside your spine and, even if it did, the medical team would notice immediately because the area of numbness would change. It is therefore virtually impossible for an epidural to injure or paralyse you.

Does the anaesthetic sometimes not work?

Rarely, a part of your abdomen or lower limbs does not feel completely numb, but this will be obvious to you and you should inform the anaesthetist. They may need to move the tube in your back slightly or ask you to change position so that the anaesthetic reaches all the relevant parts. You can be sure that, if you are having an epidural before a Caesarean section, the operation will not begin until both you and the anaesthetist are completely satisfied (following a series of tests) that you are fully anaesthetised.

Is there a risk of backache after the birth?

The studies that have been conducted to determine if epidurals lead to a higher incidence of postnatal backache have come to contradictory conclusions, with some showing that this might be so, and others claiming that back problems are more likely to be caused by a long, difficult labour or an assisted or Caesarean delivery. Postnatal back pain can also be a result of the strain suffered in latter part of the pregnancy by the lumbar, spine and pelvic regions. Weakened muscles, as well as tendons and ligaments that have been softened in preparation for birth, may also be a contributory factor. Back strengthening and flexibility exercises are the best remedy for these problems (*see* Chapter 2, p. 39).

Are there side effects of an epidural?

About one per cent of women suffer from headaches after an epidural. This is because the needle has accidentally punctured the dura, the membrane surrounding the spinal cord, and a small amount of spinal fluid leaks out, which causes pain. Symptoms are usually relieved by lying down and disappear altogether after a few days or, in the worst cases, one or two weeks. Around one in 2,000 women can get slight tingling or numbness in one of their limbs after the epidural has worn off. These symptoms can be worrying but they are temporary and usually disappear within a few days or, rarely, a few weeks.

Your anaesthetist will see you the day after your delivery to make sure you have no problems, but if you have a persistent headache at home, talk to your midwife or call the delivery suite, as you may need to return for a further consultation.

Spinal block

A spinal block works in a similar way to an epidural. However, the anaesthetic is administered into the fluid surrounding the spinal cord rather than the epidural space. Spinal blocks work almost at once and last for approximately one hour, but can only be administered once, whereas epidurals can be topped up on a regular basis. Spinal blocks are therefore used more for a Caesarean section than for labour (when pain relief may be required for longer), especially when this is an emergency and the delivery needs to take place relatively quickly.

Pudendal block

An anaesthetising spray is used to numb the skin around the area to be injected before a local anaesthetic is given to the tissue surrounding the pudendal nerves in the vagina. This is done by an obstetrician or midwife and is suitable when a forceps or ventouse delivery and/or an episiotomy is required, and no other regional pain relief (e.g. an epidural) has been given, although it is not very commonly used.

Analgesics

An analgesic is a drug that relieves pain rather than removes the sensation of it. There are certain drugs specifically used for childbirth that have no lasting effect on the babies.

Gas and air (Entonox)

Commonly called 'gas and air', Entonox is a widely used form of pain relief during labour for those who have not opted for an epidural. Entonox is a 50:50 mixture of nitrous oxide gas and oxygen and dulls the sensation of pain. It is completely safe for you and your babies. It does not, however, take away the pain of contractions altogether, but can nevertheless be useful during the first stage of labour. Using deep breaths, you inhale through a mouthpiece during each contraction so that, by its peak, the pain relief has taken effect. Since it is quickly eliminated from the body, there is no advantage to continuing to breathe it in between contractions.

Each woman reacts differently to Entonox. Some women find it helps them at least to get through early labour, and the act of breathing in slowly also calms them down and allows them to stay focused on each contraction. Others find that it makes them feel 'out of it', light-headed or nauseous, and does not dull the pain very much.

Pethidine or diamorphine

Given by intramuscular injection, these drugs take about twenty minutes to work, last for two to four hours and can help you to relax. However, when given within two hours of the actual delivery, they can depress your babies' breathing and can make them very drowsy after the birth, causing them to have difficulties feeding. They can also make women feel nauseous and very detached from their surroundings, preventing them from pushing effectively. As a result, pethidine and diamorphine are rarely seen as suitable for twin deliveries, unless labour is progressing quickly and straightforwardly.

Non-medical pain relief

Although few twin labours take place without the help of some of the above methods of pain relief, you may want to investigate some non-pharmacological ones as well, particularly for the early stages.

TENS (transcutaneous electrical nerve stimulation)

TENS machines have small electrodes that you tape to your lower back and which are connected to wires on a small, battery-operated stimulator. When you experience a contraction, you are able to give yourself a small – and safe – electrical current, via the electrodes. In theory, this stimulates production of the body's natural painkillers (endorphins), thereby reducing your pain. In practice, these machines work for some women and not for others, and they are of most help during the early (latent) phase of labour. If you are interested in hiring one, speak to your midwife.

Breathing, relaxation and massage

Pain can be exhausting and creates physical tension. The tenser you are, the more acute any pain will feel. Breathing calmly and slowly helps you to stay relaxed, as it can reduce the amount of stress hormones being produced. This allows you to focus on your contractions, but will also help you to remain calm if your labour requires medical assistance or emergency intervention.

Many antenatal classes cover breathing in labour (see Chapter 2, p. 30), but you can also practise it yourself. Slow, controlled breathing can be combined with a visualisation (mental image), music or a favourite song or repetitive chant for greater focus, but these techniques work better if you have tried them out before labour. Similarly, massage of the back or shoulders by a partner can also help relax you, although some women do not like being touched when they are in pain. You will have to show your partner what sort of massage you require and where, rather than assume they will get it right intuitively.

Water

Having a warm bath (provided your membranes have not broken) can relieve tension and reduce pain for some women. This can be a good way to pass the time during the early part of your labour, especially if it is too early to go into hospital. Once in hospital, there may be a bath or birthing pool that you can use for a while, but it is highly unusual for twins to be delivered in water as twins are usually, routinely monitored .

Other methods

Although alternative methods, such as acupuncture, aromatherapy, homeopathy and hypnosis, appear to help some women, there is no scientific evidence that they have any real effect on pain. If you would like to try one of these methods in the labour ward, check with the hospital to see if their policy allows you to do so, especially if a practitioner needs to be with you at any stage. In addition, ensure that the practitioner comes not only recommended, but is also trained and experienced in childbirth. Have at least one session with them in advance of labour to ensure that you are happy with what they are proposing to do.

LABOUR

Labour often begins spontaneously before 37 weeks in twin pregnancies. However, if you are still carrying your pregnancy and have opted for a vaginal birth, labour is likely to be induced. There are three stages of labour, which follow the same pattern in either case.

Am I in labour?

Most first-time mothers wonder how they will know when they are in labour. There are several signs that can indicate that labour is not far away, or is already in the early stages:

► Braxton Hicks (*see* Chapter 4, p. 90) contractions have become more frequent and noticeable, although not regularly spaced out.
► Vaginal discharge has become more plentiful and thicker.
► You may get a 'show' (*see* below).
► You develop lower back pain.
► Your membranes rupture ('waters break' – *see* below).

Having a 'show'

When your cervix begins to change in advance of labour, the vaginal mucus that was acting as a plug to prevent any bacteria from entering the uterus becomes dislodged and gets discharged from the vagina. This is known as a 'show'. The plug is often tinged with a small amount of blood, but this is not anything to be concerned about. If, however, you experience any actual blood loss, contact the labour ward at once.

Ruptured membranes

If you notice you are 'leaking' clear and odourless liquid, your membranes (amniotic sac) may have ruptured – commonly termed 'waters breaking'. Ruptured membranes may or may not lead to the start of labour, but you should call the labour ward as you may need to be examined in hospital. Infection can develop when the amniotic sac has ruptured, as the environment is no longer sterile, so if labour does not begin within 24 hours, a discussion is likely to take place regarding induction of birth. Some women are concerned that their membranes will rupture when they are out and about. If you are some distance from home, call the labour ward at once – depending on your situation, they may advise you to go to

your nearest hospital to be assessed. See p. 124 for information on the artificial rupture of membranes.

When to go to hospital

The signs that you are in the early stages of labour can be difficult to recognise, especially because they come in no particular order. You may get several symptoms, or only one or two. If you have noticed some of those listed above, and/or start to experience contractions, then you should call the labour ward. Their job is to advise you, reassure you and assess when you should come in to hospital. Given the additional risks of a twin delivery, they will not think you are a nuisance if you phone them even before you think true labour has begun.

Your contractions may start as mild, lower back pain, and may be irregular, occurring from five minutes to up to half an hour apart; but they should gradually increase in strength and become more regular. Depending on the advice you are given, you should plan to go into hospital when:

► contractions are regular (you need to time them – *see* Box below), gaining in intensity and the pain does not lesson with change of position
► the pain is in your lower back or upper abdomen, rather than your lower abdomen.

Bear in mind how long the journey to hospital may take (e.g. in rush hour traffic, if you live a long distance from the hospital) when deciding when to go in. If in doubt, don't wait – call the labour ward or go to the hospital.

TIMING CONTRACTIONS

You need to time both the length and the frequency of your contractions. Using a watch with a second hand, note the times that a contraction begins and ends and then calculate the length. To determine the frequency, jot down the time one contraction starts, ending the timing when the next one begins. If your birth partner is with you when you are having contractions, let them keep a note of the timings so that you can concentrate on managing the pain. You don't need to monitor each and every contraction – record them for a while until a pattern can be detected, then only start timing them again when that pattern changes.

Given the additional risks involved in a twin birth, you may be attended at some point during the birth by the following medical staff:

- one or more obstetricians (usually only one in an operating theatre)
- two paediatricians (one for each baby)
- two midwives (if labouring)
- an anaesthetist (for epidural anaesthesia or a spinal block) either during a vaginal delivery or in theatre for a Caesarean delivery
- theatre nurses (if you have a Caesarean section)
- trainee doctors/midwives (to gain experience of a twin birth); you will be asked for consent and are entitled to refuse.

Arriving at the hospital

When you decide or have been advised that it is time to go to hospital, you should make your way to the labour ward. Once there you will be shown to an examination room where a midwife will ask you about your symptoms and any contractions you may be having, and will carry out a range of tests, including measuring your blood pressure and checking the babies' heartbeat. She may then do an internal examination and, if you are in labour, you will be shown to a delivery suite where you can then change into a hospital gown or the clothes in which you plan to give birth.

The delivery suite will have an adjustable bed for you to rest or labour on, as well as a range of other equipment that will be needed to monitor you and the babies and care for them after the birth. This includes:

- a cardiotocograph, which measures the babies' heart rates using electronic fetal monitoring
- piped oxygen and Entonox ('gas and air')
- a mobile drip stand, for fluids and medication to be given via an intravenous drip if needed
- baby resuscitation trolleys (one for each baby).

The first stage of labour

Labour is commonly referred to as having three stages. The first stage is when uterine contractions enable the cervix to thin and fully dilate. This can be subdivided into the 'latent phase', when milder contractions and other signs of early labour take place

and the cervix dilates to 3 cm; and the 'active phase', when contractions increase in strength and frequency until the cervix is fully dilated at 10 cm. Sometimes, but not always, there is a 'transition phase', where the cervix is fully dilated but the urge to push – the second stage – has not yet begun.

The latent phase

The latent phase of the first stage of labour is when uterine contractions 'thin' the cervix and soften it (called 'effacement'), so that it can start to stretch and dilate. In a first labour, this latent phase, which lasts until the cervix has dilated to about 3 cm, can take eight to twelve hours, although it is not uncommon for it to last 24 hours or more. In subsequent labours, it can be considerably shorter. Although your contractions are not painless, they are usually bearable at this time, and you may be able to get some rest and have something light and easily digestible to eat and drink to give you more energy and prevent dehydration. (Once you are in active labour, you will not eat or drink until after the birth.) Unless your waters have broken, you can take a warm bath to relieve the discomfort; massage or use of a TENS machine may also help (see p. 115).

The active phase

Once your cervix has dilated to about 3 cm, you will be in 'active' labour. The uterus contracts from the top down, and in so doing, slowly pushes the presenting baby a little further down and into the birth canal. Your contractions will gradually increase in frequency, roughly from every fifteen minutes to every few minutes and, by the end of this phase, every 60–90 seconds. They will also last longer and increase in intensity.

You can expect to dilate approximately 1 cm per hour in a first labour, although the pace at which this happens varies, sometimes with little or no dilation for a while, followed by fast dilation within a short space of time. An internal examination is required in order to measure how dilated you are, and although this can be uncomfortable, your healthcare professionals will be aware of this and will aim to do it between contractions.

The transition phase

The stage when you are fully dilated but do not yet have the urge to push is known as the 'transition phrase', although it does not occur in every labour. Conversely, you may not be fully dilated but feel like pushing; you must not do this, as it could be harmful to your baby and could damage your cervix. In either situation, your contractions are now very frequent and strong, and your midwife or obstetrician will guide you about what to do next. The transition phase usually lasts for a few

The experience of the pain caused by contractions varies not only from one woman to another, but from one labour to another, so it is impossible for you to predict in advance how you will cope with it – hence the need to stay completely open to whatever situation arises during labour. This is especially the case if this is your first labour, as they are often longer and more painful than subsequent ones.

If you have not opted for an epidural at the start of your labour, you may find that adopting certain positions during the active phase allows you to cope with your contractions better than lying down. Bear in mind that the babies are likely to be being monitored continuously, which may restrict your movement. You will probably instinctively find ones that suit you, whether curled up on your side, kneeling on all fours, kneeling and leaning forwards onto some pillows (or being supported by your partner) or squatting. Squatting requires a degree of lower body strength, so it is a good idea to have practised this in advance, perhaps at an antenatal or yoga class. Walking around, if you are able to, can also be good, because gravity keeps the presenting baby's head (if cephalic) pressing down on the cervix, thus helping it to dilate.

Try to focus on getting through the next contraction only, rather than wondering how you are going to cope with all the rest, as this can create additional tension in your body – and tension makes pain feel worse. View your contraction as being the next step on a path that is leading to the birth of your babies. All you are focusing on is taking that next step, not how long it is going to take to get to your destination. Think about your breath (as you have been shown to do in antenatal classes), try to establish a rhythmic pattern of slow, deep breathing, inhaling through your nose, exhaling purposefully through your mouth, play some soothing music, visualise what your babies are doing, and employ any other techniques you might have to keep a calm atmosphere and to manage this stage of labour. However, if the contractions do become too much to bear, do not be afraid to ask for suitable pain relief.

minutes, but can be longer. Some women become tearful at this stage, and you will continue to be monitored very closely to ensure that you are not becoming too exhausted as a result of the contractions and that there are no signs of fetal distress.

> ### DID YOU KNOW...?
> The presence of meconium (the content of a baby's bowel which accumulates during pregnancy) in the amniotic fluid is one of the signs of a baby becoming distressed. If this is detected, the birth of your babies may need to be accelerated, either by an assisted delivery or by an emergency Caesarean section.

The second stage of labour

This is the stage when the baby descends through the birth canal. Contractions will be regular and strong, and you will have the urge to push. The need to monitor the babies will limit the range of positions you can adopt for delivery, but you should discuss with your healthcare professionals to find the most comfortable position for you. Your midwife or obstetrician will inform you when you are fully dilated and should start to push. It is very important at this stage that you work as a team and listen very carefully to what they are telling you to do. This is especially the case if you have had an epidural, because you may be unable to feel the start of each contraction.

In order to push effectively, take a deep breath as each contraction begins, push hard during each contraction, then rest in between. Push down into your vagina and rectum, not into your abdomen, and try to visualise the part of your body on which you are focusing all your efforts. A contraction lasts around 60–90 seconds, so you should have time for two or three long pushes. Do what feels right for you, make as much noise as you want (but don't let your energy get diverted into your screaming rather than your pushing) and don't worry if you pass some stools during this stage of pushing. It is quite common, and all the staff will be completely used to it.

Assuming the presenting twin is cephalic, the head will at some stage become visible at the peak of a contraction, although initially it will slip back up the birth canal when you stop pushing. Eventually, however, the head will stay there and 'crown'. It is important the head is not delivered too fast, so at this stage, although your perineum is stretched to its limit, you may be told not to push at all in order to avoid tearing. If it seems that your perineum is not able to accommodate the baby's head safely and there is a risk of tearing, an episiotomy may be performed (*see* p. 120).

When instructed to do so, you will push once again in order for the baby's head to emerge fully from the birth canal. It usually only requires a couple of contractions in order for the head to be delivered. After one or two further contractions, the baby's body will then be delivered as well. As soon as the baby is born, the cord will be clamped in two places – near the baby and at the other end – then cut (you or your partner may wish to do this). If the first twin is well enough at birth, and once any blood and mucus have been wiped away from the airways, you or your partner will be able to hold your baby for a short while before one of the paediatricians in attendance makes the necessary checks (*see* p. 130). If your baby is premature or has a health problem, the paediatrician may have to look after them as soon as it is delivered, although the midwives and obstetrician will keep you informed about what is happening.

Delivery of the first baby usually takes around 60–90 minutes for a first labour, and less for a subsequent one, and fetal assessment will continue throughout this time. If you push for much longer than 90 minutes, there is a danger you could become very tired and/or the baby could start to suffer fetal distress. In order to avoid this, and bearing in mind that you have a second baby to deliver as well, forceps or vacuum extraction (ventouse) may be used in order to assist the delivery of the first baby (*see* p. 122–3).

Once the first baby is born, your body then has to prepare for the delivery of the second baby. This stage can take anything from a few minutes to approximately an hour, although on average it takes around 20–30 minutes. The potential problems associated with the vaginal delivery of twins are often related to the well-being of the second twin once the first has been born. There is a risk, if the gap before the delivery of the second baby is too long, that the placenta might begin to separate from the uterine wall (placental abruption – *see* Chapter 4, p. 94) which is potentially highly dangerous; similarly, contractions often weaken after the delivery of the first baby, preventing the mother from pushing the second one out, in which case an emergency Caesarean section would be performed. In order to reduce the chances of this happening, you will be given a drug called syntocinon, via a drip, in order to keep contractions strong and regular. The obstetrician will assess the second twin to decide whether an assisted delivery (forceps or ventouse) is needed.

The position of the second twin will be assessed using external abdominal palpation (or ultrasound if required), because it can change after the delivery of the first twin. If the amniotic membranes around the second baby are still intact, the obstetrician will not break them until the baby has moved further down into the pelvic cavity. If necessary, an episiotomy will be done so that forceps or vacuum extraction (ventouse) can be used to guide the baby's head out safely. If the baby is transverse, the obstetrician will apply external pressure to turn the baby into a longitudinal (cephalic) lie. The delivery will then proceed as with the cephalic delivery of the first twin. Occasionally, the obstetrician may internally guide the second twin in order to deliver it vaginally. This requires epidural anaesthesia and the obstetrician will discuss the procedure with you in detail.

Breech delivery

If your second baby is breech, your legs will be put in stirrups, as it will be easier for the obstetrician or midwife to deliver the baby. If you have not already had an epidural, you will be given either a spinal block or, rarely, a pudendal block (*see* p. 114) in case forceps and/or an episiotomy are needed. If necessary, your existing epidural will be topped up. An epidural or spinal block also allows a Caesarean section to be done quickly, should this become the best way of delivering the baby safely.

The bottom is delivered first, and the legs are then guided out by the obstetrician, who may need to insert a finger or hand into the vagina to extract them carefully (on some occasions the legs present first). Once the trunk and shoulders have been delivered slowly and gently, forceps are often used to guide the baby's head out safely. As with the first twin, as soon as the baby is born, the cord is clamped at each end, and then cut.

The third stage of labour

The delivery of the placenta(s) makes up the third stage of labour. Post-partum haemorrhage (PPH – *see* p. 132) is more likely because the uterus is more distended as you have been carrying two babies and the area covered by the placenta is greater. Depending on the policy of your hospital, a drug can be administered – either by an injection into your thigh or via a drip – that will make the uterus contract so that the placenta(s) are delivered more quickly. Your obstetrician or midwife will then very gently pull on the umbilical cords until the placenta(s) separates from the uterine wall and is expelled, along with the membranes. This usually takes about five to ten minutes.

The placenta(s), umbilical cords and the membranes will be carefully examined (it is important that the placenta is intact and entirely removed from the uterus). The placenta(s) can help to clarify the situation regarding chorionicity and whether or not your babies are identical (*see* Chapter 1, p. 16). Once labour is over, any vaginal or perineal suturing (stitching after tearing/episiotomy) that is required will be done, either by the obstetrician or by an experienced midwife, using a local anaesthetic to numb the area if you have not had an epidural.

DID YOU KNOW…?

About 4 per cent of twin births result in a vaginal delivery for the first twin followed by an emergency Caesarean section for the second twin.

WHAT IS AN EPISIOTOMY?

An episiotomy is a small incision in your perineum (the area between the anus and the vaginal opening) that is often performed during labour. It is carried out for one of two reasons:

▸ when the perineum is not able to stretch enough to allow the baby's head to be delivered and there is a risk of tearing or delay in delivering
▸ to increase the size of the vaginal opening when forceps or ventouse are required to guide a baby out.

Uneven perineal tearing can be harder to repair and can take longer to heal than a small, straight incision. Severe tearing can also lead to other problems, such as incontinence, so if tearing seems likely you may be advised to have an episiotomy. You will be asked for your permission and, if you agree, a local anaesthetic will be administered in the form of an injection to the perineum. (Occasionally, in an emergency, there may not be time for this.) A swift cut is made either directly down from the vagina or diagonally. After the delivery, your tissues will be sutured (stitched) using dissolvable stitches.

For the first two or three days after the birth, the stitches can feel tight and very tender (*see* p. 200 for advice on reducing pain and helping healing), but with good wound management and hygiene, you should find that it begins to heal within a week. If you find that you are still experiencing discomfort or pain several weeks or months later, make sure you seek medical advice.

Assisted deliveries: forceps and vacuum extraction (ventouse)

An assisted delivery – sometimes called an instrumental or operative vaginal birth – is one in which a baby needs help being born. The use of forceps or vacuum extraction (ventouse) to assist delivery is common in twin vaginal births, and the obstetrician or midwife will work with your contractions to guide and draw the baby safely out. The decision regarding which method to use depends on each specific situation.

Forceps

Forceps can be used to rotate a descending baby's head if it is not in a good position and is slowing down delivery; or they can guide the baby down the birth canal and hence speed up the baby's birth when necessary. The spoon-shaped blades of the forceps are inserted into the birth canal one at a time in order to cup the baby's head as it crowns, and then an episiotomy is performed as the baby is guided out. This method of delivery is suitable for all babies, including premature or very small ones.

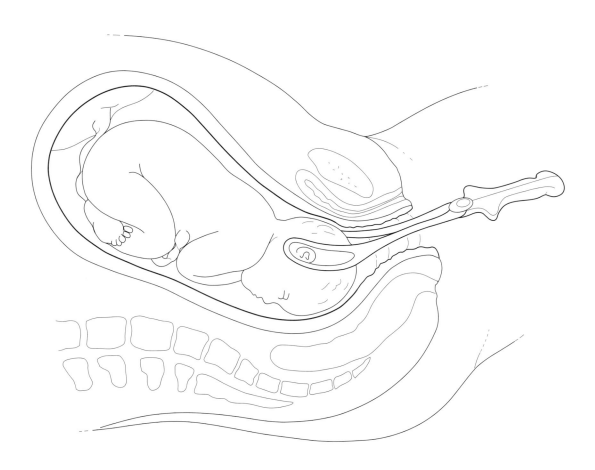

Delivery using forceps Forceps are placed on either side of the head to help guide the baby out. An episiotomy will be required to allow both the head and the forceps to pass through the vaginal opening.

Vacuum extraction (ventouse)

A vacuum extractor, or ventouse, has a suction cup attached to a handle, for pulling on so that the obstetrician can exert gentle traction to ease the baby out. The cup is placed on a baby's scalp as it descends the birth canal, but because of the pressure the cup exerts, it is not suitable for small or premature babies. Some bruising or swelling of the baby's scalp is common after a ventouse delivery, but this usually disappears within two weeks of the birth.

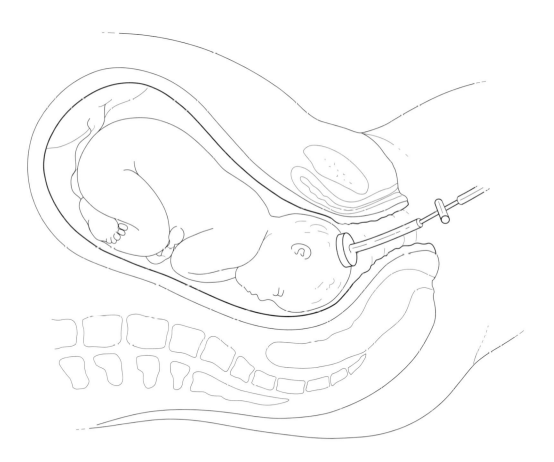

Delivery using vacuum extraction
A suction cup is attached to the baby's head and gentle traction is used, working with your contractions, to draw the baby out.

Induction of labour

Depending on your circumstances, labour can be induced (started artificially) and there are various methods for doing this.

Sweeping the membranes

If your membranes have not ruptured (your waters have not broken), this is often the first method chosen, as it can trigger labour within 24–48 hours without the need for further intervention. The obstetrician or midwife 'sweeps' one or two fingers around your cervix, causing the hormone prostaglandin to be released, which may stimulate contractions. It can be uncomfortable, as the cervix can be difficult to reach before labour has begun. You will be able to go home after this procedure while waiting to see if labour starts.

Prostaglandins

The hormone prostaglandin can be used to induce labour and is given as an oral tablet or vaginal pessary or gel. A further dose may be discussed given after six hours if necessary. You will need to stay in hospital because labour may begin at any point.

Artificial rupture of membranes

If labour is not progressing after prostaglandin has been administered, your obstetrician or midwife may artificially rupture your membranes. The fetal head will then be able to push down on the cervix and this helps release natural oxytocin into the mothers bloodstream and locally releases prostaglandin in the cervix itself. Labour is often triggered as a result of this (painless) procedure.

Syntocinon

If labour has not been stimulated using the above methods, a synthetic version of the hormone oxytocin (which causes your uterus to contract) may be given via a drip. The level of hormone can be adjusted, depending on progress. This method requires continuous CTG monitoring and you will be checked every fifteen minutes to ensure all is well with you and your babies. Induction by syntocinon often leads to more intense contractions than if labour begins naturally.

Most women who are induced go on to have a vaginal delivery. In general, though, induced labours are longer than those begun spontaneously, especially if this is a first labour and the cervix is not 'ripe' (ready to dilate) or the presenting baby's head is not engaged. In such cases, it not unusual for labour to take around 48 hours, from the first attempt at induction right through to the delivery of the babies.

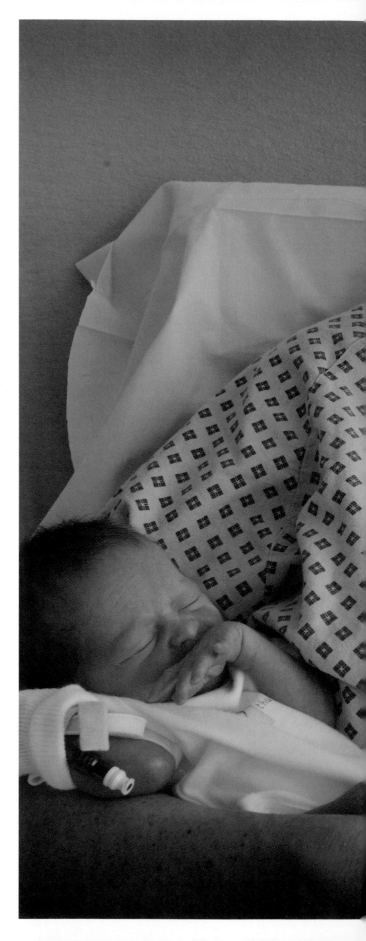

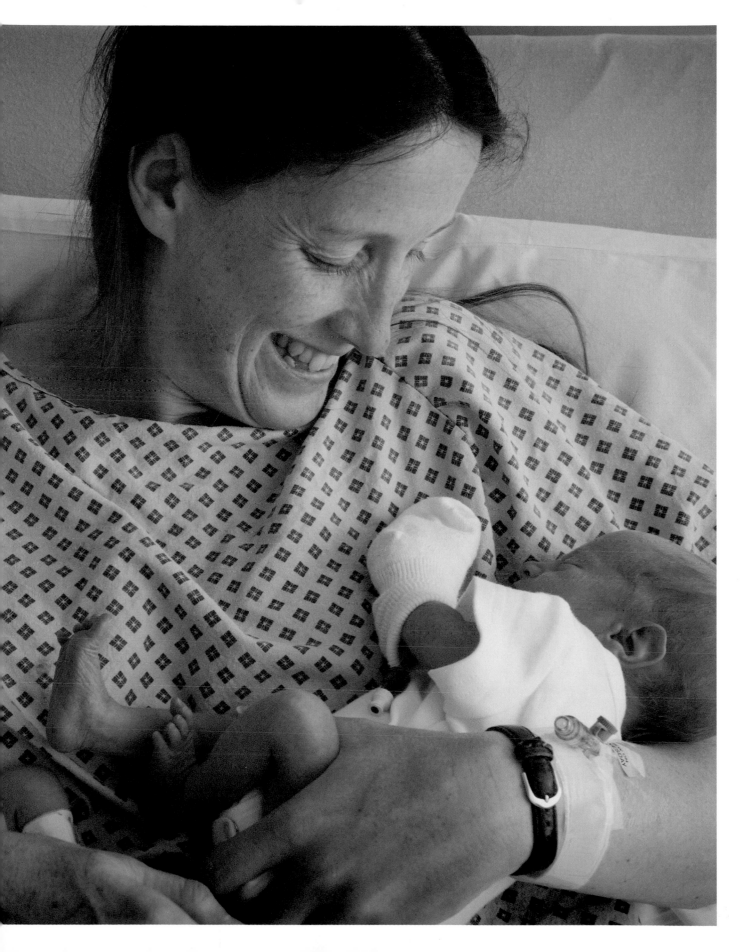

CAESAREAN SECTION

The surgical procedure used to deliver babies is usually performed while you are awake. Your lower body will be numbed, most routinely by epidural anaesthesia, so that you don't feel any pain, and you and your partner will be able to witness the birth of your babies.

You will be asked to change into a hospital gown and to remove make-up and jewellery and your pubic hair is shaved to allow clear access for the incision. Your birth partner can accompany you into theatre, so they need to change into sterile hospital clothes. If you are able to, you will walk to the operating theatre; otherwise you will be taken there in a wheelchair. It is also possible for the operation to take place in the delivery room where you have been labouring. If yours is an emergency Caesarean, you will already be on a bed in your delivery room, so you will be wheeled to theatre on this bed and then transferred to the operating table. The delivery of your babies takes only a few minutes, but the preparation (including the administration of the anaesthetic) and post-operative stitching mean that the entire Caesarean procedure takes around one hour.

Administering the anaesthetic

You will be anaesthetised in theatre or in a room next to it, either with an epidural or a spinal block (*see* p. 112 and 114). If you already had an epidural set up because you were in labour and are now having an emergency Caesarean, it may simply need topping up. You should also be offered diamorphine at the same time as the anaesthetic is given. This is an additional painkiller, which will provide pain relief for a while after the operation. It is not uncommon for women to feel anxious/faint/sick at this stage. If you do, simply tell the anaesthetist, who will give you some oxygen to breathe in through a mask and possibly an anti-emetic (to stop nausea). Once the anaesthetic has been administered, the anaesthetist will check, using a series of tests, that your abdomen and legs are completely numb. Only when you are both completely sure that this is the case will the operation begin.

A screen will be put up at chest level so that you do not see the procedure itself taking place, although if you would like to see your baby being born, you are free to ask for the screen to be taken down at any stage. A drug is given via a drip to reduce your risk of developing low blood pressure during the operation and a catheter inserted to drain away urine. You will not feel the catheter being put in, and it is usually left in place for the first twelve hours or so after the delivery, or until you are able to get up to empty your bladder.

CAESAREAN UNDER GENERAL ANAESTHESIA
The majority of Caesarean sections are performed under regional anaesthesia but occasionally, a general anaesthetic is required. This is because it is usually faster to perform than an epidural or spinal block if the circumstances require a more speedy intervention (e.g. if you have suffered placental abruption). Your partner can be with you while you are being prepared for the anaesthetic but will not be able to accompany you into the operating theatre.

Delivering the babies

After your abdomen has been swabbed with antiseptic solution, a straight, horizontal incision of about 15 cm in length is made into the lower part. The obstetrician will deliver the presenting twin first. If the membranes of the baby's amniotic sac have not already ruptured, this will be done so that the amniotic fluid can be drained and the baby can be delivered. The obstetrician may need the help of another doctor and/or to use forceps to manoeuvre the first baby's head out through the incision.

When the first baby's head is delivered, mucus, blood and amniotic liquor will gently be suctioned away from their nose and mouth, at which stage your baby may utter their first cry, just as the rest of the body is being delivered. The obstetrician will then clamp the baby's umbilical cord twice, once near the placenta and once near the baby, before delivering the second baby in exactly the same way.

After the second baby has been delivered, both umbilical cords are cut (this can be done by your partner, if requested). Depending on the health of your babies, you may be able to hold or see them briefly before they are checked over by the paediatrician (one for each baby). Afterwards, if your babies are well, they can be handed to you to cuddle or put to the breast. The doctors and midwives will try to make sure that you hold the babies next to your skin, if at all possible. If there are any concerns about the babies, they may need to go to the

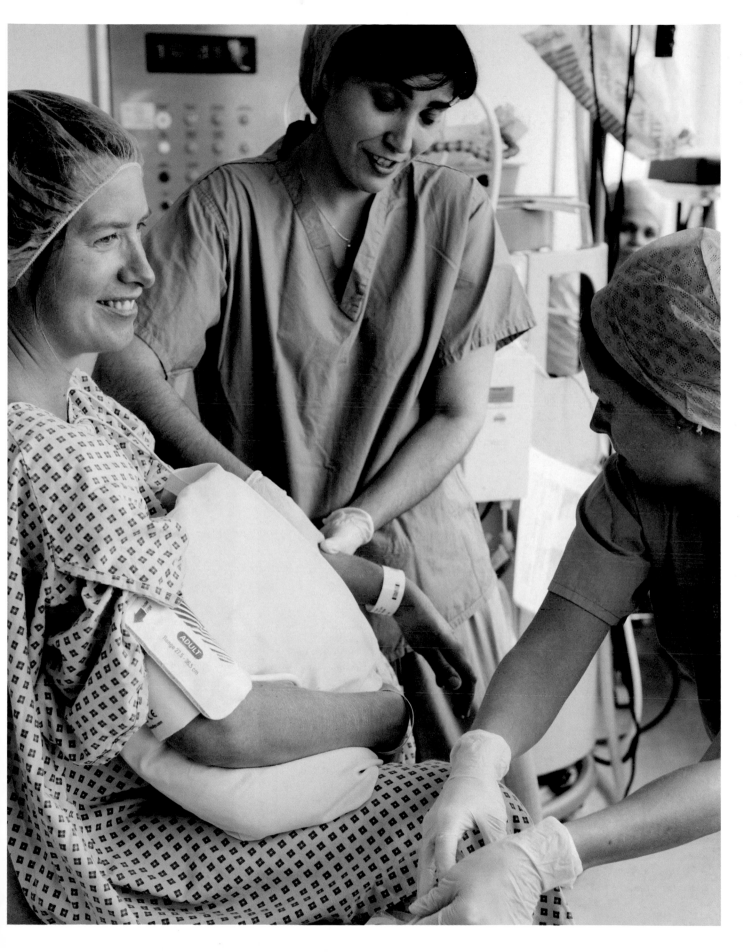

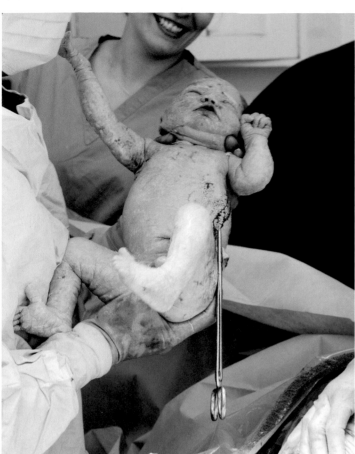

Neonatal Unit (NNU – *see* Chapter 6, p. 140). Midwives are aware of how difficult it can be for you to be away from your babies immediately after their birth, so they invariably take photographs of them soon after they are born and on each subsequent day until you can visit them in the NNU or they are returned to you on the postnatal ward.

Delivery of the placenta

While your babies are being attended to, the anaesthetist will inject you with a drug to speed up the delivery of the placenta(s) and to help the uterus to contract quickly in order to reduce the possibility of post-partum haemorrhage. This third stage of birth is similar to what happens in a vaginal delivery and is explained in more detail on p. 119 and 120. Once the placenta(s) has been removed and fully checked, blood and other fluids are cleaned out of the uterus (which is why there is usually less post-partum discharge – or lochia – following a Caesarean delivery than a vaginal one) and you are sutured. When this has been done, you will be taken to the postnatal ward.

DID YOU KNOW…?
If you are having a repeat Caesarean section, the abdominal incision will be made as close as possible to your previous one(s), so that it will look as if you only have one scar.

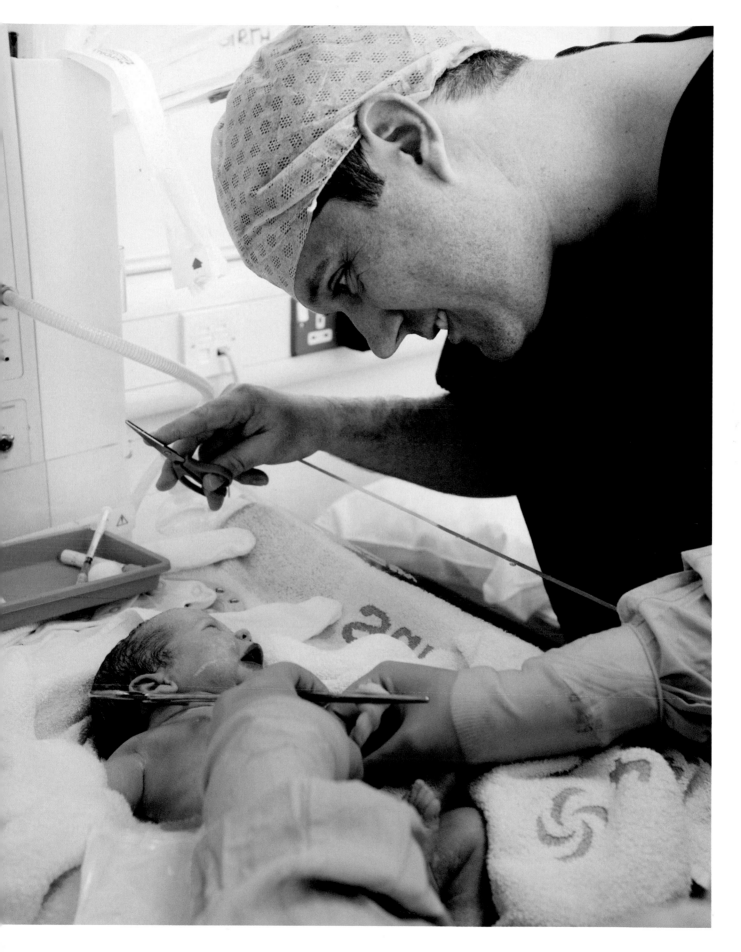

AFTER THE BIRTH

Your babies are finally here! The hours and days immediately after the birth are exciting, but often challenging and overwhelming, too. This is entirely normal and you will find that things soon settle down, but make sure that you take the time to congratulate yourself on your most amazing achievement.

There can often feel like a maelstrom of activity surrounding you and your babies immediately after delivery, particularly so with the increased numbers of medical staff needed at a twin birth. This is because you and your babies are checked over to see that you are all well and recovering as you should.

Your babies after the birth

After the umbilical cords have been cut, each baby will be dried and, if necessary, mucus is cleared from their nose and mouth. Your healthcare professionals will make sure you are able to hold the babies as soon as possible, 'skin to skin' contact helps bonding and will stimulate milk production. Afterwards, the babies will be weighed, have their length measured and are briefly checked over. They are given a wrist or ankle band to identify them, which includes their name, Twin 1 or 2, weight, date and time of birth. At this stage, babies (especially their hands and feet) are often a bluish colour, until their bodies warm up a little. Their faces are often puffy and may be marked, depending on the sort of delivery you had, and their head may be misshapen and slightly pointed if it was a protracted vaginal labour. Their appearance will soon smooth out and any marks or bruising will disappear over the next few days.

Within the first minute of their respective births, your babies will be assessed by the paediatrician using five simple measures called Apgar tests, devised in the 1950s by an American doctor called Virginia Apgar. These tests are then repeated every five minutes. The scores, marked out of ten, are used to assess the babies' overall condition at birth and to see if there is an immediate need for emergency medical care, but they do not signify what the long-term outcome might be. A score of seven and over means the baby is in good health; between four and six indicates the baby needs help with breathing; below four shows the baby needs immediate care, which could mean resuscitation or suctioning of the airways. A low initial score is not uncommon, especially for the second twin, or with twins born prematurely, after a long labour or by Caesarean section. This is why the test is repeated at five – and sometimes ten – minutes, after which time the score has often improved.

The Apgar scoring and categories are as follows:
Around 50 per cent of newborn twins are taken to the NNU. Even if this is a precautionary measure, you should prepare for the fact that you may not be leaving the delivery room or operating theatre with your babies. The medical staff will do all they can to keep you informed about what is happening, as they know how stressful this time can be for you, but do not hesitate to ask questions about anything you want to know.

SIGN	2	1	0
Heart rate	Normal (more than 100 beats per minute)	Slow (below 100 beats per minute)	Absent (no pulse)
Breathing	Regular, strong breathing	Slow/irregular, shallow breathing	Absent (no breathing)
Muscle tone	Active, good movement	Some tone, but little movement	No movement, limp
Response to stimulus	Sneezes, coughs, pulls away, cries	Facial response only (grimace)	Absent (no response)
Appearance	Normal, pink colour all over	Pink, but hands and feet bluish	Pale/blue all over

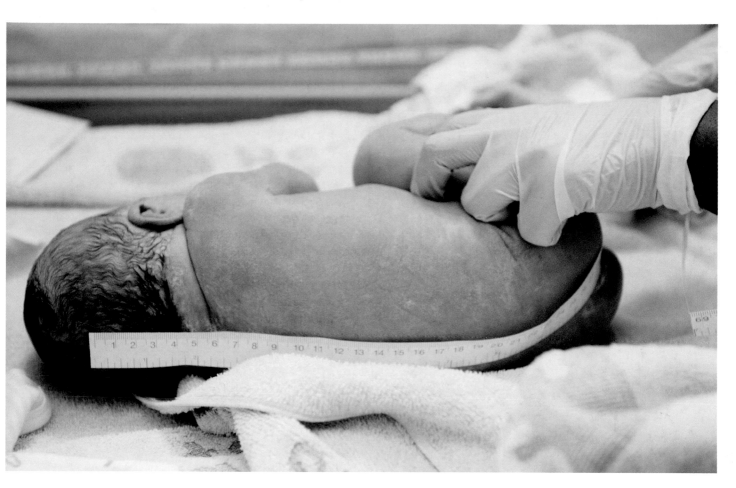

What happens to you after the birth

In addition to checking the health of your babies, your healthcare professionals will be monitoring your recovery from the birth, whether you had a vaginal delivery or a Caesarean section. How long you stay in hospital depends on the sort of birth you had, but it can range from 24 hours with a straightforward vaginal birth to three or four days with a Caesarean section, depending on individual circumstances.

After a vaginal birth

Once you have given birth and any suturing (stitching) has been done, you will be given some privacy to clean yourself up and change into fresh nightwear. If your babies are with you, this is the opportunity to be together as a family for the first time. You will probably be offered some tea and toast, or something similarly light and easy to digest. This can reduce nausea and vomiting soon after the birth, especially if you have been given drugs to induce labour or epidural anaesthetic. Eventually you will be taken to the postnatal ward, where you will spend your time until you are able to go home.

After a Caesarean section

Once your abdomen has been sutured (which usually takes

about half an hour), you will be moved to the postnatal ward. As there is a risk of developing a thrombosis in your legs after a Caesarean section, you are given support stockings to wear

VITAMIN K

Babies are born with a low level of vitamin K (the substance that helps blood to clot). A dose of Vitamin K at birth, or soon after, protects them from possible haemorrhage, especially to the brain – although this is a rare condition, it is difficult to detect and can be fatal. You do not have to give your consent for vitamin K to be administered, although concern that there was a link between the extra dose and childhood leukaemia are now known to be unfounded. If your babies are delivered by forceps, ventouse or Caesarean section, or are premature, they should be given vitamin K by injection soon after birth. Otherwise, you can ask for it to be given orally in three separate doses over the first month.

POST-PARTUM HAEMORRHAGE

Excessive bleeding from the vagina after birth is termed post-partum haemorrhage (PPH). There are two types of PPH, both of which can range from mild to severe:

▶ primary PPH, which is the loss of 500 ml or more of blood after a vaginal birth (or 1,000 ml after a Caesarean section) within 24 hours of the birth
▶ secondary PPH, which is abnormal or excessive vaginal bleeding between 24 hours and six to eight weeks after birth.

Primary PPH usually occurs because the uterus is not able to contract fast enough and/or some of the placenta has been retained, leaving blood vessels inside the uterus still pumping out blood. Drugs will be given to stop the haemorrhage and expel any remaining part of the placenta, but if the bleeding continues and is more severe (more than 1,000 ml), you may need a blood transfusion, as well as an operation under general anaesthesia to remove any retained placental tissue from the uterus.

Secondary PPH is usually caused by an infection to the lining of the uterus. Once again, this is often caused by a small piece of the placenta or membranes remaining in the womb. Normal postnatal bleeding gradually diminishes in the days following the birth, but if this is not the case, contact your doctor or midwife, as you may have developed secondary PPH. Other signs are abnormal or foul-smelling discharge (lochia – *see* Chapter 7, p. 200), a tender or painful lower abdomen, a fever or vomiting. Infection can be treated with antibiotics, but the tissue may also need to be removed from your uterus under general anaesthesia.

for a while and offered a course of injections to help prevent blood clots. Your heart rate, blood pressure, temperature and pain will be monitored regularly in the few hours after the operation and you should be offered sufficient pain relief once the epidural anaesthesia or spinal block has worn off. This can

take the form of morphine or similar, delivered as a one-off injection or via a drip that you can control yourself. However, this can make you may feel nauseous or sleepy, so after the first 12–24 hours, you may opt for oral painkillers such as paracetamol, which is routinely offered at this stage and is sufficient for many women.

If you are feeling ready, you can drink and eat, but try to eat something easily digestible initially to avoid vomiting (*see* p. 133). The midwives on the postnatal ward will be keen to get you mobile within 24 hours of the operation. This means that you can go to the toilet unaided, which allows the urinary catheter to be removed.

Your first few days after delivery

Despite the fact that you have been preparing for it for many months, the arrival of your babies can take you by surprise. Elation can quickly give way to anxiety or disorientation. This mixture of emotions is entirely to be expected: you are suddenly and permanently a mother of twins, after all, and you should allow yourself time to come to terms with this. These feelings may also be exacerbated by hunger, physical and mental tiredness and – if you had a Caesarean – post-operative pain. Talk them through with your birth partner and with your healthcare professionals too, especially if you require more pain relief. For more on the physical and emotional recovery immediately after the birth, see Chapter 7, p. 200.

Recovering on the ward

Giving birth in hospital means that your initial recovery will take place on the postnatal ward. It can be difficult to rest, given that you are likely to be disturbed not only by your own babies but those of other women too, as well their visitors. Some women opt for amenity rooms (private, en suite rooms off the ward) so that they can get some sleep and privacy. In some hospitals, priority for any single rooms is offered to twins. However, it can feel quite daunting to be behind closed doors on your own with two babies, and you may not be attended to as quickly by nursing staff, so you might, ultimately, prefer the companionship of the ward.

Ask your partner to bring in adequate refreshments, because you need to keep up your energy and fluid levels, especially if you are aiming to breastfeed. Limit visitors and restrict the length of the visits. Make sure that anyone who has a cold or any sort of infection stays away, and bear in mind that if your babies are in the NNU, visitors will not be allowed to see them, as there is usually a parents-only rule in order to limit the risks of infection.

If you have had a Caesarean section, the dressing covering your stitches will be removed after 24 hours. During this time you are likely to be more or less bed-bound and perhaps in some pain from the scar, and you may need help to pick up your babies. Take care when you try to get out of bed for the first time: you may be light-headed and feel weak, especially if you lost a lot of blood during labour or have had little to eat and drink for a while – if possible, make sure someone is with you. If you had an episiotomy during your vaginal birth, you may be less mobile than usual in the first 24–48 hours afterwards. If one or both of your babies is in the NNU, you may need to be taken there in a wheelchair until you can walk there unaided. Postnatal wards are often very busy, and it can be difficult to attract the attention of a midwife when you require one, but do not be embarrassed about requesting assistance until you are sufficiently mobile and/or strong to pick up your babies safely on your own.

Learning basic skills

Many first-time parents have little experience of caring for babies and newborn twins in particular are sometimes dauntingly tiny. You may need help learning how to care for your babies even at the simplest level, including how to change their nappies and bathe them, and how to clean and care for the umbilical cord stump until it falls off around ten days after the birth. Midwives are very used to this and will take care that you know what to do, but make sure that you do not leave hospital without feeling confident about meeting your babies' basic, everyday needs.

Your babies' first few days

For the first 24 hours or so, most babies are often very sleepy. They are adjusting to life in the outside world and are themselves recovering from the birth process. Although babies sleep for sixteen to eighteen hours of a 24-hour period during the first few weeks, they often do not both sleep at the same time, so try to rest (even if you cannot sleep) whenever they are both actually asleep. During their first few days, babies only need small quantities of colostrum, the thick, yellowish special milk that your breasts produce during pregnancy and the days immediately after the birth and before your actual milk comes in. For details on the particular properties of colostrum, *see* Chapter 6, p. 146 and information on breastfeeding and formula feeding, see Chapter 7, p. 156 and 166.

Introducing your other children to the babies

Most parents will be quite naturally concerned about the impact the new babies may have on an older child. Careful thought should be given to this during the pregnancy so that siblings are familiar with the idea of two new arrivals

and you are prepared for the first introduction. Of course, a lot will depend on the age of the older child as to how much they understand before the birth but a few points will apply to most children when they first meet their new brothers or sisters. First of all, try to plan ahead so that your older child meets you alone on the first occasion that they see you after the birth. Then you can focus your attention purely on them, by giving them plenty of cuddles and reassurance – after all, you may have been away for some time. After this, you can introduce them to the new babies. You can also arrange for your older child to bring a special present for each baby, which can be prominently displayed close to them, and for the babies each to give a present to your older child in return. If the child is older they may enjoy planning this in advance with you and perhaps also make a card. The individual presents will also start the older child off with thinking of each baby as an individual. Any visiting family members and friends should also be reminded about giving special attention to the older child and not making a lot of fuss of the new babies while they are there. You can start to involve them with helping you with small tasks such as fetching a nappy if this is appropriate so they feel involved. See also p. 212–3 for more information on how you can manage the arrival of siblings for your older child.

Going home

The moment will come when you are able to go home. On the one hand, you will be very excited, and perhaps relieved, to be going home to familiar surroundings and your own bed. On the other, you may also feel some anxiety at the realisation that you and your partner are now leaving behind the security of the hospital and the care that they can offer you and your babies, which is quite natural. For information about going home without your baby or babies if they are in a Neonatal Unit, see Chapter 6, p. 148.

When you do eventually take your babies home, they must – by law – be transported in car seats (if you are using a car or taxi). Be reassured that you will soon become confident in how to care for them, but that you can always ask for help if you have any concerns. In no time at all you will not be able to imagine life without them.

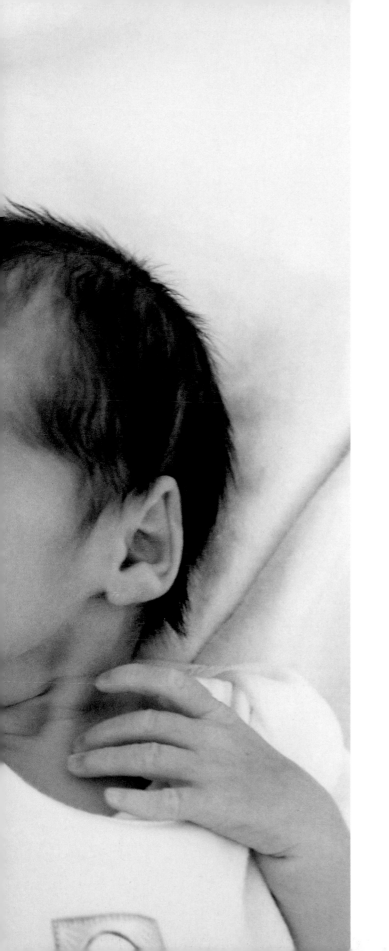

6

Premature and sick babies

Twins are likely to be born early, either because labour has begun spontaneously or as a result of the need to deliver the babies for medical reasons. Giving birth to twins born prematurely before 37 weeks, or ones who have health problems that require specialist care, brings many different medical, emotional and practical issues for parents, some of which are covered in this section.

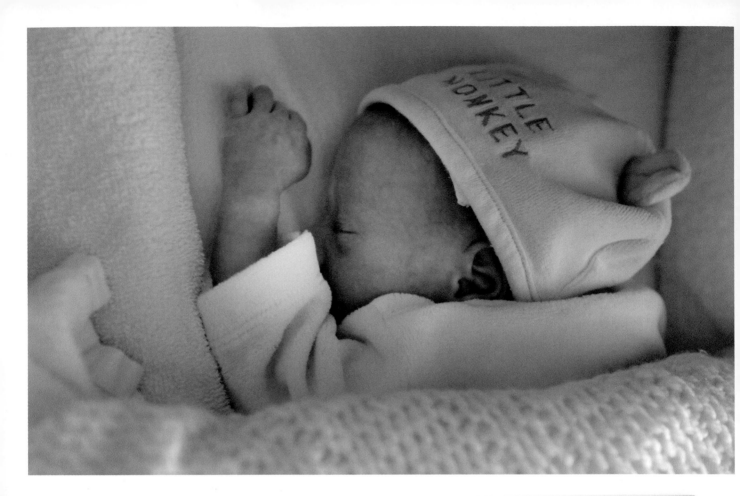

THE FACTS ABOUT PREMATURITY

At least 50–60 per cent of twins are born before 37 weeks, and up to fifteen per cent before 32 weeks. Once the babies are born, each baby will be assessed and treated individually. Two key factors in how a baby does after a premature birth are gestational age and birthweight. In addition, some babies have other health problems, identifiable before birth or soon after, that may affect their progress and outcome.

The more premature a baby is, the more assistance they are likely to require. For example, twins born at 36 weeks may be more mature but are still likely to be a little slow in learning to breastfeed; those born before 32 weeks are likely to require assistance with breathing (ventilation) and may have other health problems (temporary or otherwise); and those born before 28 weeks may have potentially life-threatening problems at birth and a poorer long-term prognosis. However, if a premature baby has a good weight for gestational age at birth, their chances of survival, and of a life with minor or no permanent health problems, improve considerably. The issue of prematurity is therefore not the only factor to take into consideration when babies are born early.

Reasons for premature delivery

There are several reasons why so many twins are born prematurely. One is that the mother goes into labour spontaneously. We still do not know what triggers labour, or why membranes rupture without warning, and it is therefore very difficult to prevent premature labour from occurring. Sometimes, if there are concerns about the health of the mother or the babies, the decision is taken to deliver the babies early (whether by inducing labour or by Caesarean section – *see* Chapter 5, p. 124 and 126), as the risks to the babies by being born at this time are less than if they remain for longer in the womb. The reasons for early delivery include:

► monochorionic pregnancy
► twin-to-twin transfusion syndrome (TTTS)
► risk of infection after premature rupture of the membranes
► pre-eclampsia or high blood pressure
► pre-existing diabetes or gestational diabetes
► bleeding from the placenta due to placenta praevia or placental abruption
► reduced efficiency of the placenta
► intra-uterine growth restriction (IUGR)
► fetal abnormality.
► genital tract infection (e.g. Chlamydia, gonorrhea)

For further information on some of these issues, see Chapter 4, p. 94–96 and Chapter 5, p. 116.

It is not possible to predict if a woman with a healthy pregnancy will go into spontaneous premature labour (although it is known that if you have had a previous, unexplained premature birth it is more likely to happen again). Similarly, there are often no indicators that an issue will develop that requires an early delivery. As yet, no medication given to women with twins to prevent pre-term delivery has been shown to have an improved outcome.

PREMATURITY AND LOW BIRTHWEIGHT

Prematurity is defined as being born before 37 weeks of gestation. There are degrees of prematurity:

Late preterm: babies born at 32–7 weeks
Very preterm: those born at 28–32 weeks
Extremely preterm: those born before 28 weeks.

Average birthweight for twins is defined as 2,500 g. For babies born weighing less than this, the degrees are described as follow:

Low birthweight: 1,500–2,500 g
Very low birthweight: 1,000–1,500 g
Extremely low birthweight: 1,000 g or less.

What happens when you go into labour prematurely

The signs of premature labour are similar to those listed in Chapter 5 on p. 116, although you may not feel much pain from contractions. If you think you might be experiencing some of these signs, call the labour ward without delay, whatever your gestation, so that they can advise you on what to do. Similarly, if you have any bleeding you must seek advice immediately.

If you are asked to come in to the hospital to be examined and it is confirmed that your labour is beginning, you may be given a drug to relax the uterus; this, together with complete bed rest for a few days, may slow down the contractions or stop them altogether. If your contractions do not cease, the doctors will have a discussion with you and a decision will be made as to whether to deliver the babies vaginally or by Caesarean section.

Depending on the gestation of your pregnancy, doctors may attempt to delay the delivery for as long as possible, as the more time that very premature babies are in the womb, the more it helps their lungs and brains to mature. Doctors will give you a steroid injection (or two, twelve hours apart), which speeds up the production of surfactant, the substance that is essential for the functioning of the lungs (*see* p. 138). Surfactant only begins to be produced at 24 weeks, continuing right up until 40 weeks. So the later babies are born, the better their lung development will be, which increases their chances of being able to breathe unassisted at birth. Delaying the delivery may also enable you to be transferred, if necessary, to a hospital with suitable neonatal care facilities. This will mean that you and your babies are both in the same hospital after the delivery and, if they are very premature, will ensure they are given the appropriate level of care from the moment they are born. For more on the outcomes for extremely premature babies, see Useful Resources.

Premature babies are at particular risk from a range of health problems, some of which are listed below. Being 'small for gestational age' increases the risks that these complications present for a baby. Many twins spend some time in the neonatal unit before they are mature enough to come home.

Breathing

Difficulty in breathing unaided is one of the common complications of prematurity, especially for babies born before 36 weeks. The more premature babies are, the less surfactant is present in their lungs. Surfactant is a substance that coats the tiny alveoli inside the lungs, helping them to stay inflated so that they have the best surface area available for oxygen to pass into the blood in sufficient amounts. If the lungs do not have enough surfactant, they are not able to supply enough oxygen and the babies can develop Respiratory Distress Syndrome (RDS). This affects around half of babies born before 32 weeks, although with proper monitoring, it is successfully treated in almost all babies. The closer to term babies are born, the lower the chances of their developing RDS.

Babies that need help with breathing may be ventilated in order to help their lungs to stay inflated and fill with oxygen (see p. 141). Artificial surfactant may also be given directly into a baby's lungs via a small tube soon after birth. When babies come off ventilation, they often do so gradually, because they initially tend to tire quickly as a result of the effort of breathing unaided. Over time, these periods of breathing on their own increase until the babies no longer need any help. Occasionally, an infection or other health setback means that a baby that had been breathing unaided once again needs ventilation, but as soon as the baby's health has improved once more, this should no longer be necessary. Some babies born very prematurely may need ventilation for longer and, in some cases, it is possible that a baby may go home while still on oxygen.

The prognosis for babies who have difficulty breathing has improved enormously in recent years. This is particularly so for those who are very premature or weigh less than 1,500 g, who had been the most difficult to ventilate safely in the past.

Jaundice

Neonatal jaundice occurs in around half of all newborns, but is particularly common in premature babies, because their livers are immature. When the extra red blood cells that are required when babies are in the womb are broken down after birth, a yellow-coloured pigment called bilirubin is produced and cleared by the liver. When levels of bilirubin are high, it is not processed fast enough and is deposited in the skin, giving it a yellowish tone. Jaundice often begins about four days after birth, and can disappear on its own. If treatment is required, it is done using phototherapy, which breaks down the pigments in the skin so that they can be excreted. The baby, wearing only a nappy and protective eye shields, remains in their cot or incubator and a special ultraviolet light is placed close to their skin. Treatment may take several days, and last for a few hours at a time. While jaundice can continue for several weeks after the birth, it usually disappears after two or three weeks. More rarely, it can be a sign of an underlying health problem, such as anaemia, infection or a liver problem, in which case different treatment would be required.

Maintaining body temperature

Premature babies have less body fat than full-term babies, and are less able to shiver (in order to generate heat for themselves) and to maintain their body temperature. For this reason, they are often placed in incubators at birth to keep them warm until they have grown and developed some fat. A baby may be in a small bed with a radiant warmer above or in an incubator. The incubator is a closed box that keeps the heat in and provides some humidity, which benefits very premature babies' skin. It has large holes on the side, like port holes, allowing you and the medical staff to touch and care for your baby.

Blood sugar regulation

Premature babies, especially those that are small for dates, are at risk of developing low blood sugar levels (hypoglycaemia), because they have a reduced stomach capacity and their digestive system is immature. For this reason, they may be given glucose intravenously and small, very regular amounts of milk. The nurses and neonatologists will make regular checks to ensure that babies' blood sugar levels are kept stable.

Infections

Immature immune systems make premature babies more prone to infections. These can lead to respiratory problems and other complications, so the staff in the NNU will be looking out for any signs of infection so that it can be treated quickly. The risk of infection is one of the main reasons that NNUs are extremely conscious of hygiene and often allow only parents (and, depending on their particular policy, siblings) to visit.

Sight and hearing

Complications relating to vision and hearing primarily affect babies born before 32 weeks and those with a birthweight below 1,500 g, although only about one in four of these babies suffers from these problems. Nonetheless, babies will be given a hearing test before they leave hospital. In the case of their sight, once they reach a certain stage of maturity, they will be screened weekly or fortnightly to ensure that any potential problems can be avoided or minimised.

Some babies can develop 'retinopathy of prematurity' (ROP), damage to the retina which is linked to levels of oxygen, and the baby's weight and gestation. It ranges from mild damage, which is the most common and causes no long-term visual consequences, to more severe, which requires laser treatment. With regular screening by a specialist ophthalmologist (a doctor specialising in problems of the eye), ROP is largely preventable.

Brain and neurological complications

Ultrasound scans of premature babies' brains are often performed soon after they are admitted to the NNU, and subsequently on a regular basis, because they are vulnerable to small bleeds from the tiny blood vessels in their developing

DID YOU KNOW...?
When you share the same environment as your babies, you make antibodies to any pathogens (germs) in the atmosphere, which are then secreted into your breast milk, passing tailor-made immunity to them.

brain. The brain and nervous system of babies born after 30 weeks are more mature and, if they have a good weight for gestational age and have no underlying health issues, it is unusual for babies to suffer from any serious neurological problem caused by these bleeds.

Babies born before 30 weeks, especially those that are small for gestational age (*see* Box below) or with fetal growth restriction (IUGR – *see* Chapter 4, p. 97), are at greater risk of a bleed in the brain. The majority of babies born before 30 weeks will recover from a bleed with little or no long-term neurological consequences. For some, however, their developmental progress may be affected (e.g. they may suffer from cerebral palsy). Some need educational support and have a range of other, more subtle difficulties. It is important that the progress of the babies is monitored, so that any problems in reaching their developmental milestones (e.g. walking, speech) can be identified and treated as soon as possible.

Babies with special needs
It is often very difficult for doctors to diagnose the extent of any developmental problem when babies are very young. A multidisciplinary team will explain to you what treatment is available and what practical steps you may need to take when your baby/babies come home, and they can also provide advice and information on the many support groups that exist. You may initially feel confused by what you have been told because you do not yet know the full implications nor the full extent of your baby's special needs. Do not hesitate to ask further questions of the medical team over the subsequent weeks and months – request information in writing if it makes things clearer for you. You will also be referred to health professionals in the community, who will continue to support you and your babies after their time in hospital.

THE DIFFERENCE BETWEEN 'LOW BIRTHWEIGHT' AND 'SMALL FOR GESTATIONAL AGE'
Being of low birthweight is different from being 'small for gestational age' (SGA), sometimes termed 'small for dates'. If you baby weighs 2.5 kg at birth, it may be described as low birth weight. However if your baby's birth weight is not appropriate for the gestational age it will be described as 'small for dates' and may be taken to the NNU until they are an appropriate weight, even though they were not technically premature.

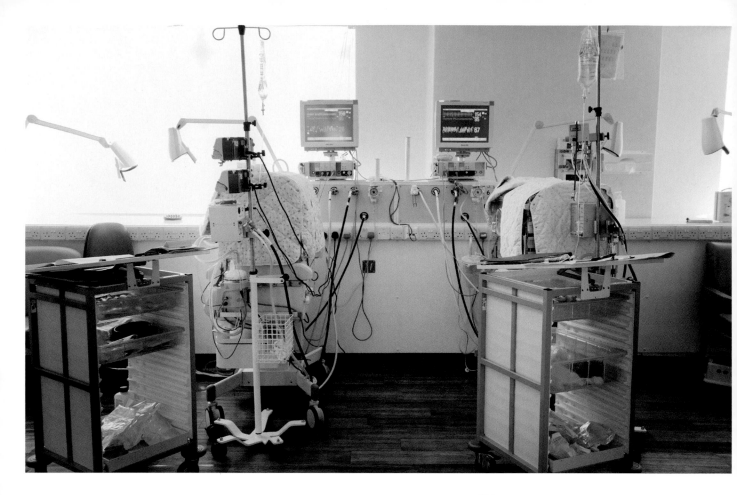

THE NEONATAL UNIT

A neonatal unit specialises in looking after premature and sick babies, offering expert 24-hour care. Neonatal care for newborns continues to improve, thanks to medical advances.

There are three levels of neonatal care: special care (formerly Level 1), high-dependency care (formerly Level 2) and intensive care (formerly Level 3). See Chapter 3, p. 50 for more information on the different types of neonatal unit (NNU). Your baby/babies will be placed in a unit suited to their care needs, and so they may have to be transferred to another hospital if your NNU is not able to offer the appropriate level of care. For example, not all hospitals have the neonatal intensive care unit (NICU) that is required for the long-term needs of very premature or low birthweight babies. Babies can also move to other levels of care within the same NNU.

Doctors and nurses on the ward will explain to you any treatment and tests they are planning for your baby/babies. Together, you will discuss your baby/babies' progress and have the opportunity to ask questions – however many times – until you fully understand the medical situation and what possible choices there might be. Sometimes, usually because of a sudden development in your baby's health, they may run certain tests or administer a certain drug or treatment before they have had a chance to discuss this with you. Afterwards, because communication and trust between you and the medical team are vital, they will ensure that they explain fully why this was necessary, so that you are happy with the clinical decision that was made.

Unless there is a medical condition that requires more prolonged treatment, most premature babies have gained enough weight and can feed sufficiently well that they are able to go home earlier than their due date.

Neonatal care: who is who

The staff caring for your baby/babies will primarily be:

▸ **neonatal nurses**: specially trained to look after premature and sick babies; the ratio of nurses to babies is extremely high in NICUs, so that the babies can be constantly monitored and cared for

▸ **neonatologists**: doctors who specialise in the care of premature and unwell babies; the most senior is a consultant, and those who work in the team include registrars and junior doctors

▸ **other health professionals**: for example, physiotherapists, dieticians, breastfeeding specialists and psychologists; these may be available if your baby/babies need further specialist help.

Equipment

The amount of equipment that surrounds a baby in the NNU can be frightening for parents until you understand why it is used. When you first see your babies, they may be attached to various tubes or 'lines', have a tube in their nose, be wearing only a nappy and a hat, and are likely to look very tiny and fragile in their incubator. The nursing and medical staff will explain the function of the various machines, and do not hesitate to ask questions as often as needed.

Ventilators

A ventilator is a breathing machine to assist or replace spontaneous breathing. Babies on some types of ventilator will have a tube reaching down their windpipe so that the oxygen reaches their lungs. The type of ventilator used by each baby will depend on their specific needs; babies can therefore be moved from one to another according to their progress:

▸ **positive pressure ventilator**: inflates the lungs by blowing in oxygen via a tube inserted through the nose or mouth

▸ **high-frequency ventilator**: provides small amounts of oxygen at high frequency (utilises a breathing rate greater than 4 times the normal rate), making the chest look as if it is vibrating; used for certain lung conditions and for very premature babies, as it is a gentler way of administering oxygen, reducing risk of damage to lungs and of RDS (see p. 138)

▸ **continuous positive airway pressure (CPAP)**: provides constant, slightly raised air pressure through two fine tubes placed in the nostrils; used for babies that no longer need total ventilation but still need help with breathing. CPAP also enables babies who can breathe on their own to maintain good levels of oxygen in their blood.

Monitors

Various monitors may be used, each attached to the baby via a thin line and a little pad stuck to a particular part of the body, such as the baby's chest or hand/foot. These monitors include:

▸ **vital signs monitor**: picks up electrical signals from the heart; changes will trigger an alarm

▸ **blood saturation monitor**: a sensor on the foot or hand detects the level of oxygen in the blood

▸ **apnoea alarm**: triggered if a baby stops breathing; premature babies, particularly very premature ones, sometimes stop breathing for short periods because their brain has not yet developed the connections that remind the body to maintain this function.

Tubes, drips and catheters

During their time in the NNU, most premature babies require medication and nutrients to be administered or blood samples to be taken, and this is done via thin tubes (lines) or catheters. Seeing these can be very upsetting for parents, but complete care is taken not to distress the babies while they are being set up.

Some premature babies cannot feed on their own, so are given breast milk or formula via a small, soft tube that is placed through their nose or mouth and down into their stomach (see p. 147). It is then secured to their face.

Plastic cannulae are often inserted into a baby's hand, arm, foot or leg, depending on where a suitable blood vessel can be found. These drips provide fluids or medication. Because babies' blood vessels are so small, it is not uncommon for the drip to be re-sited after a while. Sometimes, an umbilical catheter is used, especially in the first few days after the birth. This is a long, flexible, hollow tube inserted either into the baby's umbilical artery or vein.

DID YOU KNOW...?

The growth, weight gain and development of all babies are measured against a range of data, collated over time, to indicate an average for babies born at 40 weeks. The development of premature babies will differ from that of a full-term baby, so their milestones are calculated from the date on which they were due, not the one on which they were actually born. See also Chapter 7, p. 192.

Your role as a parent in the NNU is a very important one. Premature twins often appear so fragile to parents that they are daunted at the thought of caring for them, but the nurses on the ward will show you how you can hold or touch your babies so that they get to know you.

Touch is very important for babies, and the medical staff will encourage you to touch and talk to your babies, especially if they are having a procedure that is stressful for them. They will show you how best to do this if your babies are not able to leave their incubator. You can simply hold their hand, body or head, as they will find this very reassuring – more so than stroking or massaging, which may be too stimulating for them if they are very premature.

If your babies can be taken out of the incubators but still need to be attached to lines or drips, the staff will show you how you can hold them safely. It is better to hold one baby at a time, both for safety reasons and so that they each have your undivided attention. Ideally, you should try to have skin-to-skin contact for as long as possible (*see* right). This is a special time for you to get to know your babies and for them to experience your touch, warmth and smell and to hear your voice.

Being involved in your babies' care will gradually give you confidence in looking after them on your own. The neonatal nurses will show you how to look after your babies' needs, including how to change their nappy, dress them and clean their mouth and face (babies generally do not need bathing for some time, not least because they lose so much body warmth when they are undressed and placed in water). At first, you are likely to feel somewhat nervous, but soon you will do all this without thinking twice about it. And as a result, you and your babies will continue to get to know each other. For more information on caring for your premature or sick babies, see Useful Resources.

Kangaroo care

Kangaroo care is skin-to-skin contact that involves a baby being held directly against the parent's chest. It is actively encouraged in NNUs. The baby just wears a nappy and a hat, but is tucked inside your clothes at the front with a blanket over them (staff will show you how to do this). With their face against your chest they can smell and feel your skin and are kept as snug as possible. If possible, try talking or singing to your babies softly so that they hear the reassuring sound of your voice. Kangaroo care helps your milk production by stimulating the hormone involved in the milk ejection reflex (*see* Chapter 7, Box on p. 157). It also keeps babies happy and calm and helps them to grow, and many parents enjoy staying like this for hours, holding one or both babies at once, and creating a strong bond with their babies.

> **DID YOU KNOW…?**
> If you are unwell, the neonatal ward will advise you on whether it would be safer to stay away until you are better, not only for your baby/babies' sake, but also for that of the other sick and vulnerable babies on the ward.

> **WHEN YOU ARE ABSENT FROM THE POSTNATAL WARD**
> If you are still in hospital and are spending time with one or both babies in the neonatal unit, make sure that the staff know that you may be absent from the postnatal ward for long periods of time. Ask them to keep your meals for you, as well as any medication that you require, so that you do not miss out just because you were not there at the time they were being handed out.

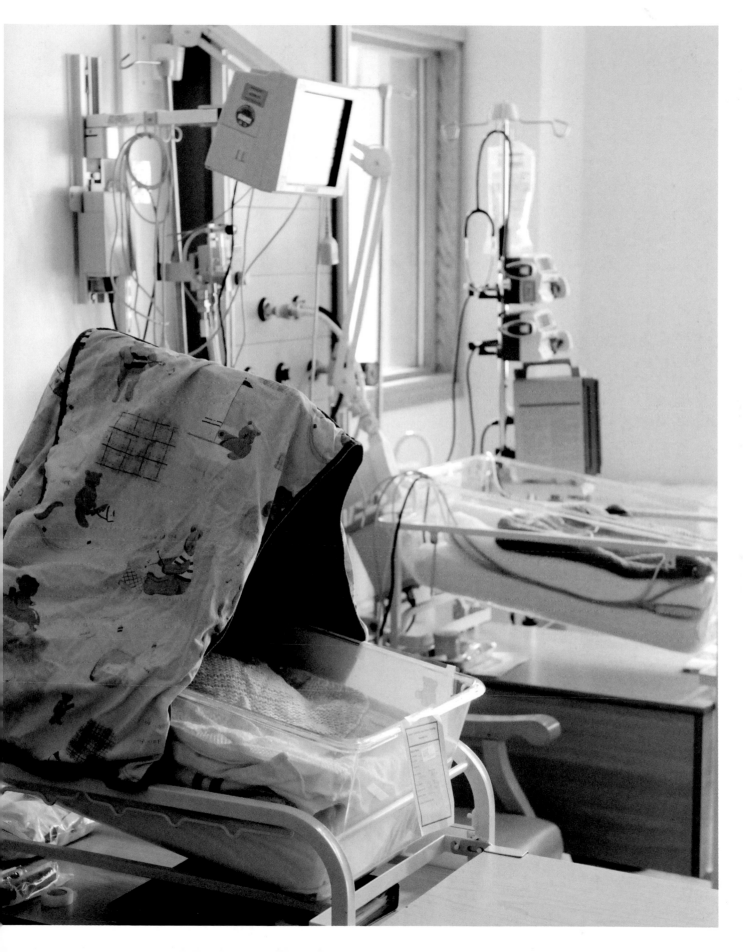

Emily's story

My waters broke when I was 30 weeks pregnant, while I was at work! It was a huge shock, as there had been no other signs of our twins making an early appearance. I was taken to hospital from the office and within four hours our boys had arrived by emergency Caesarean section. After the event, the doctors weren't able to identify a cause of my premature delivery – it was just 'one of those things' – although I had had a cold and sometimes that leads to an infection that results in the waters breaking.

My husband and I were simply not ready for their arrival and it took a while to adjust. The neonatal unit is not a place you expect to come when you prepare for being parents and I never thought it would happen to us. But we got used to it. The first time I saw my babies was two days after they were born, as I was too ill to be taken to them before then. They were in separate, open incubators at opposite ends of the neonatal unit and were covered in wires, with breathing equipment attached to their noses and feeding tubes in their mouths. It was a sight all parents hope they'll never see and I found it immensely frightening, bewildering and upsetting. And, as their mother, I felt guilty that I had somehow failed to give my children the best start.

As time went on we established a routine. I expressed milk and fed it to them through a tube. We held them when we could and changed their nappies if it was possible, eventually becoming accustomed to the wires. The nurses and doctors were wonderful and it was a privilege to meet such special people; they helped us enormously in coming to terms with the situation. Having a premature baby is two steps forward, one step back – some days are better than others – and we worried about the future and whether our babies would be healthy. But finally the day came, nearly ten weeks later, when they came home. It was strange at first, as we had got used to the hospital life and machines telling us what they needed!

Making sure babies have the nutrition required for their size and gestation is essential for their growth and development. Premature babies undoubtedly benefit from receiving breast milk from birth, and even if they are unable to suck when they are born, they can receive your expressed milk via a fine tube into their stomach.

As well as promoting brain growth and development, breast milk provides babies with the mother's antibodies – ones that they would have been receiving if they were still in the womb. These protect them from infection at a time when they are most vulnerable. The first substance you produce is called colostrum, which is ready at birth until your actual milk comes through three to seven days later. Colostrum is particularly beneficial for premature babies, as it contains a highly concentrated mixture of proteins, antibodies and all the nutrients that they need. Even if you only breastfeed for a few days, colostrum will be of enormous benefit to your babies. Although it is produced in small quantities, newborn babies do not, in any case, have the stomach capacity for anything more than a few drops at a time. The key thing is to feed a little and often. Full information on breastfeeding benefits and techniques is given in Chapter 7, p. 156.

YOUR MILK SUPPLY

Some women do find that, despite their best efforts, their supply of breast milk is insufficient for both babies. This may be a temporary issue or a more long-term one, but it is true that some women do produce more milk – and faster – than others. If this happens to you, you should discuss with the nurses and neonatologist how best to make use of your breast milk, as there are various options: for example, you may give the milk exclusively to just one of your babies (if one is unwell or smaller and weaker than the other) or you may alternate feeds (see Chapter 7, p. 169 for more on feeding options).

If you are using formula, your babies will be given a type that is specially formulated for premature babies to help with good brain, cell and immune system development. It replicates breast milk as closely as possible, so your babies receive the right balance of nutrients. Even if your babies are not able to suck from a teat at first (see below), they will be able to in due course. While they are in the NNU, the hospital will sterilise the feeding equipment that your babies are using, but you will need to know how to do so when they come home (see Chapter 7, p. 166).

Babies with the sucking reflex

If your babies are able to breastfeed from birth on their own, it is vital that you receive as much help as possible in the first few days – the staff will always give guidance and advice. This is because your babies must learn how to latch on correctly (see Chapter 7, p. 159) in order to receive the colostrum and milk they need. If they do not do this, their blood sugar levels can drop or they can become dehydrated, both of which will make it harder for them to feed, as they will be too sleepy and tired. The situation then turns into a vicious circle: the sleepier they are, the less energy they have to feed and the less your breasts are stimulated into providing sufficient amounts of colostrum and, later, of milk.

If the babies need more milk, the neonatal team may suggest that pre-term infant formula is given as a 'top-up' in the first few days, until your breast milk comes through. Do not take this as a sign that you are already failing in your efforts to breastfeed. It is simply that babies born early may need a little additional sustenance to enable them to grow as they would have done in the womb. The situation is likely to be temporary, but in the meantime, formula maintains babies' energy and blood sugar levels so that they can gradually learn how to latch on and feed efficiently.

DID YOU KNOW…?

Many hospitals have access to 'milk banks', where breast milk donated by other mothers can be given to sick babies.

Babies who need help with feeding

Twins born prematurely often do not possess the sucking instinct (which develops from about Weeks 32–4). Many also require ventilation, which makes normal feeding methods impossible. In these instances, babies need to be fed with either breast milk or formula via a soft tube (see p. 141). This also enables babies to conserve precious energy that they would otherwise have expended by trying to suck.

Expressing milk

If one or both of your babies require tube feeding, and if you plan to breastfeed, ask to express milk as soon as possible. There is usually a dedicated room in the NNU containing several highly efficient breast pumps, and bottles can be lent to you if you have not yet managed to buy any of your own. A nurse will show you how to express and how/where to store the milk (there are usually fridges specifically for this purpose). Initially, it is usual to be able to extract only a few drops of colostrum but every drop is beneficial for your babies. The more often you try to express, the more you will stimulate your breasts, producing colostrum and eventually milk. You may find that when you spend time with your babies, this stimulates the 'milk ejection reflex' or 'let-down reflex' (see Chapter 7, p. 157). In the first few days hand expressing is usually recommended so your nipples don't become sore, then you will be advised to move on to using the pump.

Start the pump at a lower setting initially, and build up the suction strength gradually in order not to damage your nipples. When your milk does eventually come through, you will probably find that you have a more plentiful supply first thing in the morning, when you are rested, so this is a good time to express. Once your babies start suckling at the breast, you should express after the feed to ensure that your breasts are fully drained and can fill up before the next feed.

Breastfeeding and expressing milk when you are at home and the babies are in hospital needs some planning and good organisation. Stress and fatigue are known to affect milk supply, so rest as much as possible to aid your production of milk. Try to keep going through this period: any breast milk at all is good for the babies.

Learning to suck

Gradually, as babies become stronger and develop the sucking reflex, they will instinctively start to 'root around' when they are held close to your breast, or they may start to suck when a (clean) finger or dummy is placed in their mouth. If you are aiming to breastfeed, try putting your baby/babies near or at your breast when they are out of their incubator and being fed. The neonatal nurses will be able to assess when each baby is

TOTAL PARENTERAL NUTRITION
Very premature babies or sick babies are given all their nutrients intravenously so that these pass directly into their bloodstream. This speeds up growth and bypasses the immature digestive system which would otherwise use up too much energy digesting the nutrients (even breast milk). This method of feeding is called 'total parenteral nutrition' (TPN) and is stopped once a baby reaches the required weight and strength and can move on to tube feeding.

ready to try to suck, either at your breast or from a bottle – you may find that one is ready for the switch sooner than the other. The switch from tube feeding will be gradual, to ensure that your babies continue to thrive: as their ability to feed and the quantity of milk being taken increases, so the volume of milk given via the tube decreases.

Colostrum is particularly beneficial for premature babies, as it contains a highly concentrated mixture of proteins, antibodies and all the nutrients that they need.

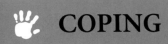

Having a premature baby/babies in the NNU is often frightening for parents. Guilt, worry about their health, fear about the future, and feelings of anger or helplessness are all common – and normal – emotions. The neonatal team will be an invaluable source of support, advice, encouragement and information.

Going home without your babies

Many hospitals have rooms for parents to stay in while their babies are in the NNU. Nevertheless, if your babies' stay is a prolonged one (*see* right), there will come a time when you need to return to your own home. If one or both of your babies has to remain in the NNU, this is likely to be a time of very mixed emotions for you, and you may feel guilty and sad at the prospect of going home without them. However, as you will already have discovered, these units encourage you to spend as much time as you wish with your babies. So you can reassure yourself that you can spend all day in the unit caring for your baby/babies in just the same way as you would be if you were at home, with the added benefit that they are receiving the best medical and nursing care. The medical and nursing staff can provide information on organisations and support groups that might be useful. (*see* Useful Resources).

Your closest family and friends will need to be told, but perhaps allocate to them the task of telling people in your wider circle, so that you do not take up time and energy informing them of what the situation is – unless you are happy to do so. The focus at such a time should be solely on you as parents, any older children and your babies.

Juggling home life (and, for partners, work) with visits to the hospital can be tiring and stressful. Even if you have one baby already back home, or older children to look after, the more you can rest, get good amounts of sleep and recover from the birth now, the better you will be able to cope with the demands of looking after two babies later on. Try to surround yourself only with friends and family who can offer you practical and emotional support, not those who take up even more of your precious energy. Delegate tasks whenever you can; for example, if you are lacking baby equipment or things for yourself, you could ask a friend or relative to get it for you.

When one baby is well and the other is in the NNU

Sometimes one baby may need care in the NNU, while the other is either on the postnatal ward with you, or is discharged and able to go home. Or it may be that one baby is looked after in one hospital, while the other is transferred to a different one for more specialist care. This situation can be very stressful and complex, practically, emotionally and psychologically, and each parent is likely to react differently.

This situation can make the bond you have with each baby different. It is entirely normal to feel very protective towards a vulnerable and sick premature baby and, as a consequence, you may find that you bond more with him/her; or it could be that you bond more with the stronger baby who is able to come home first and thus receive the benefits of your time and attention. However you cope with the situation, you should be aware that it is very common to experience psychological and emotional difficulties when one baby is well and the other not, and any feelings you may have are not unnatural. They do not make you a bad parent, but you may benefit from talking to someone about it at some stage in the future if these feelings start to impact on the way you relate to one/both of your babies. Try to discuss your worries with your partner and help each other in practical and emotional ways. You can also talk to the staff in the NNU, who will be able to refer you for more support. For more on getting to know your babies, see Chapter 7, p. 189.

Prolonged hospital stay

A prolonged hospital stay for a baby/babies means that your life will undergo a change of rhythm. Try to focus on the essentials and concentrate on what is most important: organising yourselves around your baby/babies in hospital. Get as much help as you can and, if you have other children, try to spend time with them as well so that they do not feel forgotten. If they are old enough, keep communicating with them, so that they understand what is going on and that the situation is temporary.

You should be prepared for some days to go less well than others. It is likely that you will have some setbacks, which will inevitably be worrying, so try to avoid projecting too far ahead, such as predicting when the baby/babies might come home. Keeping a diary of your journey can help you. Similarly, if your babies are sick, the neonatologists may find it difficult to be clear-cut about prognosis, because the situation could change from one day to the next.

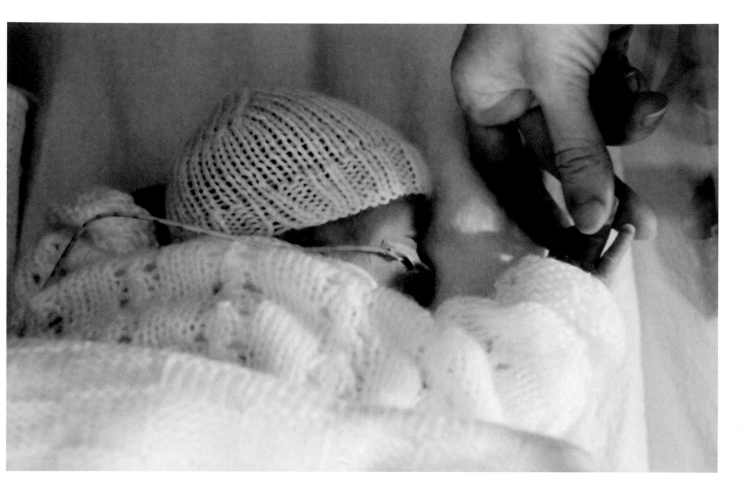

Going home from the neonatal unit

The day you bring your baby/babies home after a stay in the NNU is always a special one. You are likely to be elated that you can finally be reunited as a family, but you may also be anxious at the thought of being in sole charge of such tiny babies. Whatever your concerns, reassure yourself that the hospital staff do not discharge premature babies without being confident that the parents are able to look after them. Indeed, you will usually be left to look after your babies alone in the hospital for a day to two to help you gain confidence – you may hear this referred to as 'rooming in'. Nonetheless, do make sure that, before you bring your baby/babies home, you are clear about their everyday care, how to administer any treatment or medication, and that you have telephone numbers for the ward, as well as for your doctor and health visitor.

Once you are back home, your local health visitor will visit you regularly at first to check on your and you babies' progress and to provide advice. Your babies will probably have follow-up appointments at the hospital, but in the meantime if you have any doubts or queries concerning their health, do not hesitate to call the NNU, as the staff will be happy to help.

You may experience a delayed reaction of extreme tiredness after the babies have been in the NNU: you summon all your strength to keep going while they are in hospital, but once they are both back home you start to lose the energy that you were surviving on before. Exhaustion and anxiety can leave you more prone to postnatal depression (and mothers of twins can be at higher risk), so do try to seek help sooner rather than later if you think you may be experiencing symptoms of this common condition. For more information on postnatal depression, see Chapter 7, p. 207.

WHEN BABIES DIE

Despite many advances in the care of newborn babies and in early diagnosis and treatment for various conditions, some sadly do not survive. The death of a child, at whatever age, is a devastating experience for parents.

Grieving is different for everyone: there is no time frame for grieving and no set way of doing so. Some parents find that their emotions are powerful and almost unbearable from the start, whereas others may initially be in a state of shock or numbness. In addition, some people manage their feelings by talking to other people about what they are experiencing, while others may be more introverted, preferring to keep things to themselves. It may be that you deal with the situation differently from your partner, so you will need to be sensitive to this and accept that there is no 'right way' and 'wrong way'. You can also expect there to be bad days or hours as well as better ones and it is quite normal to experience a mixture of emotions as time goes on.

However, bereavement can be isolating: grieving parents often feel that people avoid them or are too embarrassed or fearful of upsetting you to mention the loss. It is worth knowing that support is there if you need it, both from professional counsellors and charitable organisations specialising in helping the bereaved (*see* Box). Some people also discover that certain family members or friends are of enormous support during this time – and not always those they imagined would be so.

Words from well-intentioned family, friends and medical staff, such as 'time is a great healer' or 'perhaps it's for the best', are intended to comfort, but can be extremely upsetting to hear. Yet, the reality is that, as with all bereavements, parents who have lost a baby or babies can eventually learn to live with their grief. Planning a funeral and finding ways to commemorate your baby/babies can also help you through the grieving process.

Coming to terms with your loss

Parents usually want to know why the death occurred and if there is something they could have done to prevent it – self-blame is particularly common among mothers. Not all hospitals offer a consultation after a death, so this may be something you have to request if you would like the opportunity to discuss things further. Your healthcare professionals can ask for the necessary tests to be done in order to try to explain the situation as fully as possible. This may include a post-mortem (which requires your written consent), although you should be made aware that even this may not provide all the answers.

Some couples may be tempted to try to get pregnant again immediately, but after a loss of this sort, taking a little time to recover may be preferable. Try to seek professional advice before making any decisions.

Losing one baby

Coping with death of a baby while simultaneously celebrating the birth of the surviving twin is a situation that is unique to parents of multiples. It can be all the more difficult because parents expecting more than one baby are made to feel special and there is usually an additional excitement and status that goes with a twin pregnancy. When this situation changes there are constant reminders of the loss, most significantly the surviving twin.

You may find others say things such as 'at least you still have a baby', which can leave you feeling that you should not be grieving for – or even mention – the other twin. When you are also looking after a surviving baby, you will have extremely mixed emotions – great joy and great sadness – and parents can feel very guilty for not grieving 'enough', as if they are betraying their dead baby. Conversely, you may feel guilty if you are grieving for your dead baby and, as a result, are not able to cherish the survivor. If your surviving baby is still very unwell, you may avoid becoming emotionally attached, in case that baby, too, does not survive. Parents should be reassured that all of these emotions (and others) are completely natural. You will usually be offered professional support but if not ask hospital staff or your doctor for help.

GETTING THE RIGHT SUPPORT
Many parents find that talking to a professional helps them to express their feelings, to accept the reality of what has happened to them and to find ways of living with their grief. Some hospitals have bereavement counsellors, psychologists or specially trained midwives who parents may want to speak to, at least initially. Doctors may have access to appropriate counselling services and there are, in addition, several charities that specifically support bereaved parents and children (*see* Useful Resources).

All newborn deaths (as well as stillbirths) must be registered by one or both parents within 42 days in England or 21 days in Scotland (it is not compulsory in Northern Ireland). This can be done at the nearest Registrar of Births, Deaths and Marriages, and the hospital staff will give you the paperwork you require for this. If a birth certificate has not yet been issued, this can be done at the same time. You will be given a death certificate stating your babies' names, if you have chosen them, as well as a form for the funeral director to enable a burial or cremation to take place. Most hospitals are able to offer funeral services, or you may prefer to make your own arrangements.

How your other children might grieve

Children will also grieve for the loss of a sibling(s) and there is no specific time frame for this. Children display their distress in different ways from adults (e.g. they may start behaving badly instead of voicing any sadness), so avoid imposing expectations on them. Depending on their age, they may have a limited understanding of what death is, so it is therefore important that the situation is explained to them in words they will understand; with very young children you may have to give information a little bit at a time. Reassure them that the death was nobody's fault and be prepared to say 'I don't know' when they are asking questions. You should not be afraid to show your own feelings when discussing things with them, or to talk about the baby/babies, but try to focus on their emotions. Encourage them to talk about how they are feeling, after the death and in the future. When you are dealing with your own grief, it can be difficult to support others at the same time. If you need help with this or feel that your child(ren) are very affected by the death and that this is not changing, you may consider contacting one of the child bereavement support groups (*see* Useful Resources).

Saying goodbye

It may be possible to spend time – if you so wish – with your baby/babies after they have died. While this will be very difficult for you at the time, parents who do so are grateful later on for these precious moments. If you have advance knowledge that a baby is not going to survive, you should be encouraged to spend as much time with them as possible, even if that means spending time away from the other twin –

this will not affect your long-term relationship with them. You may find it helpful to discuss with the medical staff how and where you spend your time and what you feel able to do.

Planning a funeral

Many parents find that a funeral or memorial service is a chance to finally say goodbye. Your ideas about what you feel is fitting can be discussed with a religious or spiritual leader, and professionals may be able to talk through with you what other families have found useful. If the task seems overwhelming, ask others to help. Consider also if your other child(ren) should attend the service – many value the opportunity of doing so and it can help them make sense of the loss.

If both twins have died, you may want to ask if they can be placed in the same coffin. You could put personal items there – perhaps something belonging to you or the babies, or a letter that you or your other children have written to them. Finding the right words to say at the service can be very hard, but poems and symbolic gestures, such as the releasing of balloons or birds, can be very powerful. You may want to consider the wording on the memorial plaque, acknowledging that the babies were twins or that one is survived by a twin.

Future memories

Collecting items in a 'journey box' is a wonderful way of looking back on your baby/babies' journey when newborn. You can ask staff at the hospital for anything they may have used, such as name tags, plasters or eyeshields, and often they can collect other items for you, such as a lock of hair or hand and finger prints. Photos and/or videos of the baby/babies with both parents can be a wonderful source of subsequent comfort and a photograph of the babies together can be a valuable reminder to the surviving child that they did indeed once have a twin. Some artists can produce drawings based on individual photographs of the twins if it was not possible to take one of them together at the time. Other mementoes that are often cited as being of immense help include:

▶ a baby blanket or outfit
▶ cards and letters from friends and family
▶ antenatal ultrasound scans.

Some parents plant trees or buy a particular ornament to commemorate the baby/babies, and ensure that they mark the anniversary of the birth or death in a way that is meaningful to them. For some parents, this will be the same date as the birthday of a surviving twin and some thought about how you manage this situation, as well as how it may evolve over time, is useful.

The first few months

The first few months of your babies'
lives are a very special time. However,
they can also feel overwhelming,
so you need to make sure you take
care of yourself, while you are meeting
the ongoing needs of your babies.

EQUIPMENT

Couples who know they are expecting twins need to think about what equipment they will require and, most especially, which items they may need in duplicate. As most twins are born early, it is wise to start planning essential things to buy in good time so that you are well prepared.

What to buy

Even though many parents – especially first-time parents – envisage having everything new, this can be very costly, so think about buying second-hand equipment or using hand-me-downs, as this could save you a lot of money. Your local Twins Club and branch of the NCT are good starting points, as are locally advertised table-top sales. Consider borrowing or hiring things that you will need for only a short time, thus saving your money for buying items that are longer-lasting. Family and friends can be very generous, so you could prepare a list in case they ask about what you most need or would like, thus avoiding duplication. See Useful Resources for good sources of second-hand and hire equipment.

SUGGESTED EQUIPMENT

These are things that you may find useful in the first few months and beyond. It is not a cast-iron, 'must have list', so think carefully about what might suit you. Remember, it is better to buy less than more and you can always stock up after the babies are born.

Feeding

For breastfeeding:
▸ nursing bras
▸ nursing pads
▸ breast pump (optional – can also be hired)
▸ breast milk storage bags
▸ extra pillows or cushions

For each baby:
▸ 6 250 ml bottles
▸ 6 medium-flow teats

To be shared between the babies:
▸ 1 bottle brush, with brush for teats (separate or not)
▸ knife or spatula (if formula feeding)
▸ measuring jug (if formula feeding)
▸ steriliser (steam or microwave)
▸ cold-water sterilising solution or tablets for occasional use (e.g. when travelling)
▸ 12 muslin cloths

Clothing (per baby)
▸ 3 vests/bodysuits
▸ 3–4 sleepsuits
▸ 2 pairs scratch mits
▸ 1 or 2 jackets/cardigans
▸ 1 winter hat/sun hat
▸ 1 all-in-one outdoor suit (for autumn/ winter babies)

Bathing and nappy-changing
▸ 1 baby bath
▸ 1 or 2 baby bath supports (optional)
▸ 2 changing mats
▸ nappies: disposable or cloth
▸ disposable nappy sacks (for disposable nappies)
▸ lidded nappy bucket, lined with a plastic bag
▸ cotton wool balls
▸ hypoallergenic wipes
▸ nappy cream/petroleum jelly
▸ bowl to be kept for 'topping and tailing'

Sleeping (per baby)
▸ Moses basket/carrycot/crib with mattress (optional)
▸ cot (can be shared at first) and mattress
▸ 2 sets of cotton sheets and cellular blankets
▸ 1 baby sleeping bag (if preferred)

Getting out and about
▸ 2 rear-facing infant car seats
▸ 1 double pram/pushchair/buggy
▸ 1 or 2 single pushchairs (optional)
▸ 2 outdoor blankets (not wool)
▸ 1 or 2 baby carriers or slings
▸ 1 nappy-changing bag

Miscellaneous
▸ 2 baby chairs
▸ baby-listening device (monitor)
▸ easy-to-use thermometer
▸ dummies

Having the right equipment to hand

Organising your home ahead of the birth will help you enormously in the first few weeks of your babies' lives. With a little advance planning, together with some adaptation once the babies are back home, you will be able to save yourself a lot of precious time and energy and have more time to enjoy the babies.

Arrange to have equipment in each room where it may be needed. For example, you may feed the babies in one room at night (probably the one in which they are sleeping, *see* p. 176), and in another during the day. It is a good idea to have spare cushions or pillows (*see* p. 157) for feeding in each of these rooms so that you do not have to keep transporting them from one place to another. Keep any bottles within easy reach in the kitchen – not in a low-level cupboard that you have to bend down to several times a day. Similarly, sterilising equipment needs to be easily accessed (and near the bottles).

Establishing a changing station on each floor in a house and possibly in more than one room in a flat is very helpful – bear in mind that you may be changing nappies up to ten times a day per baby, at least in the beginning (*see* p. 171). You can use a towel or the mat from the changing bag you use when going out (*see* p. 186) for one room, and keep a good stock of nappies, cream and so on at each changing station.

BABY CHAIRS

Baby chairs – either a swing rocker or a bouncing seat – are very useful when babies are young:

▸ They are a safe place to put the babies during the day while you move around the house.
▸ They provide a secure place to put one baby while you bath/feed/change the nappy of the other.
▸ Their rocking/bouncing motion can be soothing.
▸ They allow you to feed both babies simultaneously from a bottle in their respective chairs, or to breastfeed one and bottle-feed the other (*see*, p. 168).

Swing chairs are suitable for use until your babies weigh around 11 kg. Bouncing chairs can be used until your babies can sit up independently (i.e. usually for the first six months or so). Choose a model that is easy to pick up and move around your home, so that they can be of maximum use.

BREASTFEEDING

Breast milk is the best food for all babies and having it even for a short time will be beneficial to their health. Breastfeeding twins is perfectly possible: women can produce enough milk to feed two babies and you can feed them simultaneously or one at a time – whatever suits you and the babies best.

There are many benefits to babies of breast milk:

▸ It is the perfect food for babies and contains all the nutrients they need for the first six months of life. All breast milk your babies receives is beneficial, even the smallest amount.
▸ Colostrum, the straw-coloured liquid first produced by the breast and ready for the babies at birth, is especially high not only in some antibodies, but also in proteins and vitamin K.
▸ The antibodies in breast milk help to protect babies from infection and other illnesses until the babies start to produce their own antibodies at about three to four months.
▸ It protects against gastroenteritis and is also thought to reduce the risk of babies developing certain allergies, eczema and asthma.
▸ It is thought that the antibodies found in breast milk reduce the risk of cot death.
▸ It is more easily digested by the immature gut of premature babies and helps protect them from infection and other illnesses at a time when they are vulnerable.
▸ Breastfed babies are less likely to be overweight than formula-fed babies, as they take just as much milk as they need at each feed and are not overfed.

In addition, there are certain benefits for the mother:

▸ Breast milk is free.
▸ Breast milk needs no preparation.
▸ Breastfeeding is thought to reduce the risk of breast cancer, osteoporosis and ovarian cancer (once you have fed for at least two months).

Breastfeeding is the natural way for mothers to feed their babies, but it is a skill that needs to be mastered by both you and your babies. It is good to start thinking about your choice for feeding early in your pregnancy. Information on breastfeeding is given in antenatal classes, but will not necessarily address the specifics of feeding twins. So, after the birth, it helps to have support to get you started and feeling confident. While all mothers benefit from information and instruction, one of the key issues for mothers of twins is how to manage the practicalities of feeding more than one baby, and you should be given advice as to how best to do this. If midwives are very busy, maternity support staff can be an excellent source of help. Many hospitals offer the services of an infant feeding specialist. These are specially trained lactation consultants who are there to advise and support mothers who wish to breastfeed. Your midwife or health visitor should continue to guide you once you are at home, or you can contact one of the organisations that specialise in supporting mothers with breastfeeding (*see* right Box on p.157).

Breastfeeding can take a little while to establish, so don't expect too much of yourself at first. In the early weeks try to organise as much help as possible with domestic tasks so that you can concentrate on feeding your babies. Fairly soon a routine that suits you and the babies begins to emerge, and you will find that breastfeeding can be fulfilling and enjoyable. Establishing your milk supply and confidence in breastfeeding in the first few weeks will enable you to make choices about how you feed your babies as they get older. Early introduction of formula and feeding from a bottle can interfere with the establishment of breastfeeding. Later, some mothers may choose to give some expressed breast milk or formula by bottle, known as 'combined' or 'mixed' feeding (*see* p.169).

THE SPECIAL BENEFITS OF BREASTFEEDING TWINS

▸ The physical contact helps develop the unique, close bond between mother and baby. For mothers with twins, the opportunity to have one-to-one time with each baby is very special.
▸ Breast milk is free, so is a financial saving for all families, but is especially helpful with twins.
▸ It saves time: there is no need to sterilise bottles, make up feeds and wait for the formula to cool several times a day, leaving you with more time to spend with your babies.
▸ Less preparation is needed when going out (already very time-consuming when two babies are involved).

Getting started

Before you start to feed make sure you are comfortable, with your back well supported with pillows and with a drink and the telephone to hand. Check that the babies are at the same level as your breast to enable them to latch on correctly (*see* p. 159) and so that you do not have to stoop to reach them or support their weight in your arms. You may therefore need some additional pillows on your knees – especially if you are feeding the babies simultaneously (*see* p. 160). Some mothers find a special V- or U-shaped feeding cushion helpful in supporting the babies, but ordinary pillows can work just

as well. You will need to experiment to find out what suits you best, so it can be better to leave buying special cushions until you have established your preference. You may also want to consider feeding lying down, particularly at night or when you are feeling tired, or if you have had a Caesarean section and

BREASTFEEDING SUPPORT ORGANISATIONS
Not having the right support is a major reason that women give up breastfeeding. There are several organisations that offer help to breastfeeding mothers without charge. Their services can include a helpline, staffed by specially trained counsellors who have experience themselves in breastfeeding, and a website containing useful advice and information. Some are also able to offer a home visit as well. See Useful Resources for a list of contacts.

HOW BREAST MILK PRODUCTION WORKS

Milk production is stimulated by a baby sucking on the breast. It works on a principle of 'supply and demand': the more your breast is emptied, the more milk you will produce. Your breasts will produce the amount of milk your baby needs for growth. Pre-pregnancy breast size has no correlation to how much milk a woman is able to produce, so having small breasts does not mean that you will not have enough milk for two babies.

Each breast contains clusters of alveoli, little sacs in which milk is produced and stored. Ducts from the alveoli lead to the nipple. The pituitary gland at the base of the brain produces two hormones: prolactin, which produces milk, and oxytocin, which contracts the alveoli and pushes the milk down through the ducts and into the nipple. This is the 'milk ejection reflex' (MER), also known as the 'let-down reflex', and it will often be accompanied by a tingly sensation in your breasts. Triggering the MER is essential for babies to get good volumes of milk. For many mothers, the MER begins as soon as their babies start to cry, even if they are nowhere near their mother's breast. Some women have a strong MER: milk starts flowing before the baby has had time to start sucking.

Your milk will not come in until the levels of progesterone and oestrogen fall after delivery and the level of prolactin rises, usually at around three to seven days after the birth. At this stage, your breasts will start to swell and can become hard and painful, but this usually passes within a couple of days (although *see* information on Mastitis, p. 162). Because milk production works on supply and demand, if at this stage you do not remove milk from the breast regularly, supply will gradually decrease and then stop altogether. If it is stimulated by a sucking baby, milk production will continue and increase to meet the babies' needs. Some women experience cramp-like abdominal pains for the first few days after birth, and more so when they are breastfeeding. This is as a result of the oxytocin, which, as well as stimulating the alveoli, also stimulates the uterus to contract.

The milk at the beginning of the feed is known as foremilk, and is more watery and thirst-quenching than the creamier hindmilk, which comes towards the end of the feed. It is therefore important that the babies feed until they empty the breast and reach the more calorie-dense hindmilk.

find sitting up quite difficult. Lying down can also allow you to feed one baby while cuddling the other. During the day, you may prefer to be sitting on a chair or sofa and also want to have a remote control to hand for watching TV or listening to music or the radio. Make sure you have a drink beside you.

Latching on

Attaching a baby to the breast is often called 'latching on'. It is essential that this is done correctly in order to ensure effective milk removal and to avoid getting sore nipples. Because it can take some practice, try to have someone there for the first few feeds to hand each baby to you and provide general support.

With your baby at the level of your breast, turn them so their chest and head faces you. Support their shoulders in your hand and rest your fingertips on their head. Line their nose up to your nipple. You can support your breast in the other hand, either from underneath or on top, to shape it and gently brush your nipple against your baby's top lip to encourage the mouth to open wide. As your baby's head tips back, the nipple should be pointing to the roof of the mouth. Bring your baby into the breast so that they take a large mouthful of breast tissue, making sure as much of the areola as possible is inside the mouth. You may need more than one attempt at this. Don't leave the baby sucking on the end of the nipple, as this can lead to soreness: gently insert your little finger into the side of their mouth to break the suction, remove the breast and start again.

Some babies are quite proficient at finding the nipple and attaching without too much support. You can tell if your babies are latched on correctly: their mouths are opened wide covering the whole of the bottom of the areola, with the top lip turned upwards and creased over, their chin is against the breast and their jaws move rhythmically as they suck.

How often and for how long?

Every baby feeds differently, and will have different levels of hunger from one feed to the next. Signs that your babies are hungry include:

- ▸ moving their head around or 'rooting' for the breast when they are held
- ▸ moving their mouth or licking/smacking their lips
- ▸ sucking their fingers.

Crying is often one of the last signs of hunger (and don't forget that babies cry for lots of other reasons, too).

A newborn baby's stomach is very small and so they need to feed little and often. In the early weeks, the babies are likely to feed at least eight times in 24 hours, for ten to twenty minutes or longer. Since the quality of breast milk can vary on a daily basis, and even between feeds, it is important that you follow the needs of the babies, known as 'feeding on demand'. During the first few weeks, it may feel as if all you are doing is feeding, but with time you will develop more of a routine: you will begin to learn that not every cry is one of hunger and will become more aware of your babies' appetites. Remember also that frequent feeding in the early days helps to establish milk supply. Many mothers operate a modified baby-led feeding approach: instead of feeding each baby solely on demand, they feed whichever baby wakes first, then wake the second baby for a feed.

Some newborn babies are easier to feed than others. You may find that one of your babies latches on and feeds quickly and efficiently from the start, whereas the other is slower to latch on or needs more time to feed. Try to be patient and responsive. You may also feel that one of your breasts has a better flow of milk than the other, so you could make a note of which baby had which breast last time and swap sides for the next feed. As the babies get older, they become more proficient at sucking, enabling them to feed more efficiently and quickly and you to have greater time between the feeds. For information on winding, see p. 169.

Is my baby getting enough?

Unlike feeding from a bottle, it is hard to know exactly how much milk a baby is taking from the breast and this can be a worry, making some mothers question if they have sufficient milk supply. Be reassured that your babies will get sufficient milk from the breast if they are well attached, breastfeeding is comfortable and the babies fully empty the breast and come off satisfied. If you have concerns, your midwife or health visitor will be able to support you but, generally speaking, if your babies are gaining weight after the first two weeks, have about six wet nappies and pass two stools per day, and seem satisfied after most feeds, then they are getting enough.

Feeding separately and together

You have the option of feeding your babies one at a time, or simultaneously, with one baby attached to each breast at the same time. There are advantages to separate feeding:

▶ It allows you to give one-to-one attention to each baby, something for which mothers of twins often feel they have little time for.
▶ You have both hands free to attach and position one baby. Once attached, you have a spare hand to rock the other baby, cuddle another child, have a drink, etc.
▶ Some women feel more comfortable and less conspicuous feeding one baby rather than two, especially in public places.
▶ It avoids the problem of what to do when one finishes feeding before the other.
▶ It allows you to find the best position for each baby (one baby's ideal feeding position may not be the same as that of the other). One may feed more quickly than the other so treat each baby as an individual and don't compare.

There are also benefits to simultaneous feeding:

▶ It saves time and gives you more time to rest, especially at night.
▶ If one of your babies has a stronger 'suck' than the other, this baby will stimulate the MER (see Box, p. 157) in the other breast, enabling the other baby to get more milk with less effort.
▶ It avoids the disturbance of one baby crying while waiting for a feed.

For the first week or so, it is usually advisable to feed each baby separately until you are confident about your technique. This is especially the case if this is your first experience of breastfeeding. It can take a little while for your babies to learn how to latch on properly, particularly if they were born early (see Chapter 6, p. 147), and you may find that you need both hands to help them. Your other baby can be placed in a baby chair (see p. 155) or beside you until it is their turn to feed.

Once you have established breastfeeding, it is up to you whether you feed the babies together or separately. You might choose to feed them one at a time on some occasions, but simultaneously on others: if you are alone, you may prefer single feeding, but find you can feed simultaneously if there is someone around to provide an extra pair of hands. You may also change what you do over time, as your babies get bigger and heavier. Try to involve your partner from the beginning and ask visitors to come at feeding time, so that they can help you. They can:

▶ pass you the second baby if you are trying to feed two babies at once
▶ wind and settle the other baby if you are feeding them separately
▶ get you a glass of water or a snack.

Different positions for simultaneous breastfeeding

There are many different positions for breastfeeding two babies at the same time, and the principle ones are shown in the diagrams opposite. There are no rules, and you should try out different positions and do whatever is comfortable for you and your babies. You may find that one position works really well to begin with, but another is better when the babies have grown a bit, or when you have recovered from the delivery. Don't forget that you can use a combination of positions, too (i.e. you don't have to have the babies in identical positions). For example, you could have one in the cradle hold and one in the underarm hold. Ask your midwife, health visitor or breastfeeding counsellor to help you try some of the various positions. Speak to other mothers who breastfed twins, as they can offer helpful information about positions that worked for them.

DID YOU KNOW...?
Use nursing pads inside your bra to soak up any leaking breast milk and change them at every feed.

Positions for feeding twins simultaneously

Double underarm hold Each baby's head is supported by one of your hands while their body lies under each of your arms. Many women use this position when they first start breastfeeding, especially if they have had a Caesarean section.

Double cradle/criss-cross hold Each baby is held in your arms, with their bodies crossing your abdomen. This position is often used when you are more experienced and your babies have more head control.

Parallel hold Each baby is in the cradle hold, with their bodies running parallel. Babies may enjoy the closeness to each other that this position facilitates.

V-shaped hold Each baby lies on their side/front, with their body stretching away from you to form a V-shape. This position allows you to be hands-free and able to have a drink/snack, use the telephone and so on.

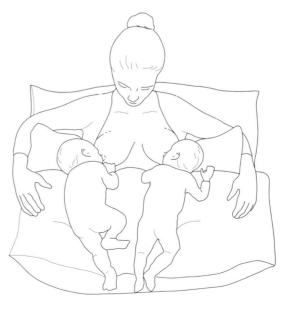

Breastfeeding complications

Incorrect latching on is the most common problem when breastfeeding and this is where it is most important to have support. If a baby does not latch on properly, complications can quickly develop, such as sore/cracked nipples and engorgement (which can lead to mastitis). Mothers should always ask for help if they feel they need more than is offered, as these problems can be prevented.

Sore breasts and nipples

If a baby does not latch on correctly, your nipples can soon become sore, or can crack and bleed. Excessively long feeding (over an hour) can also be a contributory factor, but this is often an indication of poor latching on. If you feel your nipples are getting sore, your midwife, health visitor or one of the breastfeeding organisations will be able to advise you about positioning the babies correctly and the best treatment. You may also need to check for thrush, which can cause soreness and treat any infection if necessary. Try to keep putting your babies to the breast or expressing milk throughout this time, even if it feels painful, otherwise your breasts may become engorged. To help the nipples heal, leave them open to the air as much as possible. Avoid using perfumed soap or gels on your breasts when washing.

Engorgement

Engorgement can occur when your milk comes in, at around three to seven days after the birth. Your breasts can swell up and become hard in a few hours, although this usually settles down within about 24 hours. Placing warm flannels on the breasts before a feed may help to ease any discomfort and it is important to make sure that the babies are properly latched on and removing milk well.

When milk is not being drained efficiently, it can also lead to engorgement. This can result in a vicious circle, where the fuller the breasts get, the harder it is for your babies to latch on. If your breasts become engorged between feeds, you may need to remove some milk from them, either by getting your babies to suckle or by expressing in whatever way suits you best (by hand or by pump). See p.166 for instructions on how to express breast milk. Do not drain the breasts completely, because the body will take that as a signal that it needs to fill them up again as fast as possible. Instead, empty the breasts just until they feel softer (a breastfeeding counsellor should be able to advise you on how long to do this for). Then, when it is time for their feed, put your babies to the breast and feed as normal (making sure they are latched on correctly) or, if this is not possible, express more milk to be fed to them via a bottle. Feeding little and often (on demand – see p.159) is better for

relieving engorgement than keeping to strict intervals. If you follow the above advice, engorgement usually subsides after approximately 48 hours. Remember that expressing milk is the best way to reduce engorgement. Always ask your midwife, health visitor or counsellor for advice and help.

Mastitis

If the milk from your breast is not properly drained, you may develop a hard, red and painful lump in your breast. This may indicate a blocked duct, and does not necessarily mean you have an infection. However, if your breast also feels hot and you have flu-like symptoms, then you may have developed a breast infection called mastitis. In either case you should continue to feed as often as possible from both the affected breast and the other one, feeding from the tender breast first, because the babies will be at their hungriest and more likely to completely drain it. Make sure that the babies attach well and try to massage the lump while you feed. Get as much rest as you can in between feeds and drink plenty of fluids. You can safely take paracetamol or a non-steroidal anti-inflammatory, such as ibuprofen, to help with your symptoms, but if there is no improvement within 12–24 hours, you should seek advice from your midwife, health visitor or doctor as you may need a course of antibiotics.

To prevent further episodes of mastitis, make sure your breasts do not become overfull (express a little between feeds if necessary), avoid undue pressure on your breasts (e.g. from clothing/bras, fingers pressing into them during feeds, bumps and knocks) and try feeding your babies in different positions.

Katharine's story

At the start, we went through all sorts of difficulties with breastfeeding: difficulty latching on (I had inverted nipples), pain while feeding, mastitis, and the usual worries about milk supply. However, I knew it was something I really wanted to do and, luckily, the hospital and the midwives who visited me at home were all really committed to getting me help and support to be able to achieve this. So I never gave up hope and managed to keep going on mainly breast milk for six months. I really think you have to persevere with breastfeeding and it will suddenly come right.

I was lucky that my twins didn't take long to feed, but you can be there for a while, so you need to make sure you're comfortable and have everything to hand. I liked to have two glasses of water ready, as I always got extremely thirsty the minute I sat down to breastfeed. I also kept my phone, lip salve and handcream within reach, as well as a clock to time the feed. During the night, I hated finding that I was missing something when I was all settled down for a feed, so I would leave everything out on a table in the babies' room next to where I sat, so that I could just stumble in to the babies' room, bleary-eyed, and feed.

It's so easy to get a sore back or neck from being in the wrong position. I had a special twin feeding cushion, as well as a 'V'-shaped cushion underneath to get the babies up to the right height and tons of pillows to prop me up from behind. I hadn't practised simultaneous feeding in the hospital, so it was just trial and error. I used to latch on the easier and noisier baby first. Then I had to use my arm to make sure that one didn't roll off while I lifted the second baby onto the cushion. When they're small it's possible to wind one baby by lifting them onto your shoulder or place them across the top of the feeding cushion, while you continue feeding the other one. It sounds hard, but it just takes a fair amount of manoeuvring and a lot of patience.

FEEDING FROM A BOTTLE

Some mothers feed their twins using a bottle, with their own expressed breast milk. Others choose to feed their babies using infant formula or a combination of breast milk and formula from birth or later.

Even if you feed babies from the breast for the majority of the time, you may find that also being able to use a bottle to give breast milk gives you more flexibility:

► It allows other people to feed the babies.
► It is a method of feeding in case you are not able to be present to breastfeed.
► Your babies can be fed breast milk in this way once you have returned to work (*see* Chapter 8, p. 224).

Expressing milk

If you want to feed your babies breast milk from a bottle you will need to express your milk. Expressing means removing milk from the breast by hand or by using a pump. Hand expression is the best method of removing the small volumes of colostrum produced by the breast before your milk comes in; it also helps relieve uncomfortable, engorged breasts (*see* p. 162). First wash your hands. Make sure you are sitting comfortably and your breasts are warm. Start by gently massaging the breast, working towards the nipple. With a sterilised container placed close to the breast, make a 'C' shape around your areola with your thumb on top and your fingers underneath, then squeeze the area around the nipple. Repeat rhythmically until the milk starts flowing. When the flow slows, move your fingers to a different part of the breast and repeat the pumping action.

For frequent expressing of greater quantities of milk you may need to use a breast pump. There are several different types, so look at all the information and choose one to suit you. Make sure that the funnel fits your breasts, otherwise expressing could be painful and inefficient. Small manual pumps are adequate for expressing occasionally, but can be quite tiring to use on a regular basis. Shop-bought battery-operated pumps may be good if you are able to produce plentiful amounts of milk from the start or if you are not planning to express regularly. Other mothers, however, find that the best pumps are hospital-grade electric pumps.

Although they are sometimes rather large and not very portable, they are very efficient at removing milk and enable you to express from both breasts simultaneously, which can save you a lot of time. Electric pumps can be hired at relatively low cost, either from the manufacturers (*see* Useful Resources) or from the NCT. The removable parts of manual and electric pumps must be cleaned and sterilised each time they are used. For information on expressing milk for babies that are in a neonatal unit, see Chapter 6, p. 147.

STERILISING FEEDING EQUIPMENT

Until your babies are six months old, all equipment that you use for feeding and preparing the feed must be sterilised in order to minimise the occurrence of gastroenteritis. This includes bottles, teats, measuring spoons, lids, breast pump parts and so on. Before sterilising, all items must first be washed with hot soapy water and thoroughly rinsed under the tap. (You can put these in a dishwasher but they still need to be sterilised afterwards.) It is useful to get into a routine of cleaning all the bottles in one go, either once or twice a day, morning and/or evening. After you have washed them, sterilise the bottles, teats and knife/spatula using your chosen method (e.g. steam, microwave) following the manufacturer's instructions. Equipment can be left in the steriliser until you are ready to use it, but if you do remove it, assemble the bottles fully (including the lid) to maintain sterility.

Storing breastmilk

Breast milk can keep for up to five days in the fridge at 4°C or lower, either in a sterilised bottle or in special, sterile bags (bought from chemists). It can also be stored in these bags and frozen for up to six months at –18°C or lower. Label each bag with the date and volume of milk being frozen. Freezing does not significantly affect the composition of milk and it still retains the unique protective components absent in formula.

Formula feeding

Some mothers choose to feed their babies on infant formula from birth or later. Whatever you decide, and when, is a

personal matter and you should be fully supported in the decision that feels right for you and your babies. The reasons for mothers choosing infant formula as the sole source of nourishment for their babies include the following:

► The babies can be fed by others without the need for expressing.
► You get time to rest while others prepare feeds and give the babies their bottle.

Infant formula is made from cow's milk and contains essential vitamins and minerals so that it has most of the same nutritional properties as breast milk. It is available in two forms: ready-made liquid formula, which comes in sterile cartons, and powdered formula, which comes in tins and is not sterile. Ready-made formula can be very handy when out and about or travelling, but once a carton has been opened, the liquid inside is no longer sterile and will need to be kept in the fridge and thrown away after 24 hours if it is not finished. It is cheaper (and less wasteful) to make up feeds using powdered formula for the majority of the time.

The many different brands that are available are broadly similar, although if your babies are premature, the neonatal unit staff, your midwife or health visitor can advise you on which type is most suitable. 'First infant formula' is suitable for newborns and you can carry on using this throughout the first year. Other types marketed as 'second milk', 'follow-on milk', 'hungry baby milk' and 'night-time formula', have no proven benefit and it is not necessary to switch to these, even as your babies grow. The manufacturer's instructions will guide you on how much to give and how frequently according to your babies' age, and your health visitor can also advise as to when your babies might be needing more.

DID YOU KNOW…?

The Department of Health recommends that infant formula is made up fresh for each feed, should not be kept at room temperature for longer than two hours, and that anything left over is thrown away rather than reused in order to minimise the risk of contamination with bacteria.

Making up a feed

Since powdered formula is not sterile, feeds need to be made with hot water (at least 70°C) to kill any bacteria that may be present. It is recommended that feeds are made fresh each time, but if you do need to store it, made-up formula must be kept in the fridge and used within 24 hours. As feeding time approaches, boil some fresh tap water. Bottled water is not suitable for making up feeds and avoid using water that has been boiled before as this can alter the mineral content. Leave it to cool for no longer than half an hour. When it is time to make up the feed, wash your hands and clean and disinfect the surface you are using. Pour the boiled water into the bottles, using the measurements on the side to get the correct amount for the feed. Add the powdered formula according to the manufacturer's instructions, using the measuring scoop provided. (If you are out, you can measure out the powdered milk in advance and keep it in a sterile container.) It is very important that you use exactly the right proportions of water to powder – never alter this, as it could affect your babies' health and growth. Shake the bottle well to mix the powder and water together thoroughly. Test the temperature of the feed by pouring a few drops onto the inside of your wrist. If it feels hot on your skin, wait a few more minutes for it to cool or run the bottom half of the bottle under the cold tap before testing again.

TYPES OF MILK THAT ARE UNSUITABLE FOR BABIES
Infant formula is based on cow's milk, but pure cow's milk itself should not be given to babies as a main drink until they are one year old (although you can use a little when preparing solid food – *see* Chapter 8, p. 227). In addition, the following milks are not suitable for babies under a year:

▸ goat's milk
▸ sheep's milk
▸ soya milk (unless advised to do so by your midwife, health visitor or doctor)
▸ rice, oat or almond 'milk'
▸ dried milk
▸ evaporated milk
▸ condensed milk.

DID YOU KNOW…?
Never give a young baby a bottle to hold and never leave a baby unattended with a bottle.

How to give babies a bottle

To be able to feed from a bottle your baby needs to be held in a well-supported, reclined sitting position so that they can breathe and swallow easily. You need to find a comfortable sitting position for yourself, holding the baby close to you so that you can make eye contact. Brush the teat against your baby's mouth to encourage them to open wide and allow them to draw in the teat. The bottle needs to be held at an angle so that the milk fills the teat – this prevents your baby taking in too much air. Milk flow from a bottle tends to be faster than that from the breast, so allow your babies occasional breaks from the feed so that they can bring up wind (*see* right).

Signs that indicate when your babies are hungry are listed on p. 159. The amount babies drink varies from one feed to another. If you label each bottle with each baby's name or colour-code them, you will know how much has been taken at each feed. It is not a bad thing if a little is left at the end of the bottle, as this means they have had enough. Conversely, if the babies drain their bottle quickly and still appear hungry, you can give them some more expressed milk or make up a small amount of extra formula and offer it. Do not insist, however: if they do not want it they have obviously had enough. It is more important to monitor how much formula they have in a 24-hour period, rather than whether they drink exactly the same amount every time. As with breastfeeding, many parents feed the baby that wakes first, then wake the second baby who is then fed individually.

Simultaneous feeding using bottles

While giving each baby their bottle separately means that they can receive your undivided attention, feeding them simultaneously is a time-saver and can be done whether you have someone to help you or not. There are different ways of doing this:

▸ Place one baby in a baby chair or prop them up, then place the other in your lap, allowing you to hold a bottle in each hand and retain body contact with one baby while you feed both.
▸ Place both babies in their baby chairs or on pillows and, holding a bottle in each hand, feed both babies.

▶ Feed one baby half a bottle, then put that baby down in a baby chair; feed the other baby half a bottle, then swap back. This way they are fed simultaneously and you have some one-to-one time with each.

Combined (mixed) feeding

Mothers with twins may choose to feed their babies with both breast milk and formula, known as combined, or mixed, feeding. In this way, babies continue to receive some breast milk. Combined feeding can be done in various ways. For example, you could breastfeed both at one feed (or give them breast milk from a bottle) and at the next feed give them both formula; or you could give one baby formula and breastfeed the other at one feed, and at the next feed, swap over. Some mothers breastfeed during the day and give formula at night. Bear in mind that if you are not exclusively feeding with breast milk, your milk supply will be reduced. You therefore need to breastfeed or express on a regular basis to make sure that your babies' nutritional needs are being met.

Winding

Babies often swallow air when they feed, so they will need winding after each feed, at least until they can sit up. Babies fed from a bottle (whether with formula or breast milk) tend to swallow more air than those feeding from the breast, so you may find that you need to wind them part of the way through each feed.

There are various ways of winding babies, but all involve keeping their back straight and their chin supported as you pat or rub their back gently but firmly. This releases any trapped bubbles of air in their stomach, which causes them to belch. Winding can sometimes result in 'posseting' (regurgitating a small amount of milk), so make sure that you have a muslin, bib or absorbent cloth to hand. The three most common methods of winding are:

▶ sitting the baby on your lap and supporting their chin with your hand
▶ lying the baby over your shoulder (as their stomach will be slightly compressed in this position, they are more likely to posset, so place a muslin over your shoulder before you start)
▶ lying the baby on their stomach over your lap with their face free to breathe.

CLOTHES AND NAPPY CHANGING

Changing clothing and nappies is going to be a frequent occurrence in your household, so you will want to make life as simple and speedy as possible. Outfits should therefore be practical rather than fashionable. The decision of whether to use disposable or towelling nappies is a personal one, and you will need to weigh up the pros and cons of each.

Clothing

Babies grow extremely quickly and a tiny baby at birth can double in weight in the space of a few weeks, so you only need to have a few essential items of clothing initially (*see* list on p. 154). It is easier if clothes are machine-washable and, ideally, suitable for the tumble-dryer, if you have one. Avoid synthetics and wool, and opt instead for cotton, as it is breathable and warm.

Clothes should be easy to put on and remove. A sleepsuit (babygro) is ideal, as it can be worn in the daytime, too. It is a good idea to keep a pile of sleepsuits beside each changing station for a quick change of clothing for either baby. Avoid fiddly ribbons or buttons, and choose clothes that are front-fastening and unbutton fully down at least one leg. It is easier to regulate a baby's temperature if there are several layers of clothing rather than one thick item, so you could use a vest (bodysuit) underneath the sleepsuit (which also helps to keep the nappy in place). Jackets and cardigans are also useful for extra warmth, but bear in mind that babies in modern, centrally heated homes do not need to be dressed as warmly as they did in previous generations. An outdoor suit that can be put on over existing clothing and a warm hat are useful for when you are out and about in colder weather; in the summer, babies' heads and faces need to be protected by a sunhat. It is not uncommon for babies to accidentally scratch themselves on the face and so some parents like to use scratch mits to guard against this. They can also help to keep hands warm in cooler weather.

You may be given (if not deluged with) all manner of items of clothing, both new and second-hand. (Do accept all that is offered – it can be passed on to other parents if you have too much.) Wait to see if people give you special outfits, but do remind family and friends that it is important that each baby is treated as an individual and not dressed identically (*see* Chapter 8 p. 245–6). If you do not know the sex of your babies before birth (and scans are not always 100 per cent accurate),

aim for neutral colours for the first-size clothes, because anyone seeing babies in pale blue is likely to automatically assume they are boys, and vice versa if your sons are dressed in pink. See p. 191 for a discussion on the issues of dressing same-sex twins differently.

Nappies

When deciding whether to use disposable or cloth nappies, it is important to realise that, for the first few weeks, you will get through around 50 nappies per week for each baby. Cloth nappies have developed hugely in recent years due to concerns about the environment. You may decide to use a combination of the two, depending on the situation; for example, disposables are more convenient if you are out and about or on holiday. Investing in a nappy bin (or a lidded bucket lined with a plastic bag) for each changing station, while not essential, means that you avoid frequent trips to your outside dustbin. See also p. 155 for tips on how to arrange nappy-changing stations.

Disposable nappies

Some brands are now biodegradable, thus eliminating some of the environmental concerns about using disposables. One option is to buy in bulk and you may want to have them delivered to your home. You will need:

▸ a sufficient quantity of a small size of nappy to last you for at least the first week
▸ plastic nappy sacks for the used nappies.

Cloth nappies

A big factor in deciding for or against cloth nappies is whether you will launder them yourself. Using a laundering service may save your sanity in the early weeks at least, as it avoids the work of having to wash and dry lots of nappies (*see* Useful Resources) However, the service may only come once a week, so you should consider where you could store both the laundered and the used nappies, as the odour can be quite strong after a few days. This, together with drying space, is also a factor if you intend to wash the nappies yourself. You will need:

▸ cloth nappies – up to about 50 per baby (but this depends on how often you choose to launder them)
▸ nappy liners (some are flushable)
▸ waterproof wraps or plastic pants (about six per baby) to prevent leakages.

Nappy-changing

Before you start, wash your hands and make sure you have all your equipment within reach. It is best to change the baby on a changing mat on the floor; then, if your attention has to be diverted to the other baby, the one being changed cannot fall. Starting with one baby, remove the soiled nappy and wash around the area using cotton wool dipped in plain water. For girls, wipe from front to back of the bottom; for boys, clean around the penis and scrotum, but do not retract the foreskin. Babies will still urinate when their nappy is off, so have another nappy or cloth to hand to mop up if necessary. Pat the baby's bottom dry with cotton wool or a clean towel. Barrier creams or petroleum jelly may be used, but try to air your baby's skin as much as possible to avoid nappy rash (*see* p. 196), or to reduce any inflammation should it occur. Baby wipes may be useful but they are no better than water and they are costly. When the skin is dry, fit a clean nappy according to the manufacturer's instructions, making sure that all fastenings are secure but not too tight on the baby's skin. Always wash your hands afterwards.

There are no fixed rules but, generally speaking, it is better to change your baby's nappy *after* a feed, simply because babies often empty their bowels once their stomach is full.

If you think that the odour indicates that they have filled their nappy in between feeds, or if their nappy is very wet (you will soon become expert at recognising the tell-tale signs for both events), then try to change the nappy as soon as possible.

CARE OF THE UMBILICAL CORD

After the birth, the umbilical cord will be clamped close to the navel and cut. A small stump will be left, which will dry out, heal and fall off a week or two later. Until this time you should keep the navel clean and dry to avoid infection and try to leave it open to the air for a while when you are changing your babies' nappies or topping and tailing them. If you notice that the skin around the cord is red or that there is pus or bleeding, make your midwife or health visitor aware of this so that they can advise you on the best course of treatment.

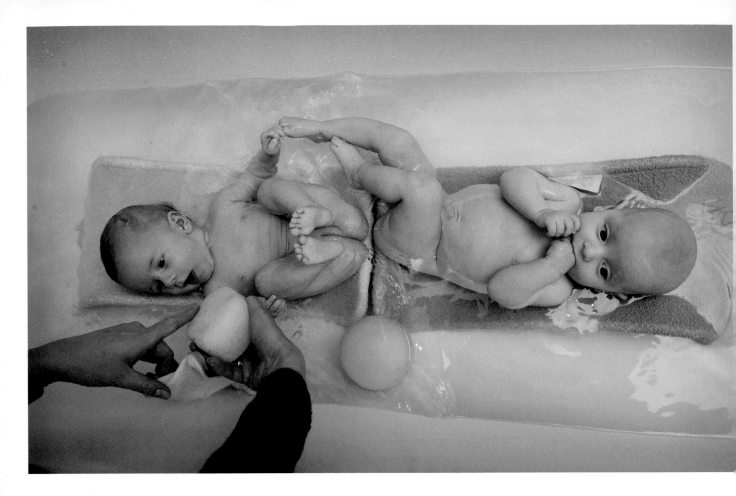

 # BATHING

When bathing two babies you will need to make sure that you are organised and that both babies remain safe at all times. An extra pair of hands will certainly help until you have established a method. However, once you have a routine, bath time can also be an enjoyable playtime for you all.

Babies do not need to be bathed every day and many parents of twins choose to bathe their babies on alternate days or two or three times a week. However, if they are not being bathed, you should 'top and tail' each baby daily (*see* opposite). Most parents find that bathing their babies in the early evening, before they put them down for the night, can be calming. On balance, it is better to bathe young babies before, rather than after the feed, and if you and your babies have had a

particularly tiring day, do the bath earlier before they (and you) become overtired and hungry.

Bath supports and baby baths

Specially designed bath supports that can be placed in the full-size bath are very useful for bathing twins, whether simultaneously or separately, as they mean that you do not have to hold the babies yourself. They cradle a baby's body in a semi-reclined position in the water, taking their weight and allowing you to momentarily attend to the other if necessary. While they provide a degree of safety, you should never leave your babies unattended in a bath support.

If you are not using bath supports, you may want to invest in a baby bath. These save water and prevent your baby from slipping around in a full-size bath. They can be put in the bath itself (some designs fit over the sides of the bath for greater ease), where they can be filled without having to transport water. Otherwise, a baby bath can be placed on a nearby solid, flat, non-slip surface. Some models come with stands, which usually makes bathing kinder on your back. You will still need to hold the baby's upper body with your hand while they are in the water.

Toiletries

Newborn babies' skins are delicate and sensitive, especially so if they are premature. You don't need to use soap – water alone is fine – but if you do so, make sure it is mild and unperfumed. A non-scented, hypoallergenic bath emollient can help to keep skin soft and hydrated – ask your health visitor or pharmacist for suitable brands. Babies' hair does not need washing with soap or shampoo every time, but when you do use it, make sure it is well rinsed to avoid drying out the scalp. When they are very young, rinsing the hair with plain water alone is usually sufficient.

Bathing separately or together?

Babies that are not yet able to sit up reliably by themselves need to be bathed one at a time, unless you are using bath supports or have someone with you who can help (*see* right). Bathing your babies separately can be rewarding, as each baby is able to receive your undivided attention. First make sure that the room is warm and free from draughts. Run the water so that it is approximately the depth of your baby's tummy, then test it with your elbow to ensure that it is neither too hot nor too cold. Have everything you need – towel, sponge, toiletries, clean outfit – within easy reach of the bath. The baby who is not being bathed needs to be in a safe place, for example, in their baby seat or on a mat on the floor, so that they can come to no harm while you are focusing on bathing the other baby.

Undress the first baby and place them slowly and gently into the water. Support them with one hand and swish the water around your baby's body with the other, taking care not to splash their face. Do not wash babies' eyes with bath water, but use cotton wool and clean water, as if 'topping and tailing' (*see* right). After you have washed the baby, lift them out of the bath and wrap them immediately with a towel. Use this to pat them dry, being careful to reach all the creases. If they enjoy it, you can massage them, making sure that they do not get cold. After you have dressed the first baby, swap the babies over so that the bathed baby is now in a secure place. You do not need to change the bath water unless the first baby was dirty, but you may need to top it up with warm water if it has become too cool. Never do this while your baby is in the water, as they could be burnt or may overheat. Undress and wash the second baby as described. Only tidy up the bathroom when both babies are dressed and in a safe place.

Bathing two babies together

If you have invested in two baby bath supports, or have someone who can help you, you can try bathing the babies together. This not only saves time, but can also be enjoyable for the babies, particularly as they grow older and are more able to interact with each other. The safety of the babies is paramount, so always make sure that they are securely in their bath support or held while they are in the bath. Remember: you must have one person per baby if you are not using bath supports. If you are bathing them simultaneously on your own, make sure that the baby that you take out of the water first is dried, kept warm and put in a safe place before you take the other out, and that the baby that remains in the water is not left unsupervised.

Bathing with your babies

Some babies are frightened by the bath experience and so it can be comforting for them to take a bath with you. Clearly, this is only practical with one baby at a time, and with your partner present to hand each one to you and see to them when they come out. The water needs to be cooler than you would normally have it yourself and you should avoid using bath products.

Topping and tailing

Some babies love splashing about in water from the day they are born, while others hate it. Babies should have their face, neck, hands and bottoms washed everyday, but you can do this by 'topping and tailing' rather than giving them for a full-scale bath. First of all, wash your hands with soap, then rinse and dry. Dip some cotton wool in warm water and squeeze out. Wash your baby's face first, gently wiping each eye from the inner corner to the outer. You must use a different piece of cotton wool for each eye to prevent the spread of any bacteria. Gently pat the face dry with cotton wool. For the bottom, wash the area with cotton wool, as you would do when changing a nappy (*see* p. 171). Dry and leave to air a little if possible to help prevent nappy rash.

CRYING

Crying is the natural and normal way for all babies to express themselves. You will soon learn to work out the reasons for the crying, but first-time parents can find it disconcerting to begin with.

Fortunately, it is rare for newborn twins to set each other off, so if one is content, they are unlikely to be affected if their sibling suddenly begins to scream. Some common reasons why babies cry are:

- hunger or thirst (this often starts as a low-volume cry but gets progressively louder)
- needing to sleep
- having a dirty nappy
- being too cold or too hot
- not feeling well
- being bored (after three months of age)
- being overstimulated
- colic/tummy ache (see p. 196)
- teething.

Try to remember that crying is a baby's only way of expressing themselves and may not always indicate a problem. However, if both babies are tired or hungry, they are likely to cry at a similar time, so being prepared by having a feeding and sleeping pattern can help. If you are satisfied that your babies' needs have been met, you then have to find a way of calming them down (see also p. 178). It can be extremely stressful if two babies are crying at once, but you can try holding both babies at the same time and walking around calmly with them, making 'shushing' noises, talking or singing to them. Putting on some music can sometimes help: classical music can be very soothing, but experiment to see what they like! Some babies like the sound and sight of a tumble-dryer or a vacuum cleaner, and many are quietened when they are taken out for a quick walk or drive in the car.

If your partner or anybody else is with you at the time, ask them to help with one baby. If you feel you are running out of patience, put the babies in their cot(s) for a few minutes and go into another room, take a few deep breaths and try to unwind a little before going back. The mere fact of not hearing your babies cry for ten minutes or so can help you to feel calmer. Some parents find that, at night, the so-called 'controlled crying' method works well for them, especially once their babies are a few months old (see Chapter 8 p. 234 for more information).

DID YOU KNOW…?

If you are breastfeeding and your babies are still on your breast after 45 minutes, yet cry when you try to remove them, then they are probably just comfort sucking (see Box, p. 159).

DID YOU KNOW…?

If you have checked all the normal reasons for crying and are worried there may be something seriously wrong, don't hesitate to get urgent medical advice.

PERSISTENT CRYING

Babies that cry a lot can make life very stressful. It is important that you have enough support, so talk to your health visitor, local support groups or call a helpline if you feel things are getting too much (see Useful Resources). Remind yourself that babies cry for all sorts of reasons and that, as they grow, they will find new ways of communicating with you.

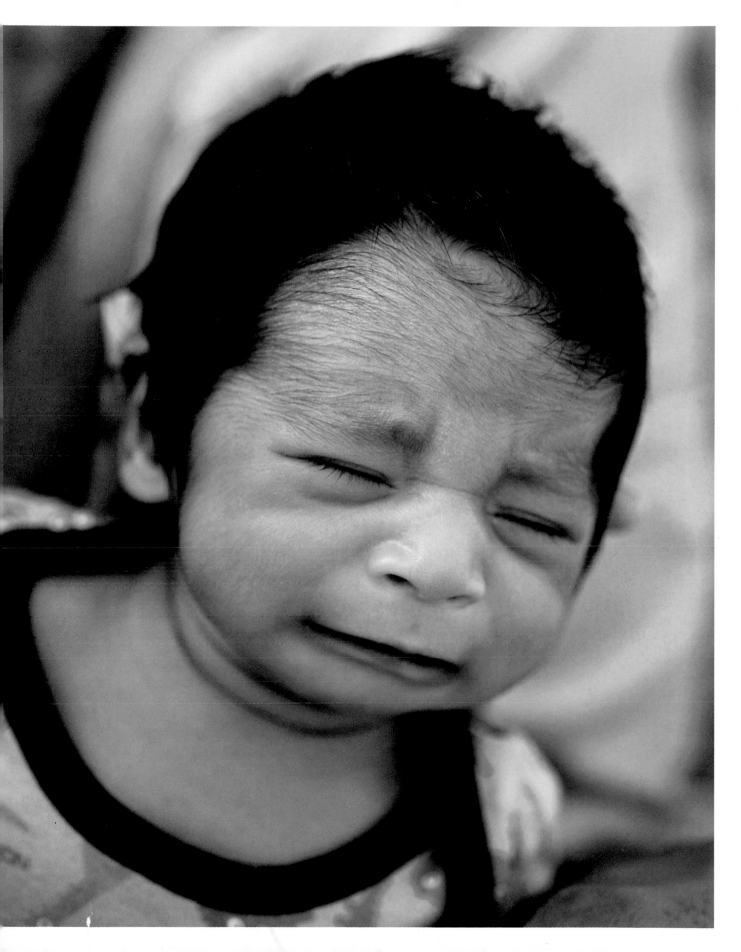

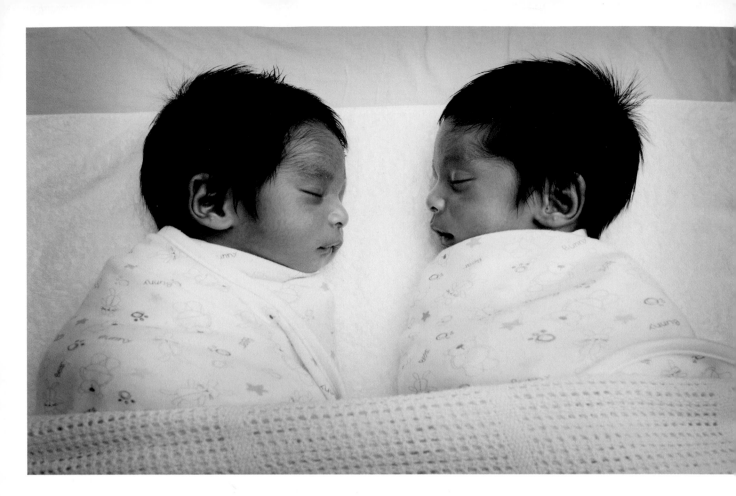

 # SLEEPING

Establishing a good sleep pattern and creating the right sleeping environment helps your babies to develop into peaceful, happy individuals and aids the well-being of the whole family. Sleep is important for parents as well as for babies, as frequent broken nights lead to irritability and exhaustion. Parents of twins need specific advice and help with getting their babies into a sleep routine.

Some babies need more sleep than others but, generally speaking, babies sleep for sixteen to eighteen hours per 24-hour period during the first six weeks. However, because they need frequent feeds when they are tiny, they tend to wake frequently. Between the ages of about six weeks and six months, babies can sleep for around thirteen to fifteen hours over the course of a day, but this can vary significantly from one baby to another, and depends on age and how hungry they are. In the early weeks, babies often do not sleep for longer than three to five hours at a stretch, but by the time they are around three months old, their maturity is such that they can start to recognise day and night-time and can go longer without a feed. By four months old, most should be able to manage at least six hours at night without waking.

However, sleep is a habit that has to be learned and a lot can be done from the start to encourage good sleeping patterns (*see* Box, p. 181). Conversely, there are certain things to avoid, as babies are very quick to develop poor habits and rather slower to 'unlearn' them. Remember that every baby is different, so what works for one may not work for another.

Your babies' sleeping environment

As you prepare your home for the arrival of your babies, you need to consider where they will sleep. The principal decision is whether they will sleep in your bedroom or in a separate room, and there are several factors that may influence your choice. (For discussion on whether to put each baby in a separate room, *see* Chapter 8 Sleep and Routine, p. 233.) There are certain reasons why you might sleep in the same room:

▸ It is recommended as the safest practice (*see* below).
▸ You will worry less if you know you can hear the babies immediately.
▸ It can be less disturbing than going to another room several times a night to change and feed your babies.
▸ It is more restful for you to feed them in your own bed.
▸ The room that your babies will eventually move to is far from yours (e.g. on a different floor).
▸ The room that your babies will use does not have adequate space to accommodate another bed/mattress/changing station.
▸ It is easier for a parent to take their turn if they know when the other parent has risen.

Other factors might lead you to decide to have the babies in a separate room:

▸ Your sleep is disturbed by every small sound your babies make.
▸ The layout of your home means that the babies' room is very close to yours, so that it is very easy to hear and attend to them.
▸ The room can accommodate a changing station to make night-time duties easier.
▸ The parent attending to the babies will minimise the disturbance to the partner who is sleeping.
▸ You have someone else to take care of the babies at night once or twice a week so that you can catch up on much-needed rest.
▸ There is room for a separate bed for the parent/carer in the babies' room.

Evidence from research has shown that sleeping in the same room as their parents for the first six months is safer for young babies. Wherever you choose to have your babies sleep, there are certain practical measures that you need to take to create a suitable sleeping environment. In addition, you need to decide what kind of bed your babies will sleep in.

DID YOU KNOW…?
Although it is important for babies to learn to go to sleep in the same place at night, you can be flexible about where they sleep during the day, such as downstairs in a Moses basket or pram.

Moses baskets, carrycots and cribs
Babies can sleep in a Moses basket, carrycot or small crib until they are around three months old. You may find it useful to be able to carry your babies to a different room when they are asleep, so the handles on baskets and carrycots are invaluable for this. Due to the size of the Moses basket, you will very soon need one for each baby, which may be more than your budget will allow. In this case, you can, of course, use a full-size cot from birth (*see* below).

Cots
If you started by using a Moses basket or crib, you will need to move the babies to a full-size cot when they appear to have outgrown it, usually by the time they are twelve weeks old. Cots are also suitable for newborns, and it can be better financially to use them from the start. You have the option of placing both babies in one cot (co-bedding – *see* Box, p. 178) or of using a separate cot for each baby. Mattresses should be new and the right size for the cot with no gap at the sides or ends.

DID YOU KNOW…?
To check if the babies are warm enough, feel the back of their necks. If they feel warm (i.e. neither cold nor hot), then the babies are comfortable.

Bed linen
Babies need very little bedding and it should be cotton rather than wool or synthetic. They do not need a pillow or a quilt or duvet of any sort. If you want, you can fit your babies' cot(s) with a cot bumper: although this is not essential, it can make babies feel more cocooned and less distracted by their surroundings, and can prevent them from hitting or scraping their head against the bars of the cot when they start to wriggle around. One cotton sheet with one or two cotton cellular blankets should be enough (depending on the season and room temperature). This is important because young babies cannot regulate their body heat – they cannot sweat, for example – because they have very little body fat. It is therefore better to add an extra cotton blanket if you think they need it than to put a wool or fleece blanket on them. See also Cot death, p. 181.

Baby sleeping bags can be very good for babies who are too old to be swaddled (*see* p. 180) and are starting to wriggle around their cot at night. They come in different sizes and togs

CO-BEDDING

One of the most common thoughts among parents is whether their babies should share a cot, known as 'co-bedding'. This is a matter of personal choice according to what suits your family circumstances and the babies themselves. There is no evidence to show that there are any greater risks when two babies are sleeping together than if they were apart. In fact, research suggests that co-bedded babies have more settled sleep and are more likely to wake at the same time, meaning that they get into similar rhythms of sleep and wakefulness. It is usually not the case, contrary to what parents might assume, that one crying baby will wake the other and, indeed, babies might even take comfort from being in the same bed.

(for different levels of warmth) and, because they cannot be kicked off like sheets and blankets, can prevent babies waking up because they are cold in the middle of the night.

Curtains and lighting

Ensure that bedroom windows have lined curtains or blinds to keep out as much light as possible (if necessary, hang an additional blanket over the curtain rail). If you can, put up special blackout blinds. Install a night light or side light (or a dimmer switch for the main light) so that you avoid excessively bright lighting during night-time feeds.

Baby-listening devices

Some parents invest in a baby-listening device, or monitor, to ensure that they can hear the babies when they are in a different room. This can be useful, for example, in the early part of the evening when you have put your babies to bed but are still up and about yourself.

DID YOU KNOW...?

You should not share a bed with your babies if you or your partner smoke, have drunk alcohol or taken any medication or drugs that make you particularly drowsy.

Settling babies

While babies need to learn to go to sleep themselves, there are certain things that can help them to settle. See also Crying, p. 174.

Dummies

You may think that you have no intention of ever using a dummy (sometimes called a 'soother'), but they can be useful to help settle babies before sleep, if yours are receptive to it. They should never be forced upon a baby and should be gently removed when the baby has fallen asleep. Breastfeeding needs to be established before you introduce a dummy (usually after one month) and thereafter you should use them judiciously rather than routinely. They can affect the growth of teeth and may also impede speech development. If you choose to use a dummy it is best to think of it as a short-term measure.

Thumb-sucking

Some babies are naturally thumb-suckers, while others never do so. Sucking their thumb allows babies to self-soothe and avoids the problem of a dummy falling out and disturbing the baby. However, if it is continued beyond babyhood, it can become a habit that is difficult to break and can lead to orthodontic problems, so you may want to think about discouraging thumb-sucking before it becomes entrenched.

Muslins and comforters

Many babies develop a liking for a particular object and, in the early weeks, a particular cloth or blanket can help to calm them so that they can go to sleep more easily. Often, this is a muslin cloth that has your smell (and that of your milk if you are breastfeeding). The advantage of having a muslin as a baby's comforter is that it can be washed and exchanged

RESTFUL NIGHT-TIME FEEDS FOR PARENTS

Wake the babies for a feed before you go to bed, so that you can get a few hours' sleep at the beginning of the night. If two babies are waking at different times in the night, this can soon become exhausting for parents, so after the first baby wakes and has been fed, wake and feed the second baby to avoid being disturbed a short time later. Before you go to bed, prepare yourself a hot drink in a flask to have while feeding to help you get back to sleep.

for another without a baby noticing. If a favourite blanket or cuddly toy gets dirty or – worse – lost, it is impossible to replace and can upset a baby or child enormously.

Muslins soon become vital for parents too, as they have many uses. As well as calming babies, they mop up dribble, milk and food; they protect bedding and prams or buggies; and, crucially, they protect clothes – indeed many parents are rarely seen without one draped over their shoulder. To soften your muslin cloths, wash them before first use and dry them in the tumble-dryer, if you have one.

Swaddling

Swaddling a newborn can also be a highly effective way of calming them and helping them to sleep. Babies feel very secure when they are wrapped tightly in a lightweight cotton sheet or blanket. You may be taught how to swaddle your babies while you are still in hospital, or you can ask your midwife or health visitor to show you once you are at home.

Why a baby might not sleep

Certain factors affect why some young babies are less able to sleep, some of which are common to all babies, while others are more specific to being a twin. Knowing what difficulties can arise and why, and establishing certain habits and routines early on, will help you to avoid them. Here are some common reasons:

- ▸ The babies might have a wet or soiled nappy.
- ▸ The babies might have wind or be too cold or hot.
- ▸ Tiny babies have small stomachs, so need more frequent feeding. Small babies typically wake every two to three hours for a feed, especially if they are being breastfed.
- ▸ You might take a little time to gain confidence in how to handle two tiny babies, especially if you are first-time parents, and to understand the reasons why they might be crying and unable to sleep.
- ▸ You might pick up a crying twin for fear that the other baby wakes. This prevents babies from learning how to settle themselves and go to sleep on their own.
- ▸ Many twins are premature and spend time in a neonatal unit. They get used to being handled, woken and fed by many different people, all of whom care for them in a slightly different way.
- ▸ If one baby comes home from hospital before the other, it can be more difficult to get both babies into a routine.
- ▸ Babies do not know the difference between night and day until they are around ten to twelve weeks old.

Cot death (Sudden Infant Death Syndrome)

Cot death, also known as Sudden Infant Death Syndrome (SIDS), is the term used for the sudden and unexpected death of an apparently well baby or infant. Cot death is very rare, but it is still the most common cause of death in babies over one month old. Most at risk are boys, premature babies and those who had low birthweight. Although the specific causes of death are unexplained, it is known that exposure to tobacco smoke (both before and after birth) can significantly increase the risk of cot death. It is therefore advisable that you give up smoking, or at least make sure that your home is smoke-free. In addition, there are some measures that all parents can take to reduce the risk of cot death:

▸ Always place the babies on their backs to sleep.
▸ Place the babies with their feet at the end of the cot, with any sheets or blankets no higher than the shoulders, so that they cannot wriggle under the covers; if they are sharing the same cot (*see* Box, p.178), babies should either be placed side by side at one end or side, or be put one at each end.

▸ If you are using baby sleeping bags, make sure they are well-fitting so that the babies do not slip down inside.
▸ Do not let the babies get too hot and keep their heads uncovered, so that they can lose any excess heat.
▸ Breastfeed your babies, if only for a short time, as research has shown that antibodies in breast milk may help to prevent cot death.

For further information, contact your health visitor or a relevant support organisation (*see* Useful Resources).

DID YOU KNOW…?

Your babies' cries will usually wake you: as a new parent, you will be highly tuned to every sound they make.

TWELVE TIPS FOR ESTABLISHING GOOD SLEEPING HABITS

1 Bath or wash your babies in the early evening, change their nappy and put them into night clothes, such as a sleepsuit, which can be easily unbuttoned in the middle of the night. Some babies enjoy a massage after their wash.

2 Feed them in the room in which they are to sleep, with the lights dimmed down.

3 Do not let them fall asleep during the feed, as they may wake soon afterwards for more.

4 Do not rock to sleep in a car seat, bouncing chair or in your arms: they need to recognise that their cot is where they sleep.

5 You can rock or gently sing to them while you are winding them, or play some music from a toy or mobile, but do not allow babies to rely on this to get to sleep.

6 Try not to stimulate them either visually or mentally during the last feed – they need to feel calm.

7 If possible, feed both babies simultaneously so that you can put them in their cot at the same time.

8 Once you put have them in their cot, say goodnight, then

walk out of the room. Avoid staying behind to stroke or pat them to sleep or to see if they go to sleep on their own.

9 During the night, do not rush to pick up your baby/babies as soon as you hear a sound. Like adults, babies wake several times during the night (we rarely remember doing so), but they need to learn to settle themselves. If they do not go back to sleep, use verbal reassurance and stroking to help settle them, but avoid picking your babies up.

10 If one or both babies do wake up properly, or if they need a feed, keep the lights dim, limit how much you speak to them, and change and feed them with the minimum amount of stimulation. The middle of the night is not the time to play 'peekaboo' with your babies.

11 Put the babies down to sleep at regular times during the day, so that they do not become overtired in the evening.

12 Make sure that if you have help, the other person always follows the same bedtime routine so that it is consistent for the babies.

Tasha's story

Running around trying to look after two babies, I remember feeling quite distraught that I wasn't giving them enough of me. I could see my friends carrying their babies around in slings all day, enjoying lots of cuddle time. I went to see a twins specialist who told me to remember a few important things: she said it was good to realise that my little ones had each other, which is very special; also, not being carried around all day meant that my babies would become more independent. I was immediately reassured. Looking after singletons can be quite isolating, I believe, and yet with twins I have never felt alone. I could hardly walk out of my front door without someone stopping to admire my babies and striking up a conversation.

She said it was good to realise that my little ones had each other, which is very special.

 # GETTING OUT AND ABOUT

Finding methods of transport that suit your lifestyle is crucial, as you need to be able to go out with your babies as easily as possible. Mothers of newborns can often be deterred from making the effort to go out and this can result in them becoming isolated. The choice of which pram, pushchair or buggy to use is therefore key.

It is well worth contacting Twins Clubs both locally and on the internet to find out what suited other families in similar circumstances. You may well find, if you ask around, that other parents with slightly older twins are only too happy to pass on their prams and pushchairs, either for free or at a reasonable price. New prams, in particular, are very costly, so do consider any other options that are offered to save yourself unnecessary expense. Some parents are able to rent a pram for the first few months before buying a (cheaper) pushchair or buggy once the babies are coming up to six months old. This should then last at least eighteen months, until the babies are well into the toddler stage.

Prams, pushchairs and buggies

Understanding the sometimes confusing differences between the many different designs of prams, pushchairs and buggies is one of your first tasks. Seek out specialist advice, as well as that of other parents of twins. Big department stores may have a reasonable range for twins, as will online suppliers. Models designed for twins vary greatly in style: many have the babies side by side, though some have them one behind the other (tandem), facing each other or even one on top of the other, like a double-decker. Some styles are easier to manoeuvre than others, so you should try them out in a shop before you buy.

Prams

In essence, a pram is a carrycot on a chassis that can be removed entirely. Prams enable babies to lie completely flat and the carrycots are therefore suitable for night-time sleeping. Some models, known as 'travel systems', also come with infant car seats that fit on the chassis. Prams are sturdier than pushchairs and buggies but can, as a consequence, be very expensive. Their additional bulk means that twin prams can be heavy to push around, particularly as the babies increase in size. However, they are suitable from birth onwards and, because they usually convert into pushchairs to allow the babies to sit up, will last until the toddler years.

Pushchairs

Pushchairs have a soft body that usually cannot be removed from the wheels and is forward-facing. While some designs allow babies to lie more or less flat, they are not suitable for longer, night-time sleeping. Pushchairs are more lightweight than prams, and are more substantial and comfortable than buggies. They are suitable until the babies are toddlers.

Buggies

Designs for buggies (also called strollers) are constantly evolving, and many are now suitable for newborns. Babies can lie almost flat but are lower to the ground and more open to the elements. Lighter and less sturdy than prams and pushchairs, they are easier to push around but may

not last as long. They fold away in an 'umbrella' fashion and are therefore the best option if space in your home is tight. They are usually better from six months onwards when the babies are getting heavier and can almost sit up.

You will need to consider the various options and think through what is likely to suit your personal circumstances best, taking into account your budget and lifestyle. To help you decide on a pram, pushchair or buggy, you should ask yourself the following questions:

▶ Will you mostly walk to places, use public transport or go by car?
▶ How easy is access to your front door? Do you have any hills/steps to climb?
▶ Can your front door, path and gateposts accommodate a side-by-side style?
▶ Can it be stored easily in your home?
▶ If you live in a flat, will it be possible or necessary to leave it in the communal hallway?
▶ How easy is it to fold? Could you do it with one hand?
▶ If you have a car, does it fit into the boot when collapsed?
▶ Can you park close to your home? (If not, you will need a model that is quick and easy to unfold so that you can transport the babies inside.)
▶ How much does it weigh? (Remember it will feel a lot heavier once it contains two growing babies, not to mention any shopping.)
▶ How easy will it be to use on public transport and in shops?

Car seats

You will need infant car seats to bring your babies home from hospital, as it is illegal (and dangerous) to carry them in your arms in a car or taxi. Car seats should be rear-facing for the first few months. After your babies reach a certain weight (around 10–12 kg) and can sit up, they will need front-facing seats. Rear-facing seats must not be placed in the front passenger seat if an airbag is enabled, as a baby can be seriously injured if it inflates. Rear-facing car seats have a handle, so although they are not light, especially once you have an increasingly heavy baby in each, they do at least allow you to carry your babies in and out of the car – since babies often fall asleep during a car journey, this can be useful. The car seats can also double up as rocking/reclining chairs for use in the home, though babies should not be left in them for long, as it is not good for their backs. If you have been given a car seat that has been used by someone else, it is advisable to check that it has not been damaged (e.g. through an accident) as that could compromise its safety.

Baby carriers and slings

Baby carriers are specially designed to fit on the front of your body, with straps over both shoulders and round your waist. (Those that you wear on your back are only suitable when the babies are older and can support themselves.) They can be a very good way of carrying a baby, both outdoors and in the home. There are some designs specifically for twins, although they will have a limited lifespan, as your babies will soon get too large to carry this way.

Baby slings are pieces of fabric that are worn across the body, generally over one shoulder, to form a pouch for babies to be put in. Again, there are designs for twins, but you may find it cumbersome to carry the babies in this fashion. Slings can be useful for supporting the baby while breastfeeding and provide a useful screen when doing so in public.

A carrier for each parent is an ideal way of getting around in situations where using a double pram, pushchair or buggy is inconvenient, or you could use a single buggy for one baby and carry the other (*see* p.185). Once they start to put on weight, babies will put a strain on your back, so baby carriers and slings are more useful for shorter trips and lighter babies.

Nappy-changing bag

A spacious nappy-changing bag is vital for when you go out. It does not have to be a specially constructed changing bag, but the advantage of these is that they have many different compartments in which you can store specific items such as bottles, nappies, creams, spare clothes (it is surprising how much you need to take with you), and they also have small changing mats incorporated in them.

You will need to consider the various options and think through what is likely to suit your personal circumstances best.

GETTING INTO A ROUTINE

Many women have babies at a stage in their lives when they have a career and/or a settled life. You are organised and feel in control of most day-to-day situations. When you have a baby – and this is especially true with twins – the change in your life can be a big shock and you may find it difficult to adjust to a completely different life that is usually much less ordered. A lot can be done to prepare yourself for the practicalities so that you can enjoy your babies and not feel overwhelmed.

It is perfectly possible to live happily without having organised or structured days, but in reality, most parents of twins find that it is extremely helpful to establish a routine and that babies actually thrive on one. Parents should not raise their expectations too high, as it will take a few weeks to establish regular sleeping and feeding times. After the babies are about six weeks old, you should find a routine developing. By the age of three months, most babies should be able to sleep and feed at reasonably set times, and by the time they are six months old they should be able to sleep through the night.

The first six weeks

The first few weeks are a precious time for parents to get to know their babies and start to find out what works best for you all. Developing a pattern for feeding and sleeping can take a few weeks for some, but will be quicker for others. Try to remain flexible and not plan too much. Relax your standards and accept that you do not need to prepare a freshly cooked meal every evening nor have a spick-and-span home – now is the time for convenience food and pragmatism. Finally, organise as much help as possible and delegate tasks to family and friends to lighten your load (see also p. 214). If you are breastfeeding exclusively, for example, your partner or a friend or relative could do the winding/changing/settling. Or they can prepare meals, unload the dishwasher, or put a wash on. This allows mothers and fathers to spend as much of their time as possible caring for their babies.

Six weeks to six months

Establishing a pattern for the day allows you to make plans around feeding and sleeping. Babies of six weeks and more usually do not take long to learn a routine – providing you and

TEN PRACTICAL TIPS FOR SURVIVING THE FIRST FEW MONTHS

1   Contact friends and your local Twins Club and NCT group for advice, support and the possibility of buying/borrowing second-hand equipment.
2   If you live on more than one floor, have one fully equipped changing station per level.
3   If breastfeeding, make sure that you have enough information and support to enable you to get started, and that there is someone you can call on for advice should you need it.
4   If formula feeding, try to establish a regular time for washing and sterilising all the equipment and for making up feeds.

5   Babies do not have to be bathed every day: 'top and tail' on days when you do not have the time or energy.
6   Forget non-essential tasks and prioritise and delegate the rest; get visitors to come at times when they can be of practical help to you.
7   Try to get out and about regularly; do not be afraid to seek help if you are feeling isolated and depressed.
8   Sleep when the babies do and take the opportunity to put your feet up whenever you can.
9   Arrange some time for yourself on a regular basis; make sure you and your partner also spend time together as a couple.
10 Relax your standards and enjoy your babies!

any others who may be helping stick to it firmly until it is established. As the babies grow and develop, the routine will evolve and you will naturally fine-tune it to suit the circumstances. But if you can get your babies into a reasonably predictable routine, one that – importantly – fits with your life as well, you will have more alert, contented babies during the day, who feed well and sleep soundly at night. You will also rediscover a little time for yourself and your partner – time that does not always involving feeding or soothing a baby at all times of the day or night – and you will keep your mood and energy levels up.

Babies aged from about six weeks until around eight to nine months should nap in between feeds (*see* Chapter 8, p. 233 for routines for older babies). Babies who are well rested during the day tend to feed and sleep better at night. If you are able to get your babies to nap together, you will find your time easier to manage, so if the babies are feeding at the same time, then they will probably also fall asleep at roughly the same time. However, if this does not happen, do not worry. You will learn from your babies what works for them individually and how you can fulfil their needs as well as yours.

Remember that, although you are in a routine, this does not have to be rigid: flexibility may be necessary and

inevitable. For example, one baby may be faster at getting into a routine or sleeping through the night than the other. Similarly, if a baby develops a cold, is teething or unwell for any other reason, you will need to adapt your normal patterns for a while. Try to resume your routine as soon as possible, however, and avoid, for example, putting the babies' lack of sleep down to a mild cold that they had two weeks before.

When they are around six weeks old, you can encourage your babies' awareness of waking and sleeping by providing plenty of stimulation for them during the day, and making night-time nappy-changing and feeding as unstimulating as possible. Give them a last feed at 10.30–11pm and, by the time they are three months old, they should be able to sleep for up to six hours without waking. When they are six months old, they do not need to be fed during the night – provided they have been adequately fed during the day and evening – and they should be able to sleep through to the morning. You may not get a lie-in, but the babies should not wake until around 6am, especially if their room is kept dark by good curtains/blinds (*see* p. 178).

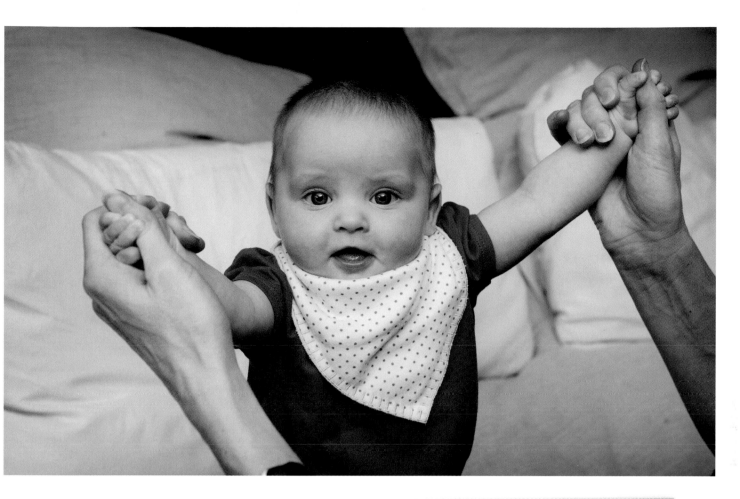

GETTING TO KNOW YOUR BABIES

Learning to know, understand and develop your emotional relationship with each of your babies is often referred to as 'bonding'. Encouraging each baby's personality to flourish individually will help the bonding process and is also crucial for their development as happy, healthy individuals.

Apart from being prepared for the range of emotions that any parent may feel, there are some key things that can help you to be the parents of twins. Holding and cuddling each baby separately from the beginning, even if only for a few minutes, will help them to get to know you and vice versa. Try to hold each of them as soon as possible after birth, but do not be anxious if this is not possible (perhaps because they need medical attention or are born early and admitted to a neonatal

unit), because you will soon develop a close and different relationship with each one. (*See* Chapter 6, p. 142 for the information about relating to the babies in these circumstances.) Some mothers don't experience the instant, boundless love that they feel they should, and it is important to reassure them that this is neither unusual nor unnatural. In the first four months, babies especially enjoy and benefit from being spoken to and sung to individually, as well as smiled at and looked at, all of which helps with the bonding process and with their long-term development. Feeding your babies yourself, whether you are breast- or formula feeding, is also an ideal opportunity to have one-to-one closeness with each of your babies.

Relating to one more easily than the other
Most mothers plan to and expect that they will treat all their children equally, so it can be disconcerting with twins to find that you may feel closer and even that you love one baby more

than the other. As Elizabeth Bryan, an authority on twins, once memorably put it in her book *Twins, Triplets and More*: 'Few of us expect to fall in love with two people at the same time …Yet this is precisely the challenge that faces the parents of twins. Many find it much more difficult that they expect.'

Feeling much closer or even preferring one baby to the other may make you feel guilty and is sometimes difficult to acknowledge, even to yourself and certainly to others. Be reassured that it is not at all uncommon, and can be caused by a whole range of factors:

▸ One baby is 'easier': cries less, sleeps better, feeds more efficiently.
▸ One baby is more easy-going or smiley.
▸ If the babies are of different sexes, you have a preference for one sex rather than the other.
▸ One baby is breastfed, the other not (for a variety of reasons); you may feel closer to the breastfed one in the early days.
▸ One baby is at home, allowing you to develop your relationship with this baby, whereas the other one is still in hospital.

Midwives, health visitors and other healthcare professionals understand that difficulties in developing your relationship with each baby can happen, so do not hesitate to seek professional advice should you need to. Partners and family should also be aware that such feelings can arise and may themselves need help with understanding how to support you. This is particularly important when one baby is allowed home and the other one is still in hospital, so that you can balance your time between the two in order for your relationship with them to develop as equally as possible.

Developing as individuals

From an early age, personality differences become evident in twins, whether they are dizygotic (non-identical) or monozygotic (identical). Seeing and treating your babies as individuals from birth is an important factor in your relationship with twins, and is crucial for helping to avoid some of the behavioural, relationship and psychological problems that may arise for them in later years. It can also help greatly with their language and social development. Although most parents recognise these facts, individuality for twins is not always easy to achieve, as 'twinship' is seen as very special. Other people often regard and treat the babies as one unit. Prepare families and friends well ahead about how to get to know and treat the babies as individuals. For more on personality development in twins, see Chapter 8, p. 245–6.

However, in the first few days after birth, one of the principal challenges you might face, particularly when they are identical, is actually being able to tell your babies apart. Planning ahead to have a soft toy or differently coloured clothes or blankets from birth will help parents, family, friends and hospital staff to know immediately which baby is which and to call each by their name. Most mothers of twins quickly learn to tell their babies apart and sometimes cannot understand why it is difficult for others to do so.

It is important to encourage everyone to treat your babies as individuals from birth. There are some practical steps that you can take to help you do this:

▸ Start preparing before the babies are born to treat them as individuals and encourage friends and family to do the same.
▸ Think carefully about their names you give them: avoid ones that begin with the same letter (Jack and John) or sound similar (Gemma and Emma).
▸ Look out for their differences, and ensure that others do too.
▸ Don't call them 'The Twins' and strongly discourage others from doing so.
▸ When speaking to/about them, vary the order in which you use their names: 'Emma and Tim', rather than always 'Tim 'n' Emma', to prevent them from sounding as if they are one person with one name.
▸ Do not dress them identically. If they are same-sex twins, you can dress them in similar designs but in different colours.
▸ Try to feed them and spend time with them on their own. Investing in a single buggy can also facilitate this (*see* p. 185).
▸ Arrange for the babies to be apart when possible (e.g. ask a family member or other helpers to look after one at a time).

It is important to encourage everyone to treat your babies as individuals from birth.

Your babies will be closely monitored to ensure that they grow and reach the various developmental milestones expected of them. Twins are more likely to be premature, and are usually born before 38 weeks, so their weight, growth and development does not always follow that for singleton babies born at 40 weeks.

Your babies' growth

From birth onwards, your babies' weight, height and head circumference will be noted down on separate charts in your 'red book' (*see* Box) so that they can be closely monitored. This data is recorded on the same charts as those for babies born at 40 weeks, but for babies born before 37 weeks, a vertical line will be drawn by your health visitor at the pre-term week of their birth – if not, you should ask for this to be done. All measurements for at least the first two years will be taken from this date, rather than the 40-week estimated delivery date (EDD) line that is printed in the books.

Recording weight is especially important in the early weeks and months to ensure your babies gain enough but not too much. At first, and especially if your babies stay in hospital for any length of time, their weight will be charted on a daily basis. Do not worry if there are small losses as well as gains from one day to the next. This is not a cause for concern, as it is normal for babies to lose a little weight in the first couple of weeks before starting to gain weight. But if the general trend is either too fast or, more importantly, too small – or if your babies start to lose weight without regaining it at any stage – then your health visitor or doctor will give you advice. Premature babies who are simply born too soon but have no other medical complication will usually catch up in weight with their full-term peers by the time they are two years old, and often sooner. See Chapter 6 for more information about prematurity.

Calculating your babies' developmental age

Average rates of infant development are based on data collected from all babies. Most babies are born at around 40 weeks, whereas twins are often born very much earlier than that. There might therefore be a difference for twins in when they reach certain developmental stages. For example, babies born at 32 weeks will be eight weeks old by the average time of gestation (40 weeks). So, when parents are told that babies first start to smile at around six weeks old, for a baby born at 32 weeks, this will probably be nearer fourteen weeks old. The same will be true of other developmental milestones and growth, at least for the first few months and years.

All babies develop at different rates, and twins are no exception. In addition, the order in which they reach certain milestones may vary from one baby to another: for example, one may sit up sooner than their sibling. Bear in mind that babies who learn to roll over, crawl and walk earlier than others are no more intelligent than those who take a long time to do so (so do not worry when other mothers boast of their children's physical achievements). For details of the development of motor skills and movement in babies, see Chapter 8, p. 244.

The Box on p. 195 provides approximate information on when you can expect your babies to reach certain developmental milestones, calculated on the basis of a baby born at 40 weeks.

YOUR PERSONAL CHILD HEALTH RECORD

A few days after the birth you will be given a Personal Child Health Record, commonly called the 'red book', for each of your babies. There are different books for boys and girls, which have different growth charts, reflecting average rates for boys and girls respectively. The red book is used to record important information about your babies, such as dates of immunisations, weight and growth measurements, and the results of routine developmental checks. You should therefore take the books with you whenever you have an appointment regarding your babies' health. You can also add information yourself, such dates of first teeth.

The six-week check

Your babies will be examined when they are six weeks old to assess their overall health and development. Your doctor or a hospital paediatrician or doctor will check:

▸ head circumference, weight and length
▸ heart, chest and breathing
▸ abdominal organs and genitals
▸ eyes, ears and mouth
▸ hip alignment
▸ grasp reflex, head control and muscle tone.

If your babies were born prematurely, the doctor will pay particular attention to their muscle tone, any breathing difficulties they may have, and their feeding and sleeping habits. Always raise any concerns you might have.

DEVELOPMENTAL MILESTONES 0–4 MONTHS

0 weeks
▸ can suck and swallow
▸ can only focus on close-up objects or faces

4 weeks
▸ start to follow you or objects as they move around their field of vision
▸ can turn the head and start to lift it

6–8 weeks
▸ start to smile
▸ greater head and neck control

3 months
▸ use arms in a more controlled manner, staring at hands, grabbing your hair, holding objects tightly, but still in hit-or-miss way
▸ may start to roll over
▸ start to make noises in response to your own speech patterns, trying to mimic your voice
▸ much more alert to environment

4 months
▸ start to drool (not necessarily a sign of teething) and increasingly make babbling sounds
▸ can bring hands together in front of body and put them or other objects into mouth
▸ can make a link between seeing an object and being able to hold it
▸ start to transfer objects from one hand to another and to improve fine motor skills
▸ can hold their head up and keep their back straight when sitting on your lap
▸ can focus close up and long distance
▸ may start to roll over (if not done so earlier)
▸ kick legs and wave arms as way of expressing emotion
▸ by now will be sucking thumb or finger (if not, will not do so).

COMMON HEALTH PROBLEMS IN YOUNG BABIES

Most babies will develop some minor health problems and you will soon acquire a sixth sense for knowing whether or not you should consult a health visitor or doctor. If in doubt, do not hesitate to do so, particularly when your babies are very young, and do not be afraid to trust your instincts, as you know your babies better than anyone else.

Jaundice

Jaundice is a very common condition among newborns in general, and especially among those born prematurely and who therefore have immature livers. See Chapter 6, p. 138 for full details of the condition. Depending on the severity of the case, your babies may be kept in hospital so that they can be placed under ultraviolet light for a length of time every day until the jaundice has improved. If the babies are only mildly affected, they may be discharged and you may simply be advised to place them in natural light for a little while every day once you are back home. This means placing them near a window, and *not* in direct sunlight.

Rashes and skin problems

A baby's skin is very fragile and sensitive. It is quite common for babies to develop slight rashes, many of which are unexplained and harmless, but which should nonetheless be checked out by a doctor. For information about eczema, see Chapter 8, p. 250.

Milia

White spots (known as milia), caused by hormonal changes, often appear soon after birth, particularly on your baby's face, but these usually disappear within a few weeks without any treatment. Avoid using perfumed bath oils or creams, as these will dry out your babies' skin and can cause irritation.

Cradle cap

A baby's scalp often becomes dry and flaky in the weeks after birth, a condition known as 'cradle cap'. Although it is unattractive, it is harmless and nothing to worry about. You can try putting unscented baby oil to keep it moisturised, but there is not much more you can do other than wait for it to disappear naturally in time.

Nappy rash

The ammonia in urine irritates a baby's skin and can cause nappy rash – some babies are more susceptible to it than others. Tips to prevent or cure nappy rash include:

► changing your babies' nappies regularly so that they are not kept in a wet nappy longer than necessary
► using cotton wool balls and water rather than baby wipes to wash the area, patting dry with a soft towel
► leaving your babies' bottoms to air as long as possible after a nappy change or bath
► applying zinc or other proprietary cream if a rash develops, as these act as a barrier between the skin and the urine (ask your pharmacist or health visitor for advice).

Colic

The common condition known as colic is thought to be caused by spasms in a baby's intestines and usually occurs between the ages of two weeks and three months. Most problems with colic arise in the early evening, just at the time when you and the babies are at your most tired. Babies affected by colic scream and cry and can be very difficult to soothe. They often draw in their arms and legs as if they have tummy ache.

The causes of colic are still very poorly understood, and babies find relief in different ways. Colic sometimes eases when they are placed across a parent's arm or lap on their tummy (but do not put them to sleep on their front), or by being rocked gently, holding them firmly and securely. Others may find that sucking on something (a dummy or finger) helps. Make sure, first, that they are not hungry. Some parents swear by gripe water or certain calming teas; others simply try to take it in turns to attend to the screaming baby/babies in the knowledge that (unlikely though it may seem) by the time the babies are three months old, the colic and the accompanying crying has usually stopped.

Vomiting

Babies will often bring up ('posset') a bit of milk after a feed, and some do so more than others (*see* Winding, p. 169). Occasionally, your baby may vomit an entire feed in a rather violent way – this is called 'projectile vomiting'. If it happens more than once, seek a doctor's opinion. However, if your baby is suddenly and continuously sick, and is unable to keep fluids down (including water), seek medical opinion without delay because babies get dangerously dehydrated much faster than older children and adults.

Diarrhoea

Before babies start eating solids, their stools are yellowish-brown and quite loose (breastfed babies usually have looser stools than formula-fed ones, and their stools have a different, less strong smell). If the stools become liquid and/or green, your baby has diarrhoea and you should consult a doctor at once, because (as with vomiting) babies can soon become dehydrated. In the meantime, simply give them cool boiled water to sip.

Constipation

When babies are constipated, you will notice that their stools become firmer and/or less frequent. Your babies may also look as if they are straining when they have a bowel motion. Formula-fed babies are at greater risk of becoming constipated than breastfed ones, but all can get a little dehydrated from time to time (e.g. due to hot weather), which can lead to constipation. If you notice a change in your babies' bowel movements, give them some additional water until things improve. You may have to do this in small but frequent doses, because babies rarely like drinking plain water at first if they have only ever tasted milk. If you are concerned, seek professional advice.

Fever

Babies and young children often develop a fever within a very short space of time and with no other obvious symptoms of being unwell. To check a baby's temperature, place a thermometer under their armpit and wait for one minute, or use an ear thermometer suitable for infants, which is an easy way of taking the temperature of a small baby. A baby's normal body temperature is 37°C. Make sure they drink plenty of fluids to keep hydrated. Prevent them from overheating by keeping clothing loose and reducing the number of layers. If they are over two months old, you can give them some infant paracetamol (although check with your pharmacist if your babies are premature and weigh less than 4 kg). You can also sponge down the babies' faces and bodies with warm water and let them dry naturally. If, after taking these measures, the babies' temperature has not fallen, seek medical advice. See also Chapter 8, for information about febrile convulsions, colds and chest problems. However, you should consult your doctor *at once* if your babies have any of the following symptoms:

▸ have a temperature over 37°C which has not responded to the above measures
▸ vomit in successive attempts to feed
▸ have diarrhoea (or nappies are dry), or stools are greenish
▸ have a cough or are wheezy

▸ develop a rash or infection
▸ are lethargic and excessively sleepy
▸ are not their 'usual selves'.

Above all, if you are concerned, always seek professional advice.

CAN TWINS AVOID CATCHING ILLNESSES FROM EACH OTHER?

Given how much time they spend together, it is not surprising that twins often catch infections and illnesses from each other. This may disrupt routines and life in general for a while (see p. 187), so get help if you can in order to cope. With more serious contagious childhood illnesses, such as chickenpox (see Chapter 8, p. 251), there is not much you can do to avoid your babies catching it from each other. This is often because by the time one baby develops symptoms, the period when they were most infectious has already passed. Try nonetheless to stick to good hygiene: for example, always wash your hands after feeding and changing one baby before you take care of the other.

Alex's story

I couldn't breastfeed at first, as my babies wouldn't latch on, so I expressed my milk, which I found physically very demanding. Having fed from a bottle from the start, the babies didn't adjust to the breast, so I continued giving them expressed milk. When we left hospital, my boys were already on an established feeding routine. This meant we had an efficient schedule when we got home: I would feed one boy, then the other, and then I would express some more. I eventually made the decision to stop at twelve weeks, as the boys were having formula as well, and having to express all the time actually limited our ability to get out and about.

Looking after twins was tough at times, but you have to realise that it's not like that forever and things change. I remember thinking it would be so much easier when they can sit up, walk, feed themselves, but the truth is, every stage has its pros and cons and you mustn't wish any of it away. The great thing is that partners, family and friends are essential. My husband had a role as soon as he came through the door after work: he was immediately given a baby and a bottle. We dress our boys separately to try to promote their own identities and to help other people identify them. Watching how they interact and play with each other is truly amazing. To see such young children playing 'peekaboo' and chatting with each other is lovely. Every mother of twins suffers from 'twin mum guilt' every now and then, thinking, 'Have I been fair?', 'Have I spent enough time with each of them?', 'I gave one a hug, I must hug the other'; but you have to just tell yourself that in the end it all balances out.

There's something very special about being a parent of twins. You experience something that not many people do and, although it is hard work from time to time, the positives outweigh the negatives. Other parents of twins are so supportive. Whenever you see each other, there's always an instant identification and it's so helpful talking to people whose children are the next stage ahead of you to give you advice.

After the birth of your babies, your body takes about six to eight weeks to return to its pre-pregnancy state. This period is known as the 'puerperium'. Many physical changes take place, including a reduction in the volume of blood and the size of your ribcage, pelvis and abdomen.

Throughout the puerperium your uterus will gradually shrink back to its pre-pregnancy size and is usually not palpable (felt externally) after fourteen days of delivery. After the birth you will have heavy vaginal discharge called lochia (this tends to be lighter after Caesarean deliveries). Lochia consists of blood mixed with tissues and mucus that was needed in the pregnancy but now must be expelled from the uterus. Usually, after a week or so, it will start to reduce in quantity. Do not use tampons until after your six-week check, both for comfort and for risk of infection. The discharge of lochia can continue for up to six weeks, but will become progressively lighter and after fourteen days will usually become significantly less blood-stained.

Recovering from a vaginal birth

A vaginal birth is the perfectly natural way to have a baby, but you still need to look after yourself as your body returns to normal. If you had an episiotomy (see Chapter 5, p. 120) and needed sutures (stitches) in your perineum, you should keep the area as clean and dry as possible until the cut has healed, which usually takes up to two weeks. Good hygiene is important, so in addition to a daily bath or shower, bathe the area regularly with clean, warm water, particularly after going to the toilet (see right), as this is both soothing and helpful to the healing process. Avoid using any soap, but if you do need to it should be very mild. Carefully pat yourself dry with a clean towel or cotton cloth.

The sutures may feel tighter in the days following the birth, by which time you may be back home. While this is not unusual, it may make sitting down painful. Many women find that using a rubber ring on a seat brings them relief, as it takes the pressure off the perineum. Ice packs placed against the area (with a clean, damp towel or cotton cloth in between the pack and the skin) can also help, as can the use of a topical anaesthetic cream or spray. Perineal sutures are usually dissolvable and so do not need to be removed. Your midwife

will check to make sure the area is healing, but if it becomes more painful or red, do ask for it to be checked again.

You may feel a little apprehensive about passing urine to start off with, so drink plenty of water to make it as dilute as possible. Afterwards, gently wash yourself with warm water – a bidet or shower may make this easier – and pat the area dry with a clean towel before using a new sanitary towel. If you have any symptoms of pain when urinating, seek advice from your midwife or doctor.

You may not need to open your bowels for a few days after delivery, but have plenty of fluids and a diet with high-fibre foods to avoid constipation.

UTERINE INFECTION

If at any stage you think something is not right with your healing process – for example, if your lochia has an offensive smell, if you develop a fever, or if your abdomen becomes/stays tender – alert your doctor or midwife. It is possible that you have developed a uterine or wound infection.

Recovering from a Caesarean section

Following a Caesarean section, you will stay in hospital for up to five days, depending on circumstances. Your incision will be covered by a dressing for five days, after which time both dressing and sutures (stitches) will be removed. Although the process may sting a little, it is fast and any discomfort should only last a few seconds. Once the dressing has been removed, wear breathable cotton knickers that rise higher than the scar to avoid any rubbing, and keep the scar clean, dry and as ventilated as possible for the first few days, until the healing process is well under way.

The skin around the incision may feel lumpy and uneven for some days and weeks. This is normal, as it is caused by slight bleeding following the operation. Eventually, the tissue will settle down and the scar will smooth out. The area around the scar may also feel numb. This is caused by very fine nerves being cut within the skin during the operation. They too will grow back over the next few weeks and normal sensation usually returns. Occasionally, the wound may leak a little

bloodstained fluid in the first few days after the operation. This is nothing to worry about. However, if at any stage the wound bleeds significantly or it becomes raised, red or tender, speak to your doctor or midwife.

You will be offered frequent pain relief while you are still in hospital, which is likely to be given by injection at first and then via suppositories or tablets. Do discuss your requirements with your midwife and make sure you are prescribed some pain relief to take home in case you need it.

Thrombosis (a blood clot) is a risk for six to eight weeks after the operation (see Chapter 5, p. 131) and so it is important to get mobile as soon as you can. If you do have painful swelling of the legs or unexpected breathlessness, you should seek immediate advice from your midwife or doctor.

The hospital physiotherapist or midwife will give you advice about postnatal exercises to help your recovery, but you will need to take things quite slowly to start with. Remember: a Caesarean section is a major operation, from which it will take a few weeks to completely recover physically.

Taking care with everyday activities

Your anterior abdominal wall and lower back will have been under considerable strain, so you are likely to feel weak and tired once you have given birth. Be careful not to start lifting heavy objects and take your time before embarking on certain household tasks that involve bending over, stretching and heavy carrying. So ask others to load and unload the dishwasher and washing machine, for example.

After a Caesarean section, you should avoid lifting heavy loads for the first six weeks, as your abdominal muscles will have been weakened by the operation. Driving may be difficult and the twisting associated with reversing may be particularly uncomfortable, so avoid it until your discomfort has gone (on average, it disappears after four to six weeks). You can, of course, lift your babies, but take care when you do so: bend your knees rather than your back, do not lean or stretch over to lift them, and if necessary, especially at first, ask someone else to hand them to you. Do not lift the pram into and out of your car boot until after you have recovered your strength, and certainly not for the first six weeks. If you feel any discomfort with an activity, stop at once.

Incontinence

Stress incontinence is the leakage of urine when you cough, laugh, sneeze or move quickly. This potentially distressing problem is not much discussed, either by women themselves or by healthcare professionals, even though it is very common to some degree both during pregnancy and in the days and weeks after the birth. Incontinence is most likely if you have

had previous pregnancies or a vaginal delivery, although others can suffer too. It occurs because the pelvic floor muscles come under considerable strain during labour, and the bladder neck can become stretched as the babies' heads pass down the birth canal. Even after a Caesarean, the weight of the babies on the pelvic floor muscles during the latter stages of the pregnancy can lead to some incontinence following the birth. Pelvic floor muscle exercises, both before birth and continued as soon as possible afterwards, will help you to regain bladder control (see opposite). If you are still suffering from stress incontinence, despite doing regular pelvic floor exercises, at the time you have your six-week postnatal check, mention this to your doctor.

Faecal incontinence may occur after all forms of delivery. Again, women at particular risk are those who have had a vaginal delivery where a long second stage has then led to complex vaginal tearing. Again, regular pelvic floor muscle exercises, begun as soon as possible after delivery, usually rectify the problem within a few days, but if you are concerned in any way, speak to your doctor about it without delay, as there may be some damage to your rectum which will need specialist help.

DID YOU KNOW…?

If you have had a Caesarean or a complicated vaginal delivery, you should wait until eight weeks after the birth to start low-impact exercises and fourteen weeks or so before progressing to high-impact forms.

Returning to other exercise

Women are often keen to return to general exercise to improve well-being and help their body to recover from the challenges of pregnancy. For the first six weeks you should concentrate on daily pelvic floor muscle exercises and walking a little each day. Do not do too much: start by walking around the block and gradually build on what you are doing over the weeks.

After six weeks it is safe to try low-impact forms of exercise, such as pilates, yoga, swimming (once your discharge has stopped and any sutures are fully healed), cycling and gentle weight training. Start slowly and listen to your body.

While the abdominal muscles are stretched during any pregnancy, it can be more obvious in women who have carried twins, so doing some gentle exercise to tone and strengthen the abdominal area can be a good idea. Start by trying to draw

Pelvic floor muscle exercises

Whatever type of delivery you had, there is one thing that you can and should begin to do as soon as possible after the birth: pelvic floor muscle exercises. The pelvic floor muscles wrap around the the bladder, uterus and bowels to give support, and help with control of and prevent leakage from your bladder and bowels. These muscles are weakened by pregnancy (due to the weight of the baby pressing down on them and the hormonal changes that occur) and by the birth itself (particularly from a vaginal delivery of more than one baby or one that involved forceps or a ventouse).

All women should begin exercises to strengthen these muscles straight after the birth and continue with them regularly for three to six months, if not for life. If performed correctly, they will enable you to gradually regain strength over your urinary and bowel functions. Specific advice will be given to you by midwives and physiotherapists antenatally and again in the early postnatal period.

While you might not think them high on your priority list in the days immediately after the birth, pelvic floor muscle exercises are nevertheless quick and easy to do and can be done anytime, anywhere. It is best to get into a habit, such as doing them by lunchtime every day or every time you do a particular task, such as feeding your baby. Incorporated in such a way into your routine, you are more likely to remember to do them on a regular basis.

There are two exercises that you should do to strengthen your pelvic floor muscles. You should aim to do both sets of exercises three or four times a day. When you first start, you may find it easier to do them lying down or sitting – only progress to doing them when standing once your muscles feel stronger.

'Slow squeezes'
Slowly squeeze the muscles around the anus, vagina and urethra – as if stopping the passage of wind or urine. Hold this squeeze as long as you can (up to a maximum count of ten), then let go. Repeat ten times, making sure you are breathing normally throughout. Start small – even if you can only hold the muscles for three seconds, you will still be getting benefit – and gradually build up the number of seconds you are holding for over time.

'Quick squeezes'
Squeeze and release the pelvic floor muscles quickly ten times, but do not hold the squeeze this time. Ensure you are breathing normally throughout. The contraction is internal, so you should not see any movement in your leg, bottom or stomach muscles, but you should feel an internal 'lift' when you squeeze.

In addition to these daily exercises, you can practise squeezing your pelvic floor muscles in the same way when you cough, sneeze, laugh, lift your baby, or carry out any other activity that is strenuous, to help prevent leakage of urine.

It is important to exercise your muscles until they are tired and not to where they are comfortable. So, when you find ten fast contractions easy, increase to fifteen, or when you can hold a slow contraction for ten seconds, increase the length of the hold to thirteen or fifteen seconds. If you are having any problems with bladder or bowel control or you are not sure how to do the above exercises correctly, speak to your midwife, health visitor or doctor, who can refer you to a specialist physiotherapist local to you.

It is recommended that women do these exercises at least once every day for ever – in much the same way that you need to brush your teeth. This may prevent problems developing in later life.

While you might not think them high on your priority list in the days immediately after the birth, pelvic floor muscle exercises are nevertheless quick and easy to do and can be done anytime, anywhere.

your tummy muscles in while you are walking and doing activities with your baby – even these gentle squeezes will help you to regain strength and tone. It is best to do any further abdominal strengthening under the guidance of a trained professional (a physiotherapist or exercise class instructor) to begin with. If you are worried that your muscles do not appear to be recovering well, speak to your doctor.

After twelve weeks or so it is usually safe to start other forms of exercise, for example, gentle running, tennis, aerobics or dancing. If you are still breastfeeding, you may prefer to stick to low-impact exercise to minimise any potential damage to joints, ligaments and the pelvic floor muscles. Remember it can take some women up to a year to recover from pregnancy – take your time and try not to compare yourself to other women you know.

Staying healthy: eating and drinking well

During these first few months with your new babies you will be very busy, but it is important that you look after yourself as well as caring for them. A nutritious and well-balanced diet is fundamental to maintaining good health and stamina (see Chapter 2, p. 32). You may find that eating little and often is easier to achieve than sitting down to three square meals a day, but avoid processed, high-sugar or high-fat foods, as these will only provide temporary energy highs and will not fill you up. It is unrealistic to expect your body to return to its pre-pregnancy size and weight within weeks of the birth. However, if you try to eat sensibly and nutritiously (while allowing yourself some treats), the weight will gradually fall off without you even noticing, simply because you will be on the go so much.

If you are breastfeeding you need to have a varied and healthy diet. You should eat three balanced meals a day and do not be tempted to substitute a sweet, convenient snack for a proper meal. You get all the minerals and vitamins you need by eating a balanced diet, but a supplement of 10 mcg of vitamin D is recommended, as it could have become depeleted by the pregnancy (see Chapter 2, p. 33). Drinking plenty is also important (and you are likely to feel naturally thirsty anyway). Water, milk or herbal teas are better than caffeinated, diuretic drinks, such as tea, coffee or fizzy drinks; alcohol will pass through into your milk and could affect your babies. Similarly, medication can pass into breastmilk, so unless you know it is safe, consult your doctor or a pharmacist before taking any.

Rest and sleep

Sleep is just as important for parents as it is for babies (see p. 176). The cliché that you should sleep when the babies do is nonetheless true, so take every opportunity to do this, even during the day. This may seem unrealistic when there are a thousand and one tasks to be done around your home, but even if you are not napping during the day, you need to find a way of putting your feet up for at least a short time. Some mothers find it more restful to breastfeed a baby lying down, for example (see p. 157). At night, you may want to arrange a 'duty rota' with your partner or a friend to allow at least one of you to have a good night's sleep. Breaks from your duties are particularly important if you are a single mother.

Your six-week check

The six-week postnatal check is an opportunity for your healthcare professional to carry out a physical examination and also for you to discuss any concerns you might have. It is usually performed by your doctor (or your community midwife or other staff within a hospital clinic). In addition to measuring your blood pressure and weight, and examining your urine for blood or protein, they will check whether:

- ▸ your uterus has shrunk back to its pre-pregnancy size and cannot be palpated through your abdomen
- ▸ your bleeding has stopped (although you could now have a period if you are not breastfeeding)
- ▸ a Caesarean or perineal wound has healed and is not uncomfortable
- ▸ your vagina and perineum are normal, and that you have no offensive discharge or pain
- ▸ there are lumps, tenderness or redness in your breasts and whether your nipples are cracked.

The six-week check is a good opportunity to discuss any physical, emotional or psychological issues you might have, however minor. These could include the fact that your perineum is still sore, your vagina doesn't feel 'right', or you are suffering from some degree of incontinence despite doing regular pelvic floor muscle exercises. You may also discuss contraception and be advised on what methods would best suit your particular needs. If you are feeling more exhausted than you think should be normal, your blood may be tested to see if you are anaemic (see Chapter 4, p. 94). This is a common problem, especially after a Caesarean section. Finally, if you think you are showing symptoms of postnatal depression (see p. 207), make sure you tell someone, as it is better to discuss this as soon as you have any concerns.

Although generally it takes six to eight weeks to physically recover from pregnancy and childbirth, every woman will be different, and for most it is a long time before they start to really feel like their normal selves. Do not worry if your recovery is still very much a 'work in progress' – you will not be alone.

 # ADJUSTING TO PARENTHOOD

Becoming a parent is a life-changing event and adjusting emotionally and psychologically to your new circumstances takes time. Experiencing a range of emotions in the early weeks and months is entirely normal.

There will be times when you feel elated at having given birth, and others (sometimes immediately after) when your life may seem very bleak. However planned your pregnancy was you should not underestimate how long it can take you to adjust emotionally. This is especially true if these are your first babies, when you have no experience of what parenthood entails. But even if you have one child already, the experience of having twins is very different.

It may be a surprise when you find that, even though these are much-wanted babies, life is not necessarily as rosy and straightforward as you thought it might be. Emotional highs and lows are therefore to be expected. Do not be too hard on yourself and try not to set the bar too high in terms of your own progress and achievement.

The 'baby blues'

However well prepared you feel, most women experience the normal mood changes that are commonly referred to as the 'baby blues'. These occur between two and five days after birth, often when your breast milk comes in, and are, in effect, symptoms of mild depression. Bewilderingly for many women, these feelings can strike at any time of the day. One minute you are fine, the next you can feel any or all of the following:

▸ tearful
▸ anxious
▸ irritable
▸ low.

You may be surprised or shocked by these emotions, especially if you have never previously suffered from them; you may also feel guilty that you do not feel more elated by the birth of your babies. Reassure yourself that these feelings are no reflection on you: they do not mean you regret having your babies and do not love them, nor that you are (or will be) a bad mother. It is simply that a mixture of hormones, tiredness and the demands of caring for your babies are – unsurprisingly – affecting your mood. The main thing to remember is that for many women, the baby blues do improve after a couple of weeks.

Make sure you communicate your feelings to your partner, who may themselves be quietly suffering from similarly shifting emotions as they adjust to their new life. If they are made aware of how you are feeling, they can start to help, namely by supporting you not only emotionally but in practical ways as well. The more they can do this, the more you will be working as team to get through what can often be a time of enormous physical and psychological adjustment.

Home alone

You are likely to have given a lot of thought to how you will care for two babies once at home, and perhaps will have planned to have some help (see p. 214). Even so, the first time you are at home caring for your babies can sometimes be daunting. If family members are living with you or close by, it is advisable to make plans well ahead about how the practical help that they may offer will work best for you all. Mothers can feel that the care of their babies is completely taken over, even though the help is given with the very best intentions; this is especially so if they are not breastfeeding. While it can be a good idea to have a visit or two lined up from a friends or relatives, do be honest about how you are feeling and ask friends and family not to come if you are tired. It may be not be very easy for you to get out of the house in the early days, so when you are ready to see people, it can be more sensible if they come to you. Do not let this lead to you providing a three-course meal, however – let them bring food, make the tea and wash up! Be honest and make it clear that although you would love to see them, it would be even better if they could help you as well, so suggest they come at feeding or bath time. In fact, it is a good idea to have a list of jobs ready for when they arrive, as most people will be pleased to give practical help. You will probably find the company of others tiring within a relatively short time, so make this clear, too.

Make sure there are friends or relatives you can call if you are feeling down or anxious: you need to know you can talk openly about any frustrations and fears you might have, and receive sensible advice if you require it. In addition, prioritise what you feel you have to get done during the day and only do the essential chores. If you still find the household tasks completely overwhelming, arrange some help if you can – then delegate! This may be to a grandparent, sibling, close friend or paid help, depending on your budget. It is also important to try and get out for a short time, even if it is not every day, to see other people. Twins Clubs or parent-and-child groups at local Children's Centres are an ideal way to meet people in a similar situation to you and to provide you and your babies with a change of scene.

Postnatal depression

Postnatal depression (PND) affects about one in ten women and studies suggest that it is more common in mothers of twins. This is because PND is thought to be linked to fatigue, anxiety and emotional adjustments, all of which are increased when caring for two babies. One of the reasons why it is important to plan ahead for your early days of parenthood is to avoid some of the physical factors that can play a part. While most women suffer from temporary mild depression ('baby blues' – see opposite), some go on to display signs of PND. Symptoms can be numerous and, as well as those listed opposite for 'baby blues', include:

- ► insomnia
- ► sudden and dramatic mood swings
- ► lack of energy and an inability to concentrate
- ► a feeling of hopelessness
- ► high anxiety
- ► difficulty with bonding with your babies
- ► feeling that life is no longer worth living
- ► loss of feelings for the babies
- ► feelings of self-harm or harm to the babies
- ► eating too little or too much
- ► no resumption of libido following the birth.

PUERPERAL PSYCHOSIS

The sudden onset of serious psychiatric problems, with symptoms similar to those of manic depression, is known as puerperal psychosis. It is rare, affecting about one in 500 women, and is an acute condition that requires specialist and urgent professional help and treatment. It is probable that your family and healthcare professionals will notice that something is not right and will ensure that you receive the appropriate care.

PND can begin at any time in the first year after birth and may last for a few months. The causes are complex and still not fully understood by the medical profession. What is known is that if you have suffered in the past from depression, you are more susceptible to developing PND; and if you have suffered from PND after a previous birth, you have a one in four chance of developing it again.

Other contributory factors are exhaustion created by the constant care that babies need (particularly if you have little practical help and emotional support) and feeling lonely and isolated, which can be a particular problem for mothers of twins, who can find it more difficult to get out and about. A traumatic or a disappointing birth experience can leave a woman feeling that she has somehow 'failed'. Problems with a previous pregnancy/birth or negative feelings about this particular pregnancy can also result in PND, as can unrealistic expectations about being a perfect mother.

Financial or relationship problems can also play their part, as can the sudden loss of freedom women experience, especially if the birth was premature and unexpected. Women can be unprepared for the sudden change in their status and this is a real shock to mental equilibrium. However much babies are wanted and planned, however frequently you are told that your life after the birth will change, it is virtually impossible for you to understand truly how it will affect you. Once you are actually in the situation, there can be some difficulty adapting to your new circumstances and sometimes women are left mourning the loss of their previous life as they make the major changes needed to get used to their new one. If you think you are suffering from PND or are at risk of doing so, there are several steps you can take to help yourself:

▸ Talk to your health visitor and/or doctor and share it with your partner, a friend or a relative. Do not be embarrassed: your situation is common and you are not to blame. By talking to others, you will be taking matters into your own hands, will feel more understood and will be taking the first step to getting better. Do make sure you are taken seriously and not simply told that 'it will pass'. Just talking about it and getting some practical and emotional support can be sufficient. Or you may benefit from more formal counselling or therapy, and in some cases medication may be prescribed.
▸ If you were a perfectionist and liked to be in control of your life before the birth, try to relax your standards, because they will cause you needless stress and misery. If you are still feeling overwhelmed by the amount of tasks you have to do (and seem unable to complete), make a list of what is absolutely necessary, and delegate them as much as possible to others. You will probably find that many of the tasks you thought were important are actually far from essential.
▸ Do a little light exercise daily (such as going for a walk) and try to make sure you leave the house at least once a day. Exercise produces mood-enhancing hormones called endorphins, which help to counteract symptoms of depression.
▸ Try to see other mothers/friends/relatives during the week, and to plan outings or visits. Socialising is good for improving your mood and for making you feel you are still a member of the human race, not simply a nappy-changing and feeding machine.
▸ If possible, arrange care for your babies on a regular basis so that you have time for *you*, and accept *any* offers of help. You do not have to do anything in particular during this time: just sitting quietly in a nearby café with a newspaper and a cup of coffee, even for a short time, can be enormously beneficial.
▸ Give yourself a daily treat. This can be as simple as a special food, a small glass of wine in the evening, or a soak in the bath once your partner is home.
▸ Do not be tempted to diet but eat varied, healthy, nutritious and *enjoyable* meals. Being calorie-deprived will make you irritable and exhausted and will aggravate your symptoms of depression.
▸ Do not suffer in silence. Speak to your family and trusted friends – you will find many of them have suffered feelings similar to yours and are only too happy to support you.

Early diagnosis and treatment will help you make a faster recovery. There are several organisations and support groups that specifically help mothers suffering from PND. Parenting websites and blogs from mothers in a similar situation can also be a great source of support. In addition, the charity Home Start offers help to families who have young children, especially those who are struggling with particular difficulties.

Partners

The birth of any baby requires mental and physical adjustments on the part of your partner as well as yourself. Your partner will inevitably be more involved with the care of two babies and, moreover, their help and support is crucial. Indeed, it is not unusual for partners themselves to be the stay-at-home carer. But even if they continue working, many welcome the opportunity to look after their babies and support you in a tangible and much-needed way. Before the birth is the ideal time to prepare for their involvement and they should be given opportunities to ask questions and voice their concerns about how to adjust to their new family.

One issue is likely to be how to cope with the pressures of work and home, with the prospect of having virtually no time

to themselves. Another is an awareness that they may lose the closeness they had with you before the birth because you – rightly – are focusing all your energy on the new babies. For some, this can become a problem, and they can (consciously or not) come to resent the babies and resent you for giving all your time and affection to these tiny, demanding human beings.

Handling newborn babies, especially premature ones who are likely to be small and more fragile-looking, can be a daunting prospect for anybody. Confidence should be built up through being involved with the babies as soon as possible after birth. Hospital staff should teach both parents the practicalities and give reassurance that even very tiny babies are extremely resilient and can actually put up with what may feel like very clumsy handling.

If partners are not fully involved with the childcare and the household tasks from the outset, many couples who were once very equal in their everyday lives find they revert to a much more traditional role, where the mother is the one who primarily looks after the babies and the home while the partner goes out and earns the money. This change in their relationship can come as a shock, and can lead to resentment in both parties: in the mother because she is no longer financially independent and finds herself doing the bulk of the household tasks; and in the partner because they feel excluded from much of what is going on at home, and is being ordered around by you in a way that never happened before. Throughout the first few months (and, indeed, thereafter), there are certain things you can each do to avoid misunderstandings and maintain harmony as a couple:

▸ First and foremost: keep communicating.
▸ Try to be patient, kind to each other and understanding of each other's needs.
▸ Remember why you fell in love – this can get very lost in the weeks and months (if not years!) following the birth.
▸ Discuss and decide before the babies are born who will do which tasks around the home and with the babies, or agree to take it in turns to do them. But be prepared to be flexible and try different things until you find what suits you both. This avoids the resentment that can build up if each of you thinks that you are the one who is always unloading the dishwasher or changing the nappies.
▸ Remain flexible and try to keep a sense of humour.
▸ Arrange to meet other families through Twins Clubs, as this can be a great source of information and help.

CONTRACEPTION

You can conceive again even before your periods have resumed and also while you are breastfeeding. Women who spontaneously conceived dizygotic twins are more likely to have another twin or multiple pregnancy. Even women who needed fertility treatment sometimes conceive naturally the next time, so it is advisable to use contraception until you are sure you would be prepared for another pregnancy. Your healthcare professionals should talk to you about this before you leave hospital and again when you have your six-week postnatal check.

Single motherhood

If you do not have a partner, planning what help and support you will have well ahead of the birth will ensure that you have time to enjoy the babies. If family and friends have offered to help, be clear about what commitment they can make and plan so that you can make the best use of their time. If you can afford paid help, think through what is best suited to your lifestyle (*see* p. 214).

Your sexual relationship

A lack of interest or desire to have sex (libido) after the birth of a baby is common in many women and can be caused by several factors: the physical recovery from the birth; exhaustion; lack of privacy (e.g., if you have someone living in with you when the babies are young); 'baby blues' and postnatal depression. In addition, many women feel that they now have a different relationship with their body, as it has physically changed after the pregnancy and birth: your breasts may be leaking milk as soon as they are touched, or you may have a Caesarean or episiotomy scar that is still healing. You may also be harbouring a resentment that you are shouldering too much of the baby care and household duties. Whatever the reason, the reality is that most women go off sex altogether for several weeks, if not months, after the birth. Given the choice between an extra half-hour's sleep and sexual intercourse, many will pick the former every time. In addition, your body may not be ready to have sex initially – indeed, it can be painful. Using a lubricating jelly or cream will help, as will plenty of foreplay. If you have an episiotomy scar, this too can make sex painful for some weeks after the birth. Wait until the scar has healed before attempting once more, and speak to your doctor if the problem persists.

You are most likely to be the primary carer for your babies in the first few weeks. As a result you can sometimes become too prescriptive about how certain tasks should be done or about what you expect of your partners or other helpers. Although you may be striving to keep in control and manage the huge changes in your life, try to bear in mind the following:

▶ There is no 'right' and 'wrong' way to do the majority of tasks, from changing a nappy to preparing a meal. It might even make your babies more adaptable if they get used to having things done in more than one way.
▶ By all means give advice, but do so in a constructive way. Praise your partner's efforts – this way, they are more likely do their fair share than if they are constantly being told they are 'doing it wrong'.

▶ Do not aim for sainthood by taking on all the childcare and household tasks. If you do, you will only have yourself to blame if it all becomes too much. Delegate as much as possible to your partner and to others.
▶ Allow your partner to have time to themselves, including the odd evening out with friends. They, too, will be feeling tired and under pressure from juggling work and home life, and a bit of time to enjoy themselves will improve their well-being. Enlist someone else to help you with the babies while they are out.
▶ Try not to reserve ALL your cuddles and kisses for the babies. A few directed at your partner will be gratefully received!

Many partners also go off sex after the birth of their babies. They, too, are likely to be tired, may feel neglected or may now be viewing you as a mother-figure rather than a lover. In addition, they may still be upset and shocked by the birth, especially if this was physically difficult event for you.

For the sake of your relationship, however, it is important during this time that you each reassure your partner that you love them and still find them attractive. Verbal reassurance is crucial, as is honest communication about how you are each feeling, because it is important that any hurt, anger or resentment do get voiced (as kindly as possible) rather than allowed to build up. But kissing, cuddling and stroking are important as well, as these ensure that you maintain a physical closeness. Try also to set aside some time together as a couple on a regular basis. This means going out without your babies – even if only for a short time – while someone else babysits at home. In this way, you will rediscover the feeling of being part of a couple, not just two parents.

Slowly, once you start to be a little more organised, rested and relaxed, and if you keep up a physical connection between you, you will hopefully regain your desire for sex. While there are no rules and you should do what ever you feel is right for you, sex is nevertheless a habit, and people can get out of habits quite easily. There may be a time, therefore, where you both have to make a concerted effort to start again. Only you know what is best for your relationship, but if lack of sex leads to tension between the two of you, then the problem needs to be addressed before it damages your relationship.

Sex after having babies is usually very different. It is often less frequent, but it can become more intimate and intense because pregnancy, birth and parenthood have given you an additional and unique closeness.

Try to set aside some time together on a regular basis. In this way, you will rediscover the feeling of being part of a couple, not just two parents.

Other children

If you have older children, you are likely to be apprehensive about how they will adapt to having two new babies in their lives. However much you try to prepare other children for the birth of siblings, and however excited they initially appear at the prospect – an excitement that can extend to the first few days or weeks after the babies' arrival – the fact remains that for most children, the birth of a sibling, and most especially twins, is a huge change in their lives. If you have had only one child up until now, that child will have had the undivided attention of both parents. The arrival of newborn babies will inevitably shift much of the parents' time and attention to their care. Suddenly, having had all their parents' kisses, cuddles and time, existing children can feel sidelined and 'second best'. Grandparents and other family and friends may go straight to the new babies, where once the older child had been the focus. Unsurprisingly, children can become jealous and try to remedy the situation in a variety of ways: they might start to behave in an attention-seeking manner or throw tantrums. They may also act in a more baby-like fashion. For example, if they were already drinking from a cup, they may want to return to a bottle, no longer be clean if they were potty-trained, or want to be carried everywhere when they are perfectly capable of walking. However, there are many steps that you can to take to help prepare an existing child for the arrival of new babies and how you do so will depend on their age:

▸ Keep routines and their daily life unchanged as far as possible (e.g. continue reading to them at bedtime, or taking them to their various activities during the week).

▸ Arrange for special trips or time on your own with them, so that they can have one-to-one time with you and/or your partner.

▸ Ask a friend/relative/godparent to spend time with them so that they can feel they are the focus of that person, to counterbalance the attention the babies are receiving from others.

▸ Anticipate that other people can, unintentionally, make such a fuss of the new babies that your existing child/children can feel totally overlooked. Encourage them to pay attention to older children, too. Some adults will already be aware of this need and may even bring a little gift for the older child as well as the babies.

▸ Buy your child a gift from each of your babies, and buy something that your child can then give to each baby in return (e.g. a small cuddly animal that can become their 'special' toy).

▸ Ask your child to become your helper in a specific task – not a chore, but something that they might enjoy doing (e.g. fetching small items such as nappies). Do not coerce them, but rather make them feel as if they are in partnership with you, so that they feel valued and special.

▸ Do not make any changes that will disrupt their everyday lives while they adapt to the arrival of their siblings (e.g. avoid moving them out of their cot into a 'big' bed, moving them into a different bedroom or trying to potty-train them).

▸ Because the older sibling is confronted from the start with a 'unit', it is important to create opportunities to change the dynamic. Try, on occasion, to take the child out with just one of the twins, possibly sharing a double buggy, so that they can bond in a unique way with each of their siblings.

▸ Be aware that your older child may attempt to hurt the babies. Young children will not realise the consequences of their actions and will not be consciously aware of why they are behaving as they are.

▸ Avoid making a big fuss if your older child comments that they want to put the babies in the bin or return them to the hospital or to your tummy, as this is very common.

▸ Above all, reassure them that you love them just as much as before. The best way of doing this is to give them lots of cuddles and kisses, tell them verbally (assuming they are old enough to understand) and make sure they spend time with you on their own.

Older children have a better understanding that will allow you to communicate with them openly, so try to explain what is happening (e.g. why the babies are currently taking a lot of your time). Plan how can you involve them with the care of the babies and encourage a rewarding relationship with their siblings by letting them spend time alone with one baby at a time. For information on introducing an older child to their siblings for the first time, see Chapter 5, p.133.

HELP AND CHILDCARE

What help or childcare is available and what you feel you will need depends on your personal circumstances, but exploring all the options and planning ahead before the babies are born is always a good idea. The golden rule is to never turn down any offer of help, even if making the best use of it needs some organisation.

Start off by thinking who will be available and what kind of help they could give you. Ask yourself the following questions:

- ▶ Will your partner be at home and, if so, how long is this likely to be for?
- ▶ If you are a single mother, will your parents, other family or friends be able to stay with you when the babies are born?
- ▶ What voluntary or local authority help may be available to you as a family with twins?
- ▶ If you wish to use paid help, think carefully about what type would be most beneficial within your budget?

The early days after the birth are a very special time for you and your partner to get to know your babies (see p. 189) and many couples prefer to have this intimate time to themselves before enlisting help. In both the short and longer term, your parents and those of your partner can be a great help, but it will depend on where they live and their age as to the commitment they can make. Friends and other family members may offer to help with shopping, washing, preparing a meal or basic housework. People often prefer to be told what needs to be done, so do not hesitate to give them specific tasks – it will be more rewarding for them and of more benefit to you.

The sort of childcare you opt for depends on your own circumstances, what family and other help is available and whether you are planning to go back to work. Whatever you decide, however, it is advisable to think about your needs in plenty of time so that you can find the solution that suits you. See also Chapter 8, p. 258 for information on managing life after returning to work.

Paid childcare is not cheap, and some options are more expensive than others. Nurseries or childminders may be affordable with a singleton, but once you factor in having to pay *per child*, you may decide that they are not financially attractive. Speak to other mothers for recommendations of good local nanny agencies (which may also have doulas, maternity/night nurses or au pairs on their books). Some magazines are a good source of childcare advertisements, as are local newspapers and, if you have one, your local Twins Club. With all forms of childcare, it is vital that you follow up all references and speak to recent employers or (in the case of childminders and nurseries/crèches) existing parents. The following childcare options are suitable from birth onwards:

- ▶ maternity nurses
- ▶ night nurses
- ▶ doulas and mother's helps
- ▶ nannies (live in or live out).

The following childcare options are more suitable once babies are a little older:

- ▶ registered childminders
- ▶ au pairs
- ▶ nurseries/crèches.

Maternity nurses and night nurses

Maternity nurses help the mother to care for her babies – they do not normally get involved with the household tasks – and are the most expensive childcare option because they usually cover 24 hours a day, six days a week and live in. Generally speaking, maternity nurses need to be booked several months before you actually give birth. You should always interview potential candidates to see if you get on, because you will be seeing a lot of each other and it is important that you have a good working relationship – but with your own personal boundaries clearly defined.

Maternity nurses are usually employed for between two and eight weeks, although you may want them to do a few nights or days rather than be with you all the time. When arranging the period of employment for a maternity nurse, remember that your babies may be born earlier than expected. You might want them to start as soon as you and the babies are at home, or you may prefer to delay their arrival to give you and your partner time together. You may also have other have relatives coming to help in the initial few days and so would prefer them to start at a later date.

The first two or three weeks are the time when you get to know your babies and start learning about parenting. Your needs and the demands of your babies will evolve over this time, so what you require from your maternity nurse will also change. You will soon get used to what suits you all as a family. Most valuably, maternity nurses can care for the babies at

Parents of twins are not entitled to any benefits or grants from the government beyond what is available to all parents. At the time of publication, all families are entitled to a tax-free payment for children called Child Benefit and there are separate rates for each child in your family. If you have no older children, the higher rate of child benefit is payable for the twin who was born first and the lower rate will be paid for your second twin. If you have an older child, the lower rate will be paid for each twin.

If you were already getting a benefit or tax credit before your pregnancy, you may qualify for a Sure Start Maternity Grant. This is a one-off lump sum, which you do not have to pay back, and is awarded *per baby*. See Chapter 8, p. 257 for information on Statuary Maternity Pay.

night, bringing them to you for breastfeeding, which will enable you to sleep for a longer stretch.

As their name implies, night nurses help you with night-time duties, in much the same way as a maternity nurse. However, they then go home during the day, as they do not live in. They, too, can be helpful in the first few weeks when you may be feeding more than once a night.

Doulas and mother's helps

The rise of doulas is a recent phenomenon. From the ancient Greek word meaning 'woman servant' or 'caregiver', a doula is an experienced woman who offers (non-medical) emotional and practical support to a woman (or couple) before, during and/or after childbirth (*see* Chapters 4 and 5). They 'mother the mother', which in turn helps the whole family to enjoy the experience of having babies. This is particularly useful if you have no relatives living nearby. Doulas can be hired for the postnatal period alone and work flexible hours, agreed in advance, to suit the mother. This can range from a few visits to fixed hours for a period of six to eight weeks. They usually charge an hourly fee or, if hired for pre-and post-birth, often offer a fixed-price package. Doulas have usually had children themselves and have good knowledge of childcare, but they are also happy to help the mother around the house. There are doula qualifications in the UK and a non-profit association,

Doula UK, which has a register of qualified caregivers (*see* Useful Resources). Nanny agencies may also have doulas on their books.

Nannies

Nannies can live in or live out and look after your children in your home. In the past, live-ins were cheaper than live-outs, but this difference has been eroded in more recent years. Nannies may have qualifications such as an NVQ level 2 or 3, a BTEC in childcare or an NNEB qualification, but none of these is obligatory to work as a nanny. You can hire a nanny to look after your children exclusively or you can share them with another family. The basis on which you nanny-share can vary: you might have a nanny on certain days, while the other family has them for the others; alternatively, the nanny might look after your babies plus a child/children from another family at the same time. This makes sharing a nanny cheaper than having one employed solely by you.

A nanny's salary is paid net of all tax, National Insurance contributions and other benefits, which must all be paid by you, the employer. These can easily add another 30 per cent to the wage bill. It is not surprising that employing a nanny is beyond the means of many families, although with twins, this option may start to look more cost-effective than some of those listed on page 216.

It is important to start off on the right footing by laying out employment terms very clearly. Communication, honesty and respect are key to developing a good relationship.

It is important to start off on the right footing with a nanny by laying out employment terms very clearly and making your wishes known. Communication, honesty and respect are key to developing a good relationship. Employers who regularly arrive home late are among the common gripes among nannies, as are what they deem to be unreasonable demands that have not been agreed upon prior to employment. Ideally, try to store up goodwill so that, when there is a crisis or you need a favour, your nanny will be happy to oblige. Remember that they are an employee, not a family member who is happy to do extra for nothing. Pay overtime if necessary – it is worth it for peace of mind. If possible, try to include babysitting one evening a week in the contract, to allow you to go out on a regular basis. Give warning of when this evening will be – your nanny has a life, too! There are books and websites with further advice on employing nannies and drafting contracts (see Useful Resources), and if you are hiring one through an agency, check the small print in advance. Finally, speak to other mothers for further tips and advice, especially those that are relevant to the area in which you live.

Registered childminders

Childminders look after children in their own home rather than yours, and are paid by the hour and per child. This can make them expensive once you calculate the costs for two babies. They often look after other children as well, including their own, so if yours are unwell, they may not be able to care for them until they are better. In addition, their hours are often less flexible, and they may not be able to accommodate your needs if, for example, you work late on certain days. Your local council will have a list of registered childminders, all of whom will have been thoroughly vetted (which includes an inspection of their home).

Au pairs

These are young women and men who have come to the UK to improve their English. They live with you, have their own room, receive board and lodging, as well as a small amount of money (speak to local nanny/au pair agencies and to friends to get an idea of what this amount should be). They are not allowed to work more than fifteen hours a week and – according to the Home Office – are not employed by you, but are considered members of your family. This can mean, for example, that they have meals with you. In return, they undertake childcare duties and light household tasks. Many do not have particular experience of looking after babies, so it is better to use au pairs when your babies are a little older, and to limit their duties to general household tasks and to *helping* you with childcare, rather than being left in sole charge.

Au pairs are often hired when they are still abroad – there are specialist au pair agencies and websites that allow you to do this. Always speak to them in advance, as an email exchange will not tell you how good their English is. Clarify as much as possible in advance of their arrival what you require them to do. Au pairs will expect to have several hours off during the day to go to language classes, as well as evenings to themselves, unless pre-arranged by you. Once again, respect and communication are key, and they should not be seen as young people whom you can make use of for very little money.

Nurseries and crèches

Nurseries are run either privately or by the state. Good ones are usually very oversubscribed and, as with childminders, they charge per child (although they may give a small discount for a second child). This can make them very expensive if you have two children. Many nurseries take babies from a very young age; crèches tend to take them only after they are a few months old. Nurseries will look after babies full-time or part-time, whereas crèches usually take them for a few hours at a time on an ad-hoc basis. All crèches and nurseries are very tightly regulated when it comes to safety and the ratio of carers to children, but do ask local mothers for recommendations, as this will provide useful feedback as well. When you visit a possible nursery or crèche for your babies, ask about staff turnover, as this gives a good indication of how happy the work environment is. The advantage of good nurseries is that they provide a stimulating, sociable environment for your children and are reliable, whereas if a nanny is unwell, you will have to cancel going into work or make last-minute arrangements with others. Conversely, if your babies are unwell, the nursery will not accept them, so you will be left calling in favours or taking time off work. Many nurseries do not stay open late, so if your job requires you to work into the evening, or if getting there before closing time is going to be a constant, mad rush, it may not be a suitable childcare option for you.

8

The first year

Your babies will reach many important
milestones during their first year.
You, as parents, will also undergo
many new experiences, which will
make this first year of your babies'
life exciting and fascinating but,
at times, challenging as well.

EQUIPMENT FOR OLDER BABIES

Between the ages of four and twelve months babies change fast, as do their needs. The equipment you need during this period will evolve, and you will have to organise your home so that it provides a safe, enjoyable and stimulating environment as the babies grow into toddlers.

The amount and variety of equipment for older babies is as enormous, if not more so, than that which is available for newborns, and it can be equally overwhelming and costly. As ever, try to resist buying too much, accept offers of gifts or hand-me-down equipment (as long as it is safe and in good condition) and try to buy second-hand where appropriate and possible. You are likely to be more relaxed in your own home if you are not constantly worrying about the special vase on the shelf or the precious bowl on the coffee table. You will also be freer to encourage your babies' natural curiosity and desire to explore the world if you have eliminated the more obvious dangers in their immediate environment. However, while there are certain essential points to bear in mind, there are endless potential 'danger spots' in every home and it is never possible to eliminate completely the risk of accidents. It is easy to become paranoid as a parent, so it will be up to you to decide where you draw the line.

That said, there is no doubt that having twins increases the chances of an accident occurring, as you have two mobile babies to keep an eye on. It is also much easier for two babies to get themselves into a dangerous situation, unwittingly or not, simply because one can end up pushing or clambering up on the other. You should try to make your babies aware as early as possible of certain dangers (they will respond to your tone of voice even if they do not understand the actual words). This will ensure that they respond at once to certain commands and to the word 'no', not only in your own home but also, importantly, when you are out and about with them.

Stairgates

If you have stairs or rooms that you want to prevent your babies having access to, you will need to install stairgates. Fit a gate at the bottom and top of each flight of stairs, and use gates that screw into the wall; they will leave a hole when you finally remove them in a few years' time, but they are safer, as they will resist the pressure of two or more toddlers pushing against them more effectively than spring-loaded ones. Spring-loaded, moveable gates are more useful for creating temporary, sectioned-off safe areas, say at bath time or mealtimes.

Playpens

Playpens are ideal for providing a safe playing area for older, more mobile babies, and are large enough to accommodate two babies. They are also particularly useful when you have

SUGGESTED EQUIPMENT FOR OLDER BABIES

Listed below are suggestions for what you may find useful as your babies become older and more mobile. See the relevant sections in this chapter for more information on each item.

Home safety
- stairgates (2 for each flight of stairs)
- playpen
- fireguard for each fireplace (if required)

Weaning (per baby)
- high chair
- 2 plastic bowls
- 4 plastic spoons

- cup with training spout and handles
- 1 plastic bib or 2 bibs with sleeves

Bathing
- non-slip bath mat

Sleeping
- 2 cots (if not used from birth)

Travelling
- 2 forward-facing car seats
- 2 travel cots
- child-view mirror for the car

to attend to one of your babies specifically (e.g. change their nappy) or carry out a task that will divert your attention from your children for a short time, such as answering the front door. Some babies are happier to be in playpens than others, but ultimately, as long as you provide them with toys, you will at least know that they are in a safe environment. It is often good to have the playpen in the room in which you will spend a lot of time, such as a living room, or near the kitchen area. You can then keep an eye on your babies while you carry out essential tasks. Travel cots make exceptionally useful, mobile playpens (before they are able to climb out!).

Safety gadgets

There is a vast amount of safety equipment on the market, some of which are more helpful than others. The following is a list of options to help you choose which are likely to be most suitable for your needs. Most are cheap to buy and easy to fit, and can reduce the worry of trying to keep an eye on two increasingly curious, mobile children in your home:

- **Door stoppers**: gadgets that fit around the width of the door (top or side) to prevent it shutting on little fingers. Useful if it is difficult to keep doors shut or wedged/tied back.

- **Cupboard and drawer latches**: prevent babies and toddlers from opening cupboard doors and drawers. Useful in the kitchen/bathroom to prevent access to cleaning fluids, sharp objects, medicines and so on.
- **Corner cushions for furniture**: small plastic fittings that soften corners sharp-edged furniture, such as low tables.
- **Electrical socket inserts**: plastic inserts that fit over sockets and prevent little fingers from being inserted into the holes.
- **DVD/CD/digibox protectors**: fits over the slot in the front of the equipment to stop small items being inserted through the 'letterbox'.
- **Fireguards**: essential if you have a real/gas fire or a wood-burning stove. Secure them to the wall with hooks so that they cannot be moved by the babies.
- **Toilet seat lock**: useful for hygiene purposes, but also to prevent babies from tipping themselves into the bowl or dropping in objects that could block the toilet.
- **Hob/oven/cooker knob guards**: shields to protect your children from burns and from turning on the appliance.

General safety

In addition to the specific areas mentioned above, you will need to secure certain features of your home that are potentially dangerous. If you have not done so already, now is definitely the time to invest in a small domestic fire extinguisher and smoke alarms. Never leave your babies on their own in a room where a fire has been lit. It is easier for twins to clamber up to windows and onto higher surfaces using their sibling as a co-climber. So, windows should have safety catches or restrictors so that they cannot be fully opened. Some parents install bars on windows above the ground floor, although this is not essential. Ensure that you tie up dangling curtain or blind cords, as these are a strangulation hazard. Check that any glass doors are fitted with safety glass (it will be labelled with a kite mark). Avoid placing rugs on slippery floors.

Once they are about ten months old, babies can haul themselves up to a standing position by holding on to the furniture and start to walk around it (known as 'cruising'). Furniture can usually bear the weight of one toddler, but if two toddlers do this at the same time, there is a greater risk of the piece of furniture tipping over onto them. Free-standing items, such as small bookshelves, cupboards and televisions, should therefore be fixed to the wall.

House plants can be messy if pulled over and are, in some cases, sharp or even poisonous. The Royal Horticultural Society (*see* Useful Resources) supplies a list of potentially harmful plants, but any that you have at home are best kept out of reach of your babies. Pet litter must also be kept well out of the way of babies once they are mobile – consider moving it to another room if necessary or placing litter trays in a separate, zoned-off area (*see* section on stairgates).

Ground or eye-level cupboards and drawers become irresistible to young children. Sharp, breakable objects and, crucially, medicines and household cleaning products must be kept in cupboards or drawers fitted with safety locks (*see* list opposite) and preferably high up and well out of reach of babies and young children. Conversely, putting some non-breakable plastic containers or miscellaneous pots and pans in a floor-level kitchen cupboard can often provide lots of safe fun for babies, especially when they are armed with wooden or plastic spoons with which to make a noise. This will then satisfy their curiosity and also allow you to do whatever you have to do in the kitchen, at least for a few minutes.

From around the age of four months, babies start to grab at things and put them in their mouth. Once they can sit up and then crawl, babies seem to develop a beady eye for any piece of dirt or dust on the floor, and before you know it, they have picked it up and tasted it. However, small objects, particularly coins or small pieces of toys (perhaps belonging to an older sibling), can be lethal and you must be alert to anything that could potentially be swallowed and become a choking hazard. If you start to be aware of this when your babies are not yet mobile, you will be in the habit of not leaving anything lying around on the floor or within their reach by the time your babies are old enough to start exploring the world around them. Be careful, as well, with the contents of any wastepaper bin – plastic bags are a particular suffocation hazard and should be disposed of safely.

Any sharp or breakable objects should be kept from babies and toddlers, so they do not poke themselves or each other. Loose wires or cables should be tucked well away. Kettle flexes should never be near or hanging off the edge of a kitchen work surface, as these can be grabbed by a cruising baby. Avoid overhanging tablecloths (which can be easily pulled off) and keep chairs tucked in to prevent babies climbing up onto the table. Get into the habit of using the back burners on your hob first, rather than the front ones, and always turn any pan handles towards the back so that, once again, these cannot be reached. When carrying hot liquids (e.g. in a mug or a pan), never carry them over a baby.

FEEDING AND INTRODUCING SOLIDS (WEANING)

The gradual change from a total milk diet (whether breast milk or formula) to one that includes other forms of food is known as weaning. During the first year, milk or formula still forms the basis of an infant's diet, but by the time they are about six months old, babies will be ready for some 'solid' food.

Breastfeeding older babies

Breast milk changes to meet a baby's needs, so what you were producing when your babies were newborn will be different in composition from the milk you produce for your four-month-olds. This means that the nutrients and any other factors, such as helping with immunity from diseases, are right for the babies at the stage they have reached.

Breastfeeding when you return to work

If you are breastfeeding and want to continue doing so when you go back to work, your employer is legally obliged to make this possible for you (*see* Useful Resources for further information). However, they must be informed in writing of your plans before your return to work so that you can both find ways to implement them. These include setting aside a suitable place and sufficient time for you to express your milk (*see* Chapter 7, p. 166). Many women find that they can feed at home just in the morning and evening without their milk supply being unduly affected. But if your breasts become engorged during the day, you will need to express while at work. If your babies have been breastfed exclusively up until now, you may need to express twice during a full working day for around twenty minutes. Keep the milk cool in a fridge or cool-box, so that it can be given in a bottle at a later stage to your babies. If you have fed exclusively from the breast up until

INFANT FORMULA AND ALLERGY TO COW'S MILK

Parents whose babies have been breastfed exclusively are sometimes concerned about switching from breast milk to infant formula, because they fear their babies may become allergic or intolerant to cow's milk (babies should not be given normal cow's milk as their main drink until they are one year old). Similarly, the increasing prevalence of eczema and asthma in babies is often blamed on an 'allergy' to milk. In fact, asthma is much more likely to be caused by inhaled allergens in the environment (e.g. house dust mites, mould, pets, cigarette smoke).

It is important to understand that allergies and intolerances are two entirely different conditions: a milk allergy is a response by the antibodies in the blood to what is perceived as a harmful substance, whereas an intolerance to milk occurs when the gut is not able to produce enough of the enzyme needed to process the lactose (sugar) in milk. This results in loose, watery stools and is usually a temporary condition. Genuine allergy to cow's milk is rare, affecting around five

per cent of infants under the age of one. It can manifest itself in many ways, including rashes, diarrhoea and vomiting, but most babies will outgrow their allergy by the age of six and 90 per cent by the time they are adults.

If you suspect that your babies have either condition, they must be tested by a qualified immunologist or specialist allergy or gastrointestinal doctor, who will usually work with a dietician. It is not advisable to consult a nutritionist who, aside from not usually being medically qualified, does not have access to proper medical testing. Equally, never use over-the-counter tests. It is important to take the advice of a medical team before changing any baby or toddler's formula, as this can have very detrimental effects if it is not nutritionally suitable (e.g. anaemia, weakening of the bones poor growth). Switching to soya-based infant formula is not necessarily the answer, as it, too, can cause allergies or intolerances (particularly in babies under six months); goat's milk is not nutritionally suitable for babies and young children.

now, it is a good idea to give an occasional bottle of expressed milk to your babies well before your return so that they get used to feeding this way.

Stopping breastfeeding

Many women know how long they want to/can breastfeed for and the length of time they continue doing so depends on many factors. Currently, the recommendation is that mothers breastfeed exclusively for at least six months, if possible. Making the decision about when to stop breastfeeding is entirely personal and will depend on a range of individual circumstances and situations for the mother, babies and rest of the family. Mothers should be fully supported and not feel guilty when they decide to stop completely, at whatever stage of their babies' lives.

When you have a good milk supply and decide to stop breastfeeding you will need to do so gradually. If the babies are less than six months old and exclusively breastfed, the usual way is to substitute one breastfeed for a formula feed each day and allow the breasts to adjust to this before making another change. If you are breastfeeding only one baby at every feed, alternating babies in a combined feeding approach (*see* Chapter 7, p. 169), you should alternate breast and formula feeds so that, once again, your breasts get used to the new, lower demands. Gradually cut down breastfeeds one at a time until your milk has dried up completely. Often the first morning feed is the last one to be dropped because your body will have replenished its stores of milk during the night.

Babies who have never sucked from a teat before may initially resist switching to feeding from a bottle, especially if done by the mother. This is partly because they miss the comforting smell and feeling of closeness derived from skin-to-skin contact during breastfeeding. In addition, the technique for sucking from a teat is different from that required to breastfeed, so babies need to learn a new technique, as well as get used to the new taste and consistency of formula. Getting a partner or other adult to give the first few bottles can be helpful, and can mean that the babies no longer associate feeding solely with you.

Introducing solids (weaning)

Weaning is the term used to describe the process of transferring babies from an all-breast milk or -formula diet to a mixed diet involving solid food. Once babies start having solids, they derive many of their nutrients from the food they eat. However, weaning is a gradual process, and breast milk or formula continues to be a necessary and significant part of your babies' diet throughout their first year and until they are well into their toddler years. In general, babies will be ready to start taking other foods at about six months old, but if your babies were born prematurely, your health visitor will be able to give advice as to the best time to begin. There are a number of signs that will help you to judge when the babies are ready, but there are no rigid rules and what you instinctively feel should be taken into account. There is no reason why twins should be ready for weaning at the same time as each other, so be prepared for one baby to be ready sooner. Signs include:

- ▸ starting to need night feeds once more, having previously slept through
- ▸ no longer seeming satisfied by a breastfeed or bottle and requiring feeding more often during the day over a period of a few days
- ▸ starting to grab at objects to put them into their mouth, or starting to chew things
- ▸ showing interest in the food you are eating, either by licking their lips or by trying to reach it.

Although it will be easier for you if you try to wean them at the same time, be prepared for one baby to take to it more readily than another. This can happen, for example, if there is a big size discrepancy between them, or if one baby spent longer in hospital than the other.

If you want to continue breastfeeding when you go back to work, your employer is legally obliged to make this possible for you.

Weaning equipment

When your babies are ready to start transferring to solid foods, there are some pieces of equipment and tableware that you will need.

High chairs

Once your babies are able to sit up, they can use a high chair. There are many different styles of high chair on the market and you will need one for each baby. Some are height-adjustable and/or have removable trays, allowing babies to eat directly at the table; others can be converted into chairs when the babies are older. Whichever model you choose, it will need to be sturdy, as it will come in for much wear and tear and wiping down, and should be easy to wipe down.

Bowls, utensils and cups

Non-slip, microwave-safe plastic bowls are the most practical tableware, while plastic spoons are best suited to babies' mouths and easiest for them to use when they start to feed themselves (see p. 228). Unless one of the babies is unwell, you do not have to have separate spoons or bowls for each baby until they start to want to feed themselves.

Plastic cups and beakers with lids are suitable for drinking water from about six months old (you can also use them to give breast milk or formula). Those with handles encourage babies to drink from them on their own (under supervision), and the spouts are particularly suitable once babies have teeth; those with valves also prevent spillages. Remember, never leave a baby to drink alone with a bottle or cup as they can choke. Babies who are using bottles will need fast-flow teats as they get older, as their suck is much stronger. Remember that by the time the babies are six months old, you will no longer need to sterilise feeding equipment.

What to feed and how much

The first time you give solids to your babies, ensure they are not tired or too hungry. It is usually better to feed babies solids before they have their milk/formula, but you may want to give them a little milk/formula first to take the edge off their appetite, so they are not ravenous and frustrated at trying something different.

While they are termed 'solids', the first foods that you give your baby will be smooth, liquidy purées. After the age of seven to nine months, depending on how long they have been on solids, babies can move on to lumpier purées, even if they do not yet have any teeth. As the babies progress, you can start to give them 'finger foods', that is, foods they can pick up and eat separately: breadsticks, grapes, meat, raw foods (e.g. pieces of fruit and vegetables). Until they have teeth, these will need to be cut into very small pieces or slices.

Start with giving solids once a day. Baby rice is a good food to begin the weaning process with because it is smooth and bland. It is better to introduce one new taste at a time, waiting for your babies to get used to it before moving on to another. Gradually move up to a pattern of breakfast, lunch and dinner (usually at the time of the late afternoon feed). Infant rice, porridge or other cereals can be given at breakfast; and at lunch and dinner you could try puréed vegetables and fruit, such as carrot, potato, parsnip, broccoli, apple, pear and mashed-up banana. Do not add any salt when cooking the vegetables, or add it to any food after cooking, as a baby's metabolism is not able to cope with it in the way that an adult's can. For any food that needs to be mixed with milk (e.g. cereals, mashed potato), you can use breast milk, formula or a small amount of cow's milk.

You may find it useful to purée a quantity of a few different foods and freeze them in ice cube trays. They can then be

SYMPTOMS OF FOOD ALLERGY

If your baby suffers a food allergy, you will generally see a physical reaction within 20–30 minutes of their eating the food. Depending on the severity of the reaction and how much of the food your baby has eaten, symptoms will include some or all of the following:

▶ a rash, commonly on the face, spreading over the rest of the body
▶ itchy skin
▶ a cough
▶ runny or blocked nose
▶ sore, red and itchy eyes
▶ vomiting or diarrhoea
▶ swelling of the lips or mouth/tongue/airways
▶ difficulty breathing.

The last two symptoms mean that your baby is suffering an anaphylactic reaction to the food and needs to have treatment urgently.

defrosted as and when required, thus avoiding the need to prepare food for each feed. However, as your babies' appetites increase you may find small plastic containers and freezer bags containing enough for two are more useful, because ice cube-size portions will quickly get used up. When you first start weaning, try one cube of food (or the equivalent) per baby and build up according to your babies' needs. While it is important not to assume that twins will have the same tastes and similar appetites (they are individuals, after all, and not necessarily more alike than other siblings), you should avoid giving entirely different foods to different babies simply because one of them does not like a particular food. This will be the slippery slope towards them becoming fussy eaters and your becoming their food slave. Babies should learn to eat what they are given, even if they only taste it.

Once they start eating solids, remember to give babies sips of water to drink as well, to make sure they do not become dehydrated. Avoid giving them juice, as it will encourage their taste for sweet things, which can damage their teeth once they come through. Many babies do not like water at first, but try to persevere until they are happy with it – if they are truly thirsty, they will drink it.

EGGS

Eggs can be given after the age of six months as long as they are hard-boiled. A small number of babies have an allergy to eggs, although this may only be to the loose or raw forms. Start by feeding your babies a small amount of well-cooked egg and if you think there has been a reaction (see Box above), ask for a referral to an allergy clinic. Remember that eggs are contained in lots of foods (e.g. pasta, biscuits), so check ingredients carefully. Children usually grow out of an egg allergy by the time they are three years of age.

Home-made or ready-made?

In the past, there were clear benefits to feeding babies home-made as opposed to commercially prepared baby food. The former was nutritionally more balanced and tasted better. This is no longer the case and there are advantages and disadvantages to both, especially when feeding two babies. You may find it helpful to do a mixture of the two forms of solid food. However, do not offer unfamiliar food when you are out as it may get rejected.

Home-made food

There are certain benefits to home-made food:
- It is cheaper and less wasteful in the early stages.
- You can vary the amount and consistency to suit your babies.
- The babies get used to the food that you eat yourself, so that family mealtimes become simpler as they get older.

However, there can also be drawbacks:
- It can be fiddly/leaky to transport.
- It is difficult to keep free from contamination or keep cool on hot days and so on.

Ready-made baby food

Commercial baby food is subject to regulations to ensure that it is nutritionally balanced and healthy for infants. There are certain benefits:

- It is convenient when you are in a rush or have run out of home-made food.
- It is useful when travelling.
- It is safe: a sealed jar or packet is sterile.
- It is made to high standards and now incorporates a variety of ethnic flavours (e.g. korma, stir-fry).

Nevertheless, there are some drawbacks:

- It can be bland and too uniform in texture as your babies progress.
- It is more expensive than home-made food.

Learning to feed themselves

It is an important part of each child's development to explore their food and learn to feed themselves. Feeding twins inevitably takes more time, and so you might at first feed them with a single bowl and spoon for greater efficiency. However, as soon as they are ready, give them each a bowl and spoon so that they can start learning how to do it for themselves (even though you may continue to help them).

Initially, weaning can make a considerable mess, particularly once the babies start to wield the spoon, so be prepared for food to end up in their ears, eyes, up their nose – indeed, anywhere but their mouth! Feed your babies in your kitchen or dining area rather than in your living room, and place newspaper under their high chairs or (if your babies are not yet sitting up) baby chairs. That way you can simply gather up all the paper at the end of the feed rather than spend time and energy wiping down the floor or plastic mats. Plastic bibs with a scoop-like tray at the bottom to catch spills (sometimes called 'pelican' bibs) are best, as they can simply be emptied out and/or rinsed at the end of each feed, whereas fabric ones will need regular washing. However, bibs with fabric sleeves are useful for protecting the babies' clothing.

Feeding time, especially when you have lovingly made the food yourself, can easily become a very emotive experience. The process of eating or even refusing to do so can be a way of seeking attention, which is more common in twins as they have to compete for one-to-one time with you and their other carers. Babies soon discover that they can play with their food, cause a fuss if they do not like it, and generally make mealtimes extremely stressful. Although it is much easier said than done, the calmer you appear to your babies, the more relaxed these mealtimes are likely to be. If your babies really just do not want to eat, you should never force feed them.

TIPS FOR HAPPY MEALTIMES
- Use plastic cups, bowls and spoons.
- Avoid introducing more than one new food at a time.
- Do not introduce new foods if your babies are very tired and hungry.
- Encourage your babies to start feeding themselves, either with a spoon or with their fingers, even though this will make a mess.
- Once they are more able to feed themselves, try to eat with your babies whenever possible, so that they copy what you do.

Food allergies and intolerances

Allergies tend to run in families, so if a parent has a food allergy or suffers from eczema, asthma or hay fever, their child is more likely to suffer from an allergy/allergies as well, though it is not possible to predict which ones. In their effort to limit the risk of their babies developing allergies, these parents are often anxious about what they should feed them. The foods that most commonly cause allergies in babies and young children are:

- ▸ eggs
- ▸ nuts
- ▸ peanuts (these are not nuts but pulses)
- ▸ sesame seeds
- ▸ fish
- ▸ shellfish.

In the absence of reliable information from large-scale scientific trials, the advice should probably be to avoid giving these foods to babies under the age of two if you or your partner already suffer from true allergies (or asthma and eczema). If you do not, there is no reason for you to limit your children's diets. The same advice applies to wheat, to which increasing numbers of adults appear to be intolerant (true wheat allergy, as seen in coeliac disease, is rare): offer it to your babies unless there is a clear medical reason not to. (For the difference between an allergy and an intolerance, *see* Box on p. 224).

One of the alleged benefits of waiting until babies are six months old before weaning them is that they are less likely to develop food allergies or eczema because their immature immune system will be more developed. Yet there is now considerable uncertainty whether the link between early weaning and developing allergies and/or eczema now even exists. In the end, the choice of what you feed your children and when is yours, and should be taken on the basis of medical consultation, rather than scaremongering stories in the media. Babies and children thrive on a varied diet, and the more they are introduced to a wide range of foods, textures and tastes when they are young, the lesser the chance that they will become fussy eaters. For more information on childhood allergies.

Victoria's story

When I look back, I realise I found weaning quite difficult. I've always enjoyed cooking and I loved making different concoctions for my twins but, when it comes to food, Toby and Georgina are chalk and cheese. Toby was and still is, at the age of six, very interested in food. Georgina was much harder, hating all the things children are supposed to love – like bananas – and always wanting purées to be as smooth as possible, whereas Toby wasn't bothered by the odd lump. I found it very hard catering for their different wants and needs, and mealtimes became quite fraught, even for Toby.

Having battled with trying to spoon-feed two babies, when teeth finally began to emerge and they wanted to feed themselves, I ditched the blender and decided to embrace finger food. That's all I gave them for a few months. I cooked pasta, fish and vegetables so they were soft, put it all on plastic plates in front of them and hoped for the best. I think the variety of shapes and colours was much more appealing to Georgina than the 'mush' I'd been making and it was lovely to watch them both discover proper food at last. As I became less stressed, they began to eat better. I am sure the fact that I was more relaxed helped them enjoy their food more.

SLEEP AND ROUTINE

From about the age of three to four months, babies are mature enough to sleep for longer periods of time. This means that if you establish a regular night-time routine and are consistent in your approach, your babies will learn to fall asleep on their own and to soothe themselves so that, when they wake at night, they are able to get back to sleep. They will then become good sleepers at night and happy, contented babies during the day.

Unless your babies were born earlier than 34 weeks, by the time they are four months old they should be able to sleep for at least six hours without waking. At six months old, babies no longer need feeding in the night and should be able to sleep through until morning (around ten hours). To help with this, you could wake the babies and give them a feed before you go to bed. Even though older babies might be drinking from a cup during the day (*see* p. 226), many still like this final feed to be from a bottle. After the age of five months, babies who still demand a feed during the night are probably just waking out of habit and should be given increasingly diluted milk so that, within approximately a week, you are simply giving them water. They should soon stop demanding a night feed. If they are genuinely hungry rather than comfort sucking (*see* Box on p. 159), this may be a sign that they should be on solids (*see* p. 225).

Your babies' sleeping environment needs to be conducive to good sleep (*see* Chapter 7, p. 176). From about three months old they are likely to sleep better in their own cot, if they are not already doing so, as they will be getting too big to share. They may also appreciate having their own personal area, although many enjoy having their cots placed close together to allow them to communicate. Some babies are happier to transfer to a cot than others, so be prepared for one to be more unsettled and to take longer to adapt to the new sleeping arrangements than the other. If older babies are still in your room, they can be disturbed by others snoring, getting up or going to bed at different times from them, so consider moving them to their own room when they are six months old.

SAME ROOM OR SEPARATE ROOMS?

Sharing a room is usually not a problem for twins. On the whole, babies do seem able to sleep on even if their sibling is wakeful. If your babies normally sleep in the same room but one is keeping the other awake on a regular basis, it might be better to separate them, if only temporarily. Equally, there is nothing wrong with each of your babies sleeping in separate rooms of their own on a permanent basis, assuming you have that option and if one consistently sleeps better than the other.

Establishing good practices

The first thing is to ensure that your babies learn to fall asleep by themselves, because without this, they are likely to be poor sleepers. The tips provided in Chapter 7 for establishing good sleep habits (*see* Box on p. 181) are applicable to babies of all ages. In addition, consider the following when the babies are four months and older:

- ▸ Carry out the same bedtime routine each night.
- ▸ Change the babies into fresh night clothes (even if they have been wearing a sleepsuit in the day), as this helps them to understand the difference between night and day.
- ▸ Start reading simple, short books to them to create a moment of calm before putting them to bed (they will still also enjoy a lullaby).

Whatever routine you adopt needs to work for the rest of the family as well as for the babies, otherwise it will cause you stress and resentment. Avoid getting yourselves into a situation where the night-time routine is so drawn out that it takes over half your evening, leaving you and your partner exhausted and ravenous.

During the day, older babies need to have a regular routine, stimulation (including outings and activities) and sufficient food, once they are weaned, to ensure better sleeping at night. Regular naps, usually after each feed, help to avoid babies getting overtired in the evenings, which (perversely) can prevent them from getting to sleep. However, by the time your babies are a year old, they will only need about two hours' sleep during the day, so you need to adjust their daytime sleeping schedules to ensure that they sleep at night.

Tackling sleeping problems

You will find plentiful advice about how to avoid or tackle any sleep problems, but not all of it is helpful for twins, so any difficulties you might have should be considered on an individual basis. Problems can arise when both you and the babies have unwittingly got into a particular habit. For example, if your babies have learnt to fall asleep in certain circumstances – perhaps in your arms or sucking on a bottle – then they will associate this activity with falling asleep. If they wake in the night, they are then unable to settle themselves because they find they are in a different situation from the one they associate with sleep. They start to cry, at which point parents often come in to soothe and settle them, thus rewarding crying.

Leaving your babies to cry

Assuming that there is nothing actually causing your babies to cry (they are not teething, unwell or uncomfortable – see Chapter 7, p.174 and Did You Know? opposite), the question is how you choose to deal with the crying. If you do not mind that your babies wake, cry and cannot settle during the night, then do not let others tell you it is a problem. If you are happy and able to continue in this way, then there is no reason for you to change. Some parents have their babies in bed with them or in the same room as them for many months, if not years, either for part of the night or the whole of it. If this is what works for you, then you should feel free to carry on.

KEEPING A SLEEP DIARY

If one or more of your babies has difficulty sleeping, consider keeping a sleep diary for a week in which you note down nap, sleep and feed times. You may see a pattern emerge that you could alter in order to improve the situation. Also, speak to your health visitor and other parents, as they may have helpful suggestions.

Methods that help your babies to settle themselves

While some are happy to leave their babies to cry, many parents find that months of interrupted sleep have a cumulatively harmful impact on every aspect of their lives. In addition, they may start to notice that their babies are not rested or thriving in the way they feel they should be if they were sleeping better. It is this desire to improve their babies' sleeping habits that leads many parents to adopt a more structured approach.

This approach is often called the 'controlled crying' method, although there are other ways of referring to it, and there are many books available on the subject. However it is described, the approach involves training babies to self-soothe so that they learn to fall asleep on their own. When they start to cry, the intervals at which you return to reassure your babies become increasingly spaced out, and you are discouraged from rocking them, picking them up or feeding them in order to soothe them. Only verbal reassurance and a little stroking are advised before you leave the room once more. Consistency and determination are required by both parents, and whether or not you try this approach depends on you, your style of parenting and your particular situation. But invariably the method is successful – often surprisingly quickly.

DID YOU KNOW…?

You will soon get to know instinctively whether you think your baby's crying is unusual and you should investigate further. A change in your baby's usual cry, such as to a high-pitched, scream-like noise, could be a sign of your baby being unwell or in pain and you should seek medical opinion (see p.251 for more information).

A change in routine

When babies are unwell, their sleep routine usually suffers. This can also happen when there is a change in their life, such as moving house, or going away to an unfamiliar environment (e.g. on holiday). Whenever this is the case, try to return to your babies' normal sleeping schedule as soon as possible, rather than allowing them to develop a different routine (or lack of one), which they can do very quickly. You should be the one establishing their routine, not the other way round. Some parents continue to blame minor illness or travel for why their babies are 'unsettled' for weeks afterwards, thus ensuring that new (bad) sleep habits develop that can then be difficult to break.

OUT AND ABOUT

As your babies grow older, getting ready to go out can take some time. You will need to pack food and nappies, plus toys for entertainment, comforters and other miscellaneous paraphernalia. Being well organised and calm will help to facilitate these trips.

Adjusting to this new notion of time will help to avoid you feeling stressed at the mere thought of going out with your babies. Accept that things are going to take longer, plan to do less and try to minimise the amount of preparation you need to do immediately before going out by having a nappy-changing bag ready packed with all the things you need (you could do this while your babies are asleep). Internet shopping for routine, everyday items and presents can be a life-saver for parents of twins, allowing you to save your energy for more pleasurable outings.

Car seats and car safety

Once babies can sit up (at around six months old), and/or weigh over 9 kg, they should be put in a front-facing child seat whenever travelling in a car. These are designed to go in the back seat and will last until a child weighs 18 kg. Never fit one in the front, as airbags released in the event of an accident could seriously injure a baby. Some seats are suitable for up to 36 kg in weight, and others have detachable backs so that the seat can be used as a booster for older children.

In the car

You might find it useful to buy a child-view mirror that clips underneath your rear-view mirror, making it easier for you to see what is going on in the back of the car without having to turn round. Ensure that the rear car doors are fitted with child locks that are activated at all times. This not only prevents doors from being opened while the vehicle is moving, but also electric windows from being meddled with. Remember that a toy or another object can become a missile to be thrown at another child or, more dangerously, at you while you are driving – remove any larger, hard objects from reach. On a warm day, the metal parts of seat restraints can become extremely hot, so take care when handling and placing against your babies' bodies.

Local trips

You will soon get to know which of your local shops can easily accommodate your double pram, pushchair or buggy, and which have facilities for feeding and nappy-changing. A trip to the local playground needs more thought when you have two babies, as it is much harder or impossible for both of them to use many pieces of play equipment at the same time. Nevertheless, the playground and the exercise it brings are important for babies, so you need to decide how best to do this. Since time apart allows your baby greater space to develop as an individual, you could arrange for a family member to take one of them to the playground, while you focus on an activity with the other. Or you could ask someone to come with you and each take charge of one baby. If you are on your own, keep one baby safely strapped in their pushchair or buggy, perhaps with a toy for entertainment, while you push the other on a swing or support them on a slide or climbing frame. Things the babies can do simultaneously, such as play in sand pits, are often a welcome source of enjoyment. Using public transport or making short trips in the car both need planning. You will need to ask yourself the following:

- Do you have toys and comforters ready?
- Is there a chance of your trip taking longer than usual and interfering with your twins' feed and sleep times?
- Do you have extra feeds/food/nappies with you in case you are delayed?
- Can you park the car close to your destination so that babies can be easily transported if you have not brought your pushchair/buggy?
- Will the parking space have enough room to open the doors on both sides of the car so that you can put your babies in and out of their seats easily?

As ever, being prepared and not allowing yourself to become over-anxious will help to make any trip more enjoyable.

> **DID YOU KNOW...?**
> While they are still small enough, place your babies back-to-back in an infant playground swing. This overcomes the problem of trying to push two swings at once and also gives the babies firm support.

Longer trips

Travelling with two or more babies requires advance planning and an ability to anticipate (where possible) the unexpected on the day itself. Whether you are travelling by car, train or plane, aim for practicality above all else. For example:

- Always pack more nappies and feeds than you will need – better to have too many than too few.
- Use disposable nappies and packets of wipes.
- Pack a full change of clothing for each baby – older babies can suffer from travel sickness.
- If your babies are eating solids, make sure you provide them with food you know they like – now is not the time to experiment.
- Do not be too precious about feeding them home-made food if it is going to be complicated to transport and warm up. Jars of ready-made baby food come into their own in these circumstances.

Travelling by car

When planning your journey, bear in mind that you may need to stop frequently, perhaps at least every two hours. Allow plenty of time for nappy-changing and feeding, and make sure you take the babies out of their car seats for long enough so that they can move around a little and stretch out. Many service stations in the UK and abroad have microwaves for heating up milk or food, but take care that is thoroughly reheated and shake or stir before use to prevent 'hot spots'. Where possible, try to keep to their schedules for feeding and sleeping, but if your babies are sleeping, keep driving rather than stop for a break. Once your babies are a little older and can hold objects, remember that they can also drop them, so any comforters or favourite toys need to be securely attached or easily reachable in the back of the car, otherwise you may soon have a screaming baby distracting the driver. Nursery rhyme CDs can soothe or entertain babies (though they might have the opposite effect on their parents) and so are good for long car journeys.

Travelling by train

If your babies are not yet sitting up, you can keep them in their car seats/buggy, provided you are at the end of the carriage. Otherwise you will probably have them on your lap. This can be tricky, as they will find it harder to sleep and can become tired, especially if the journey is a relatively long one. Try to have some toys to bring out at various intervals – ideally a mixture of new (for the novelty factor) and favourite ones (for the comfort factor). If the babies are weaned, put a few finger food snacks on the table or tray in front of you to keep them occupied. If you have someone else with you, walk each baby around the train at regular intervals, as they often enjoy the movement and will find the change of scene interesting. Finally, avoid evening train journeys if possible, as your babies are likely to be more tired and grumpy than if they travel earlier in the day.

Travelling by plane

Travelling by aeroplane with twins is quite difficult if you are on your own, and this section assumes that you have someone to accompany you. Until the age of two, babies do not need their own seat and can sit on an adult's lap. The confined space of an aircraft can make babies fretful and many also dislike the extension belt that must be used for take-off, landing and during any turbulence. Babies under six months old, however, often travel better than those between six months and three years old, as they are less aware of their surroundings and are unlikely to get as bored. On short-haul flights, try not to book evening departures: these are more likely to get delayed and babies can be very unsettled if their sleep routine is disturbed.

Some airlines can supply carrycots for young babies to use during long-haul flights (although not for take-off and landing or during turbulence). These need to be booked well in advance and are allocated on a first-come, first-served basis. Some carriers (especially national airlines) allow you to book an extra seat for a child under the age of two at a reasonable cost, so that you can put your babies in their own forward-facing car seats secured to the seat. Some airlines also have a limited number of their own infant seats (make sure you request them in advance).

Most airlines will allow you to take your buggy to the departure gate before loading it into the hold. Some may even allow you to take it on board with you. If the buggy is put in the hold, make sure the cabin crew request that it is taken out as soon as the plane arrives, so that you do not have to walk through long airport corridors holding the babies as well as all the other paraphernalia. Take-off and landing often cause an uncomfortable build-up of pressure in your babies' ears, which can result in a lot of crying, so get them to suck on a bottle (of water or milk) or on a dummy, as this will help unblock their ears. As with train journeys, you should have toys and snacks at the ready to keep the babies occupied. Be aware that you will not be able to eat or drink much yourself, simply because of the logistics of trying to use a tray in front of you while holding a baby on your lap. You may find it easier to pack a snack and a bottle of water, which you can consume at a time that suits you best.

PLAYING

Babies are by nature inquisitive and learn a great deal from playing. Although it can sometimes feel as if you never have enough time to play with your babies, it is nonetheless important that you devote a little time each day to doing so. And if you can do this on a one-to-one basis with each of your babies, they will benefit even more.

If you can, set aside some time to play with whichever baby wakes first (hopefully it is not always the same one); or, if you bath your babies with the help of another adult, one of you can bath a baby while the other plays with the other one (alternate who looks after which baby). A few minutes each day of individual play will also help your babies to develop their sense of identity and strengthen their relationship with you. If you have older children (rather than toddlers), they can also be encouraged, under supervision, to interact on an individual basis with their siblings, and this can strengthen their bond. Language acquisition is also helped if babies have eye contact and individual attention, so you should try to find even small opportunities every day to play with each of your babies on their own (see p. 248 for more on language development).

The sort of activities and play your babies are able to engage in will depend on their age. When babies are under one year old, there should be no sense that a particular activity or toy is suitable for a particular gender – their taste in play will not begin to manifest itself until they are toddlers. Wherever possible, rotate the toys your babies play with so that they can develop a range of different skills.

One toy or two?

Ensuring that each child has their own toys from the start is an important part of developing the individuality of twins. The question of whether babies should each have their own set of toys – thus duplicating a good many of them – is one that parents tend to resolve on a case-by-case basis, depending on their budget and the amount of room they have at home. When they are under one year old, many toys can be shared, especially as they will not be gender-specific. However, it is important for twins to develop the notions of ownership and individuality, as well as that of sharing, so in some cases they should each have their own toy, even if it means you have two of the same.

DID YOU KNOW…?
Bath time provides great opportunities for play once the babies can sit up, but make sure you fit your bath with a rubber mat to prevent the babies from slipping. Never leave babies alone in the bathroom.

Playing: when and at what?

As your babies' development progresses, so will their types of play. Avoid buying too many toys and remember that simple items can be just as entertaining, if not more so, than an expensive ones. Charity shops and table sales are ideal for picking up second-hand toys cheaply, and many areas have a toy library, where toys, books, puzzles and larger play items can be borrowed at a reasonable cost. The following activities are based on the developmental stages of a baby born at 40 weeks gestation. See also Box on p. 242 for a suggested list of suitable playthings.

Four to six months

By the time they are four months old, you will be able to hand things to your babies and sit them in a baby chair with a small tray in front of them containing toys and other objects.

READING TO BABIES
It is never too early to start reading to children and you should try to read to one child at a time whenever the opportunity arises. Even very young babies respond to bright images and the rhythm of your voice. At this stage, 'touch-and-feel' board books are ideal, and as they get older they can more easily turn the pages themselves. Older babies can listen to longer stories and may relish a variety of different types of books (this is when libraries become invaluable), as well as continuing to enjoy one or two particular favourites. Pick something that you enjoy reading, too, and the experience will be even more beneficial. Reading a story at bedtime can help establish a good sleep routine (see p.233), but having a book to hand at any time of day – even when out and about – can help improve a baby's mood and provide an invaluable diversion.

LIST OF SUITABLE TOYS
You may want to consider getting one or two items from each section of the list:

Four to six months
- rattles and teethers
- soft toys with a crinkly surface or squeaks and rattles inside them
- musical toys and shakers
- wooden spoon and plastic bowl
- toy mirror
- baby gym
- playmat
- mobile

Six to nine months
- cloth or board books
- toy phone
- baby door bouncer
- activity centre or bar
- push-along toy
- car/truck/train
- bath squirters and cups (empty plastic bottles will do just as well)
- simple lift-out shapes puzzle

Nine to twelve months
- shape sorter
- stacking bricks or cups
- musical instruments (e.g. xylophone, drum)
- cardboard box to sit in
- ball (large enough not to be swallowed)
- pull-along toy
- bead frame
- small inflatable paddling pool

Encourage them to look at what they are seeing and to touch and stroke it. If they have to stretch to reach the object, it will encourage their curiosity further. A mobile is useful entertainment for when they are lying down. Toys that have different shapes, textures and bright colours or that make a noise are good, but babies will also gain pleasure from ordinary wooden or plastic kitchen utensils (such as spoons or bowls). Babies start to laugh and giggle during this time, which makes playtime a lot more fun. By the age of six months, they will be rolling over, so lying down on playmats or under a baby gym is good stimulation. If you have not done so already, start singing or playing nursery rhymes and other songs to your babies. You can sing badly – they will not know any better! Songs which involve actions are especially fun and mother-and-baby groups that you take them to might have a special singing session.

Six to nine months
Babies will be sitting up during this time and, by the end, most will be crawling or 'bottom-shuffling'. Baby door bouncers that you fit to the frame encourage their increasing physicality, while giving you peace of mind that your babies are safe and in one place. Once babies can sit up and become better co-ordinated, play opportunities increase. They can watch other children and adults playing, they start to copy you and to place objects more accurately (e.g. one block on top of another) and can watch you turn the pages of a 'touch-and-feel' or 'lift-the-flap' board or soft book (see Box on p. 241). Babies put any unknown objects in their mouth as a way of helping them to discover what it is, so make sure any toys they have cannot be swallowed. Their sense of humour and their understanding that other people are separate from them continues to develop, so that by nine months, babies discover the game of hiding and uncovering objects and, soon after, the game of 'peekaboo'. Bath toys that squirt or cups that the babies can use to pour water make bath time more fun – if you can spare a few extra minutes and are tolerant of splashes.

Nine to twelve months
Babies' language is starting to emerge, and with it an understanding of simple instructions (e.g. 'Where's Daddy?'). They will be able to stack objects, put them inside each other and also enjoy knocking them down. Shape sorters, stacking bricks or cups are ideal at this stage. Babies will make an increasing mess and noise when playing (many enjoy toys that involve banging or pushing a button to make a sound) and, as long as you can bear it, this should not be discouraged. Babies have fun playing in sandpits and (fully supervised) in paddling pools. They will be pulling themselves up, cruising and (in the case of some) walking, so need to watched the whole time as they continue to explore the world around them. Pull-along toys develop their mobility and they will also enjoy climbing in and out of boxes. Take them to activities and toddler groups where they can move and climb around in a safe environment and learn to interact with babies who are not their siblings.

 # YOUR BABIES' CONTINUING DEVELOPMENT

All babies develop at different rates, whether they are singletons or twins. If twins are premature, especially if born before 34 weeks, parents should be aware that their babies' development may be a little behind that of singletons.

The time at which babies reach certain milestones can differ, even between twins. It is more helpful to parents of premature twins, especially those born before 34 weeks, to consider whether their babies' development is appropriate for the date at which they were due rather than their actual birth date.

Motor skills and movement

A baby's development of movement – or 'motor development' – always takes place in the same order, from the head downwards and from the central part of the body outwards.

Babies first gain control of their head and neck, allowing them to hold their head up; then their upper limbs and trunk, so that they can start to use their hands; they then gain greater control over their abdomen, enabling them to roll over and then sit up; finally, they gain control over their legs and feet, allowing them firstly to crawl, then to stand and eventually to walk. During all this time, they are also gradually developing the fine motor skills in their hands and fingers.

However, the age at which babies reach these developmental milestones can vary enormously. Monozygotic (identical) twins tend to reach milestones at a similar time, where as the development of dyzogotic (non-identical) twins can be more varied. Some babies roll over at four months, and sit at six; others stand up without ever crawling. As a guideline, the developmental stages listed opposite occur at approximately the following ages for babies born at 40 weeks gestation. For information on babies four months and younger, *see* Chapter 7, p. 192.

DEVELOPMENTAL MILESTONES: 5–12 MONTHS

5 months
- can voluntarily grasp and let go of objects, though not always with accuracy
- increasingly laughing and interacting with others and making feelings clear

6 months
- increasing control over upper torso
- may be able to sit up with some support (back may still be rounded and position not secure)
- can reach out to grab things and may drop them deliberately
- test objects out by putting them in mouth
- can hold spoon/large pieces of food and put in mouth, albeit messily
- much more alert to surroundings and to people, and can distinguish between angry and cheerful tone of voice

8 months
- can sit unaided
- grasp objects between thumb and index finger, so can eat some finger food and engage in more varied activities

9 months
- crawling or 'bottom-shuffling' along the floor using arms
- will take objects when offered
- may point to objects they want

10 months
- can pull themselves to standing and may start 'cruising' (taking steps while holding onto furniture)
- can wave goodbye, play 'peekaboo'

12 months
- increasing confidence when standing, and may walk unaided
- can pick up tiny objects (and put in mouth)
- can pick up and drop objects at will

DID YOU KNOW…?
It is important to remember that there is no link between the age at which babies reach these generalised developmental milestones and their future intellectual or sporting ability, whatever others might imply.

Follow-up checks

Well baby clinics take place in doctor surgeries, health centres and community halls. They are run by your local health visitor and are places where you can go to have your babies weighed and checked, as well as getting information and advice. You do not need to book ahead for this and the informal setting is ideal for meeting other parents. Taking twins to the clinic to be weighed and measured can be stressful and many parents soon begin to reduce the number of trips once they are satisfied that their babies are making good progress. However, certain visits to health clinics are inevitable, such as when your babies are being vaccinated or having their developmental checks, so on those occasions, try to bring another adult along to help you, as the visits will be longer than usual. You will need to book two appointments – one for each of your babies – and, if possible, aim for the start of the session when the clinic will be more likely to be running on time.

Your babies will have a check-up when they are between seven and nine months old, at which their physical, developmental and language progress will be assessed. As well as measuring and weighing your babies, the doctor or health visitor will carry out certain checks covering:

- hearing
- sight
- social interaction
- gross motor skills.

As with your babies' six-week check, this is a good opportunity to mention any concerns you might have about these or other aspects of their physical and mental development, such as feeding and sleeping.

Personality development

The personalities of twins have always been a source of fascination to others. This is especially the case with identical twins who share the same genetic make-up, but even then nurture does play its part in shaping the individual characters.

It is therefore important for parents to be aware of this so that they can raise happy, independent children who have a strong sense of their own identity.

People make a greater fuss of twins and treat them as special. As a result, if the children have not been prepared in their early years to see themselves as individuals, it can be difficult for them, when they are older and have to go out into the world on their own, to adjust to being just 'another person'. So, the earlier twins are treated as individuals, the better it will be for them and for their confidence. For ways to encourage separate identities, see Chapter 7, p. 191. In addition, as the babies grow older:

▶ Continue to observe their differences and to point these out to other people.
▶ Let them pick clothes for themselves, as it will allow them to explore their own tastes.
▶ Give different hairstyles to same-sex twins, especially if they are identical.
▶ A friend or relative could be assigned to each twin to spend time with them individually.
▶ Make sure they do not always have to share clothes, toys and other possessions. A notion that each twin has 'his/her' toys (at least some of them), for example, helps them to recognise their individuality.
▶ Encourage their different tastes and friendships, but also allow them to have the same ones if they choose.

As twins get older, they often want to differentiate themselves from their sibling. Yet they are often prevented by others from developing their own identity and, instead, are constantly being reminded that they are part of a pair. For example, people may call them 'the twins', they may openly admit that they cannot tell them apart and they may assume that they have the same interests. Parents, out of convenience, often prefer that their children take up the same activities, have the same friends and attend the same schools.

Some twins relate well to each other from the start, but others do not; their closeness can also depend on their gender and whether or not they are identical. The sheer amount of time that twins spend together, particularly in their early years, means that they inevitably form a very special relationship. If parents are not vigilant, twins sometimes become over-reliant on each other and this can limit their ability to form friendships and relationships. Try whenever you can to organise separate play dates and arrange for them to pursue activities that they each have a particular interest in. Consider asking for them to be put in different classes, if possible, when they go to school.

The personality of each baby starts to appear at a very young age and even identical twins will not behave in an identical manner. Parents should be mindful of these differences and avoid thinking of their babies as a single unit. Paradoxically, in their attempt to differentiate their babies, parents often unintentionally attach labels to each baby: for example, one is 'the quiet one', the other is 'the noisy one'. These labels can often stick and, before long, become an accepted characteristic, even though children often grow out of these early traits. Sometimes, a label given to a young child – energetic and sporty versus a quieter and more cautious sibling – can prevent twins from exploring other sides of their personality, because they feel their sibling has already acquired that label. There is then a subconscious unwillingness to take over that characteristic or to compete with their sibling. As twins grow up, it is easy for parents, again unintentionally, to praise each twin in the areas that they each allegedly excel in, which entrenches the twins' view that they are 'only' good at this and should not try to rival their sibling in their own special area of ability.

Twins are usually very close, even if their personalities are quite different, and are an enormous influence on each other, especially in the early years. Although this closeness is very special, it is vital that they are each encouraged to develop as an individual and to explore all areas of their personality, whether their sibling has those characteristics, tastes or talents or not.

TEETHING

Although babies grow teeth at different times, and some are even born with them, most babies usually get their first teeth at any time between six and twelve months old. Their first teeth are usually their top or bottom front teeth (the incisors), followed by their molars. When teeth are on the point of coming through, babies can get a bit grumpy or feverish, will have flushed cheeks and may chew on rattles, hands or anything hard that can soothe their gums. Special teething rings or gel can be given to ease their discomfort, as well as infant paracetamol to alleviate pain. You should start to clean your babies' teeth as soon as the first tooth comes through. Wipe each tooth gently with a clean, damp flannel. Once your babies are over one year old, you can use a soft toothbrush and a very small amount of toothpaste.

Language development

Language acquisition is one of the most fascinating parts of child development and parenting: how do babies make sense of all those sounds they hear and order them into a language? This topic has an added dimension when there are two languages spoken at home (see Box). It is known that twins are slower than singletons to acquire speech. This is more likely to be the case if they are premature, of low birthweight and/or are boys (girls are faster at acquiring language). During their first two years, twins can be several months slower than a similar-aged singleton at developing language. However, if you have concerns about language development at any time, you should always seek professional advice rather than assume it is because they are twins.

There are several factors that are thought to contribute to the initial delay in the language development of twins:

▸ Parents interact less with their babies on a one-to-one basis, and therefore have less eye contact with them.
▸ Parents tend to speak in shorter sentences to twins, probably through lack of time, and use less complex language.
▸ Parents are more likely to speak to one baby but be looking at the other, or their actions may not match their words because they are busy attending to something else.

The differences in speech acquisition manifest for twins themselves in the following ways: they are older when they say their first word; and their sentences are shorter and simpler; their vocabulary is smaller. However, once children start school, differences in speech development usually disappear, so there are no long-term repercussions.

It is estimated that, when they are young, babies need to hear a word 500–600 times before they will say it for the first time themselves. The following are some of the stages that babies go through during their first year as they slowly start to understand and acquire speech:

▸ By three or four months, your babies are making sounds back to you and trying, in their own way, to imitate your voice.
▸ By seven or eight months, they are babbling and starting to make syllable sound such as 'goo' and 'ga'.
▸ By ten months, they can respond to their names and those of familiar people.
▸ Between ten to twelve months, they will start to say 'mama' and 'dada'.
▸ By the time they are one year old, they can respond to simple instructions (e.g. a request to give a particular toy) and babbling is more expressive.

There are certain measures you can take to stimulate your babies' speech development. Maximise your eye contact with them, as this is vital in language acquisition: you will know that you have their attention and they will be able to watch and copy the shape of your mouth and try to make the same noises. Ensure that, as much as possible, your language matches your actions so that they can make a link between the two. Try to repeat words or phrases your babies are trying to say, thus enabling the babies to hear them more frequently and correctly. Make time for each baby to speak to you. Sometimes, one baby's speech develops more than another's or one is more chatty, and mothers find themselves addressing this baby more than the other, quieter baby. Try to make sure that you divide your time equally between both.

MORE THAN ONE LANGUAGE?

It is increasingly common for children to be brought up in a household where more than one language is spoken. If each parent has a different mother tongue and chooses to speak to their children in this language, this can (though not always) cause a slight delay in language development. However, the advantages of knowing a second language from birth outweigh any temporary disadvantages. The fear that babies will become confused between the languages is groundless. If each parent is consistent and speaks only their language to their babies, the babies will very quickly work out that each parent, in effect, has a different 'code' and they will easily adapt to this. Moreover, up to the age of six months, babies can distinguish between fine differences in sounds that allow them, in later years, to speak the language with the accent of a native speaker. After this age, babies' ability to recognise these minute differences in pronunciation gradually disappears. This is why, when children learn a second language later on at school, they always do so with the accent of their mother tongue. Parents who are able to bring up their babies with two languages should therefore be encouraged do so from birth.

By the time your babies are four months old, you will know them well enough to notice any slight change in their well-being. It is common for them to develop minor illnesses, fevers or rashes, but you should not hesitate to consult a doctor if you have any doubt about the severity of the condition. It is always better to err on the side of caution with children, especially when they are not yet old enough to speak.

Try to get help with looking after your babies if one of them is ill, because this can be a particularly exhausting time for parents: the baby who is unwell will need more looking after, while the other can suddenly become more demanding of attention and may, in any event, become unwell soon after. Indeed, when one of your babies is ill, it is not worth going to great lengths to try to prevent the other from catching the illness. In all likelihood, your attempts will prove futile and you will tire yourself out in the process. Other than observing good hygiene, you should therefore continue as normal.

Colds and chest problems

It is estimated that children catch between six and ten colds per year. Colds are viral infections and so cannot be helped by antibiotics. The main inconvenience for babies is that it often gives them with a blocked nose. This can make it difficult for them to feed and sleep well, and can turn them into grizzly, unhappy babies. Raise their cot a little at the head end to help ease congestion at night. A few drops of a eucalyptus-based decongestant on the bottom sheet of the cot, on their sleepsuit (never on their skin) or in a room vaporiser can also be highly effective. If the symptoms persist beyond a week, ask your doctor to prescribe some suitable decongestant nose drops.

Chest infections can often follow colds. If a baby starts to show signs that their breathing is affected or they develop a cough, consult your doctor. Babies' lungs are immature, especially those of premature babies, so chest infections can quickly develop and can sometimes become more serious.

Bronchiolitis

Bronciolitis is one of the most common chest infections in babies, affecting up to one-third of infants under the age of

one. It is caused by a virus, so is not responsive to antibiotics, and it results in the smallest airways in the lungs (the bronchioles) becoming inflamed. This reduces the amount of air entering the lungs, making it harder for a baby to breathe. Initial symptoms include a slight fever, a dry persistent cough and difficulty feeding. Your baby will then become wheezy. Most cases of bronchiolitis disappear within one to two weeks. However, some babies (especially premature ones) need hospitalisation, because they require help with their breathing.

Skin rashes

Skin rashes are often unexplained, difficult to diagnose and invariably not serious. They can even be caused by changes in clothing material, washing powder or fabric conditioner, but should nonetheless be checked out by a doctor to rule out a more serious problem.

Eczema

Around one in five children suffers from a dry skin condition known as eczema. Typically, the skin is red and itchy, and in more severe cases can weep, crust and bleed. It is non-infectious and can appear anywhere on the body, even the face, but is often found in the creases of the elbows and backs of knees. Eczema can be relieved by applying unperfumed emollient cream to your baby's skin to allieviate dryness and prevent cracking, and your doctor may also prescribe a topical steroid cream to control flare-ups. Scratch mits can be used to prevent babies from scratching, as broken skin is vulnerable to infection. Most children grow out of eczema by the time they are seven.

Vomiting and diarrhoea

If a baby is taking solids and begins to vomit and/or have diarrhoea, the most likely explanation is that they are suffering from a viral or bacterial infection affecting their stomach and intestines. You should stop food and milk for 24 hours, give plenty of water to sip at regular intervals, as well as a dose of oral rehydration solution (glucose, salt and water) specifically for babies. This can be bought from a chemist and does not stop vomiting or diarrhoea, but does prevent babies becoming dehydrated as a result. You may need to administer this over a period of time if your baby is unable/unwilling to drink much. The problem usually improves within 24 hours, after which you should reintroduce milk gradually (water down the first feed), followed by solids. However, if you are at all

MENINGITIS

Meningitis is an infection that causes an inflammation of the layers surrounding the brain and spinal cord, and there are two types: viral and bacterial. Viral meningitis is the most common form and, while it can make babies very unwell, it can also be mild and most people make a full recovery. Many bacteria can cause bacterial meningitis, some of which also result in septicaemia, a severe infection of the blood. While this form of the disease can be successfully treated with antibiotics, early diagnosis is vital, as it can be life-threatening and leaves many with permanent disabilities.

Symptoms for bacterial meningitis do not appear in any particular order, but in babies include:

- a high-pitched, untypical cry
- moaning, irritability, dislike of being held
- tense or bulging fontanelles (soft spot) on top of the baby's head
- poor feeding/refusing food/vomiting
- drowsy, floppy, unresponsive behaviour
- stiffness of neck and dislike of bright lights
- convulsions (fits)
- fever, but with cold hands and feet
- pale, blotchy skin
- **IMPORTANT:** a rash of tiny 'pin prick' spots, which do not fade when a glass tumbler is pressed against it – this is a key symptom of septicaemia.

While babies receive the Hib, Meningitis C and Pneumococcal vaccines as part of the UK's routine vaccination programme for babies and infants there is still no vaccine to prevent all forms of the disease. Meningitis progresses rapidly in babies, so if in any doubt, trust your instincts and act fast: go to your nearest doctor or hospital emergency department at once. See Useful Resources for sources of more information about meningitis.

worried – for example, your baby seems very floppy, has a fever and/or is unable to keep even water down – consult your doctor at once, as babies can become dangerously dehydrated very quickly. For information on constipation, see Chapter 7, p. 197.

Febrile convulsions

Babies often develop a fever even if they are not actually ill, and their temperature can rise quickly. A young child's brain sometimes finds it difficult to cope with a sudden rise in temperature and, for about one in 35 babies and young children, most commonly between the ages of six months and three years, this will cause them to have a fit (convulsion). They lose consciousness, go rigid, roll their eyes and have jerky limb movements. Once they regain consciousness they are very limp, pale and sleepy. Fits are rarely dangerous, although they are worrying for the parents when they occur, but 30–50 per cent of children who have one fit will go on to have subsequent episodes. Should your baby have a fit, try to stay calm, turn their head to one side and protect it underneath, but do not restrain them or put anything in their mouth. Try to lower their temperature as detailed in Chapter 7, p. 197. A fit usually lasts a few minutes, and you should call your doctor once it has ended. Almost all children who have febrile convulsions grow out of them during childhood.

Infectious diseases

Babies can catch infectious diseases at any age, although those who are breastfed will gain some immunity (if the mother herself is immune) for the duration they are fed. Vaccination is recommended for babies and is routinely offered for the serious and highly infectious diseases of measles, mumps and rubella (MMR) between the ages of twelve and eighteen months. Before then, however, they are able to catch these diseases, which are becoming more prevalent once again because the level of immunity in the population has fallen in recent years.

Chickenpox

Chickenpox is a mild illness that is most common in children under ten. While a vaccine does exist, it is not part of the UK's free immunisation programme (except for high risk cases, such as the siblings of very ill children). It causes a rash of red, itchy spots that become fluid-filled blisters. These then crust over into scabs, which will eventually drop off. Chickenpox is very contagious, but it is most infectious from one or two days before the rash appears, so if one baby has chickenpox, it is highly likely that your other baby will already have become infected. If you think one or both of your babies has contracted chickenpox or has been exposed to the virus, seek medical

251

advice. When caught in the first year, chickenpox is usually milder than when caught later on in childhood or in adulthood, but premature removal of scabs by excessive scratching can cause permanent scarring. Symptomatic relief for itchy skin can be given by applying calamine lotion or cream, or ask your pharmacist for advice. If your babies will tolerate them, you could put them in scratch mits, particularly at night.

Measles
Measles is a highly infectious viral illness and can be very serious for a young baby. It initially manifests itself by a fever, cough, runny nose, grey-white spots in the mouth and sore eyes. A rash appears three or four days later in blotches of small flat spots all over the body and the fever rises significantly. See your doctor immediately if you suspect your child may be infected.

Mumps
Mumps causes no symptoms at all in about a third of cases, while others experience swelling of the glands under the jaw, leading to ear pain and discomfort while eating. Complications in infants are rare, but you should visit your doctor for a diagnosis in any case.

Rubella (German measles)
The symptoms of rubella are usually mild: babies will be 'under the weather' for a day or so, and will develop a non-itchy pink rash within 24 hours. It is difficult to diagnose accurately in young babies, but if a pregnant woman catches it, the consequences can be catastrophic for her unborn child – receiving a diagnosis will alert you to the need to avoid newly pregnant women.

YOU AND YOUR FAMILY

Having children will inevitably alter the relationships in your family. As your new lifestyle evolves over the next few months, you will need to think about finding time for yourself as an individual, as well as time with your partner. And if you have other children, finding enough time for them is also vital for the health of your family unit.

Looking after yourself

Continuing to get enough rest and sleep is just as important as your babies grow older. Their increasing mobility means that the physical demands on you will be greater, but once your babies start to sleep through the night, caring for them usually becomes more manageable. However, if you have had lots of nights with little sleep, the effects can linger on for some months – but they will eventually ease and you will start to feel more energetic once more.

Once you get your babies into a routine during the day, you will also find little pockets of time for yourself. As a result, the routine will become as important for you as it is for them. You might not be able to sit down to watch an entire DVD uninterrupted, but you could have a quiet lunch and a quick read of the newspaper while your babies are having their afternoon nap. Short breaks such as these are often enough for you to recharge in order to take on the rest of the day. It is also important to keep up good eating habits, as this will help boost your energy and mood. Do not skip meals, and stick to a nutritious, balanced diet with plenty of fluids. Too much alcohol, however, can leave you feeling drained the next day. See Chapter 2, p. 32 for more information on healthy eating.

As was the case when the babies were very young, you should still try to prioritise tasks and avoid setting yourself too high a standard. Nobody is going to judge how good a mother you are according to how many adventurous meal combinations you are concocting for your babies, for example, or whether your home is super-tidy. Think about what really needs to be done to keep you and your babies happy and healthy – after all, this is the most important thing. Organise yourself as much as possible, but do not worry about the non-essentials or about what others might think of you.

Losing your baby weight

You should have a nutritious, balanced diet while you are breastfeeding. However, if you are no longer breastfeeding and you have not lost weight that you gained during pregnancy and would like to do so, then you need to think sensibly about how to do this. Do not be tempted to 'crash diet'. When your body is significantly calorie-deprived, your metabolism goes into 'starvation mode' and slows down because it thinks food is going to run out. It becomes harder and harder to lose the weight and you risk piling it all back on (and often more) as soon as you start to eat normally again. Similarly, if you cut out whole groups of foods, such as carbohydrates, you will start to crave them and the chances are that you will give in sooner or later, undoing all the good work you might have achieved.

The best way to lose weight is to lose it *gradually*, by eating healthily but sensibly. You should aim to lose around 500 g per week. Trying to lose more than this when you are looking after your babies is likely to leave you exhausted and ill-tempered. Allow yourself some treats, whether it is a glass of wine at the end of the day or a biscuit with your tea, but avoid slipping into bad habits. The other essential to losing weight is to burn up more calories by exercising. This can be done simply by walking whenever you can, rather than driving everywhere. If you can find someone to look after the babies, you could attend a regular exercise session; there are classes that allow you to attend with a baby (e.g. a mother-and-baby yoga class), but make enquiries in advance to see if it would be practical to attend with two.

Making new friends and finding support

If you worked prior to having children, your social life probably took place mostly in the evenings. Women at home with babies find that they have to build a network of local 'daytime' friends. Finding new friends can take a little time, but the sooner you start, the sooner you will start to build that essential support group of empathetic mothers who, in months and years to come, will provide you with friendship, advice and much more besides. This is especially important if you are a single parent, as it is vital for you to be able to share experiences and discuss any difficulties you may be having with others who understand.

You may not know many other people with twins and it is also more difficult for you to get ready to leave the home, to meet up with others, to find suitable activities, or simply to go out and do some shopping. However, as mothers of twins are more prone to feeling isolated, it is vital that you find ways of keeping in touch with the outside world. Your local Twins Club can suggest suitable activies to do with twins and with other mothers in your area.

Remember that caring for two or more babies is demanding, so you need regular breaks away from them. (This does *not* make you a bad mother: it makes you a normal person.) Being cared for occasionally by others can also benefit your babies, as it can help them to develop their individuality, become more adaptable and learn social skills that will help them to become confident about the outside world. In Chapter 7 p. 207–8, information and advice is given on how to reduce feelings of isolation and postnatal depression (the two issues are not always linked, but if you are feeling isolated, you are more likely to develop postnatal depression). Once your babies are three to four months old, there are other things you can do to help yourself:

▶ Accept all offers of help with looking after the babies. Delegate and, if you can afford to, consider paying for help so that you can have a break. Do not feel guilty about seeking help, especially for childcare or housework, even if you have not gone back to work (*see* Chapter 7, p. 214 for more about sources of help).
▶ Get your babies into a routine or pattern that suits you as soon as possible. The more rested and organised you are, the easier it will be to cope with the increasing demands of two toddlers.

▶ When you have some time for yourself, make sure that you use this to do something pleasurable, not to catch up on household tasks.
▶ Seek out the company of others and build up a network of other local mothers. Try to avoid travelling long distances on a regular basis with your twins, as this is can be tiring.
▶ Search out local activities to do on a regular basis with your babies (e.g. a mother-and-baby group).
▶ Arrange for regular babysitting. This can be vital for maintaining your relationship with your partner and for your own mental well-being. If you cannot afford to pay for it and do not have family close by, consider offering to babysit for a friend so that she can do the same for you.
▶ Remember: a happy mother will have happier babies!

Spending time with your partner

While looking after young babies can be all-encompassing, it is important to find some time for yourselves as a couple. Simply having an uninterrupted dinner with your partner at home can be wonderful, but there is nothing like an evening out, even if it is just a quick trip to the local pub, to enable you to talk in a way that is often not possible when you are at home. Although this does need to be organised in advance for the babysitting – the joys of a spontaneous evening out are no longer possible once you have children – it will be well worth the effort. Usually, couples find they are more relaxed and open with each other and return home in a better mood than when they left.

The importance of sharing the care of your babies and general domestic tasks with your partner does not diminish with time. If anything, it increases once your babies become mobile, need more entertainment and less sleep. Communication between you and your partner remains key and the advice provided in Chapter 7, p. 208–12 for the first three months of your babies' life is still relevant when they are older. In essence, kindness, flexibility and, where possible, a sense of humour are vital.

Rediscovering a sex life

Spending time together, communicating on a daily basis and being aware of each other's needs usually mean that you will resume your sex life spontaneously, although it may not happen for several weeks and even months. If you are concerned about your sex life when your babies are six months old, however, you should try to discuss the situation with your partner. Choose a time when you are both calm and undistracted, using words and a tone that are neither hurtful or accusatory. It may be that one of you (or both) has lost the desire for sex for various reasons, and this needs to be explored.

Even if you are not having intercourse, you need to maintain a physical connection with your partner: try to keep touching, kissing, cuddling or stroking each other, rather than reserve all these marks of love and affection for your babies. In the end, it may be that you start again simply because you feel you should, even if you are not yet feeling a burning desire to do so. As long as both partners take things slowly and do not feel pressurised, it is undoubtedly better for the health of your relationship that sexual relations resume.

Other children

Despite any initial excitement, as time progresses most children experience some difficulties adapting to having a sibling (*see* Chapter 7, p. 213). And when twins are involved, those difficulties can be magnified. Children over the age of three seem to cope better, as they are able to do small tasks and play with the babies. They often relish the chance to make the babies laugh and enjoy being a source of fascination for them. Older children are also more likely to have found their place in the world and to feel safer in their relationship not only with their parents but also with other people, especially if they are already at nursery or school. However, children under three can easily feel left out of a family unit that now appears

to be largely made up of their parents and the new babies, with little time and attention left for them. If parents are not careful, twins can start to dominate family dynamics, with life revolving around them to the detriment of an older child.

A sibling's feelings may not be obvious from the start, and they may be too young to voice what they are thinking, but it is very common for the initial euphoria to have given way to feelings of jealousy and resentment by the time your babies are a few months old, and especially once they are mobile. As time goes on, it is therefore even more important that you spend time on your own, ideally every day, with any older siblings. It is better for them to have a few minutes of undivided attention – for example, reading them a bedtime story – than half an hour when you are dividing your attention between them and the babies. Try to boost their self-esteem by telling them that they are the special or clever one for having two babies and draw attention to any ways in which the babies try to emulate them. Similarly, encourage grandparents and other willing relatives or friends to make a fuss of older children and to take them out for special treats.

Safeguarding toys

As soon as your babies start being able to grab things, ensure you keep any older children's toys well out of the way. In the case of small toys, this should be done for reasons of safety. But cherished toys or carefully assembled constructions should also be safeguarded. Having a special thing 'spoilt', even if not on purpose, can increase any feelings of jealousy and resentment in your older child(ren) towards these younger siblings, who have invaded their space so entirely and so successfully.

Maternity leave

The question of when to go on maternity leave depends on a range of factors, most especially your health during the pregnancy. Twins are likely to be delivered by about 37 weeks, and 50–60 per cent are born before then, so you should inform your employer that your maternity leave will need to start earlier than they may be expecting.

The legislation concerning maternity leave and statutory maternity pay (SMP) changes regularly, as does that relating to any benefits you can claim during pregnancy and once your babies are born. The best ways of finding out about these issues is to consult the Department for Work and Pensions, the Citizens' Advice Bureau or Maternity Action, which is a national charity providing information regarding all aspects of pregnancy and maternity rights (*see* Useful Resources for websites). If your employer offers more generous terms of payment during maternity leave, you will be made aware of this when you inform them you are pregnant.

During your maternity leave, you are entitled to Statutory Maternity Pay (SMP) either from your employer or, if you do not qualify for SMP, Maternity Allowance (MA) from Jobcentre Plus (contact the above organisations if you are unsure). In order to claim SMP or MA, you need to provide your employer with a Mat B1 certificate, which you can obtain from your doctora or midwife no earlier than twenty weeks before your due date. This confirms your pregnancy and your expected date of delivery (EDD). Your SMP or MA cannot begin earlier than eleven weeks prior to your EDD.

During your pregnancy, you are entitled to take reasonable, paid time off to attend antenatal appointments and classes. You may also benefit from certain employment or health and safety rights linked, for example, to your working conditions (check with your HR department, your union or Maternity Action).

Employment rights during pregnancy and maternity leave

Below are some of the key employment rights to which you are entitled. There are others, so check with the organisations listed for detailed information.

▶ All workers are protected against sex discrimination if you are dismissed or treated unfairly because of pregnancy or childbirth, or because you have taken maternity leave or exercised any of your maternity rights at work.

▶ You have the same maternity rights whether you are a full-time or part-time employee, and whether you have a permanent or fixed-term/temporary contract.

▶ If you are self-employed or doing casual work, you do not have the right to maternity leave, but may still get maternity pay and have other rights.

▶ It is illegal to make a woman redundant because she is pregnant or on maternity leave.

▶ If you are made redundant for other reasons during maternity leave, your employer must offer you suitable alternative work. If there is none, they must pay you notice and redundancy pay in the same way that they would if you were not pregnant.

▶ You are still entitled to maternity leave if your babies die after the birth or are stillborn after the end of Week 24.

▶ During maternity leave, you have the same statutory rights as other employees (e.g. regarding annual paid leave, notice period in your employment contract, redundancy pay after two years' service).

If you are an employee

There are many issues to consider when deciding when to stop work, how much time to take off and whether to return after the birth. Clearly, financial and other personal considerations will play a large part in your deliberations.

Before you tell your employer that you are pregnant, work out how your job could be done in your absence and think about drawing up a document to present to them. Try not to undersell yourself (a common female trait), but remain flexible about considering options your employer may suggest to cover for your absence. Avoid going for the 'cheap' option, where another colleague 'takes over' your job: this implies that your job can be done by someone else *on top* of their current responsibilities and could leave you vulnerable on your return. It could also lead to bad feeling from the other colleague if they have become overwhelmed with work; conversely, if they have enjoyed the enhanced role, they could resent your return. The 'fill-in' person could have made mistakes that you will then have to rectify, or have left you with a mammoth in-tray on your return. A better option is to suggest outside help, or that a colleague(s) switches roles for a while.

It is best to wait until your pregnancy is well established before telling your employer you are pregnant (currently, the latest time is the fifteenth week before the babies are due). Unless you are absolutely certain that you are leaving after the birth, inform your employer that you intend to return. If in the end you decide not to, you will simply resign as you would do if you were leaving your job for another reason. You will not have to refund any SMP, but you may have to refund any pay that was in excess of SMP. Consider how long you want to take off, although this is not legally binding and you can change your mind later. Your employer may have a generous maternity leave package, but bear in mind that an extended absence could affect your career prospects.

You have the right to ask to return to work part-time or flexi-time and your employer is obliged to consider your request. However, they also have a legal right to turn it down, provided they do so in writing and cite valid business reasons. If necessary, outline a plan for them explaining how this might work in your particular job (e.g. job-sharing). It might be that your company has not previously had to consider such a request and could, with proper advance planning, be receptive to your proposal.

If you are self-employed

Women who run their own businesses are growing in numbers and have different considerations when they are pregnant, especially when expecting twins. While you should wait until your pregnancy is established before telling clients and other colleagues, it is not possible to physically hide a twin pregnancy for as long as you can a singleton pregnancy (which is sometimes until halfway through). You will therefore need to work out at an early stage what you will offer your clients and colleagues as a 'solution' to your absence – continuity is important and others will not want to feel you are abandoning them. The question of SMP and maternity leave does not arise; instead, if you are not to lose clients and potential income, you will have to decide how soon and on what basis you start work again. During the pregnancy and after the birth there are certain things you need to consider:

- ▸ Work out if it is possible or necessary for someone else to take over some or all of your responsibilities.
- ▸ Learn to delegate as much as possible and as soon as possible. Pay for extra help if you can.
- ▸ Technology enables you to stay in touch as little or as much as you want after the birth. Decide, therefore, how much you want this intrusion in your life at a time when you are likely to be tired and focused on your new babies.
- ▸ If you plan to work from home after the birth, decide where you will draw the line in terms of hours and circumstances. Are you happy to be available at all times? Some women are, while others prefer to separate out their personal and professional lives.
- ▸ If you work from home, keep your work environment separate from your babies' living environment, especially if your childcare is also based at home. A nanny's job is made harder by the regular, unannounced appearance of a parent. Similarly, you will not want to be distracted or made anxious by each cry or tantrum of your children.

- ▸ Avoid telling clients that you cannot deal with them because you are, for example, at an antenatal class or a toddler playgroup. Simply say you are unavailable: they do not need to know why, and thinking you are in demand is better than thinking your priorities do not lie with them.

Rights for partners

Partners are defined as anyone with responsibility for a child, such as husbands, biological or adoptive fathers and same-sex parents. They have no legal right to take paid time off to accompany the woman to antenatal appointments, though with warning, many employers do allow this. Partners can take Statutory Paternity Pay and, currently, up to two weeks' paid Paternity Leave if they give correct notice to their employer. In addition, unpaid Parental Leave is also available for both parents up to a child's fifth birthday (*see* Useful Resources for more information).

Studies are regularly done to try to shed light on whether working mothers benefit their children or not. In the end, the answer tends to depend on two key factors: first, if the quality of the childcare is good, then children are more likely to thrive, whoever they are looked after; and second, if a mother is happy and fulfilled, there is a greater chance that her children will be as well. If you have decided to return to work after the birth of your babies, the big question, whether you are an employee or self-employed, is how long to take for maternity leave. It is especially important to consider this if you are an employee, as self-employed women may be able to start work gradually and on a more ad hoc basis. There is no right or wrong answer to this question, as each woman will be different. For many, financial considerations are the most important factor in how soon they return to work.

Babies whose mothers return to work before six months may become more adaptable. If they are looked after by an experienced nanny or a good nursery, they will probably soon get into a routine and be doing a range of activities where they meet other children, perhaps earlier than if they were still being looked after by their mother. Some mothers think that the longer they wait to go back to work, the harder it will be to leave the babies, not just for you but for them as well. Babies go through a phase at around nine months old where they can become quite clingy, and this could coincide with the time when you are leaving them for the first time, adding to any distress and guilt you might be feeling about going back to work.

On the other hand, you may want to delay starting work until after they are six months old for a range of reasons: you will have weaned your babies yourself; they will (hopefully) be sleeping through the night, allowing you to feel more rested during the day; and you will finally have had a chance to enjoy your babies a little more after the demands of the first few months. Ultimately, only you will know your own situation and, together with your partner, be able to arrive at a decision that works both for you and your babies.

Whatever you decide, be prepared to be flexible when it comes to your work–life balance. What you imagined might work for you when you were pregnant might not turn out to be the case once you have had your babies. Many women change their mind concerning their plans for work once their babies are born and it is difficult to anticipate how you will feel at this stage of your life. Even as your babies grow and become toddlers (and thereafter, for that matter), your views on what works best for you and your family are likely to evolve, so do not worry if you have not got everything sorted out and perfect from the start. You are not a superwoman, and those who look as if they might be are usually worrying in private about falling short in one or several areas of their life, and/or are surviving thanks to an expensive army of paid helpers. Whatever you decide, if you are happy with the choice you have made, the chances are that your babies will be too.

Managing life once you are back at work

Many women have mixed emotions about going back to work after the birth of their children, especially their first-born. They may be keen to get back to a world where they are having adult conversations, are making use of their skills and their brain, and have some control over their day. On the other hand, many privately wonder if they are doing the best for their children by having them looked after during the day by someone else, however good the childcare might be. And they are sad at the thought that they may not be the first to witness the many milestones that their children will reach, such as their first words or their first steps.

Ultimately, you should reassure yourself that babies are extremely adaptable and, if the childcare is good, there is no reason why yours will not thrive in this new environment. After all, in many cultures, babies and children are raised not

> **DID YOU KNOW…?**
> Pregnant women and new mothers are entitled to free prescriptions and NHS dental care for one year.

Whatever you decide, be prepared to be flexible when it comes to your work–life balance. What you imagined might work for you when you were pregnant might not turn out to be the case once you have had your babies.

just by the mother but by a wider network of women. And the point about the milestones is that your babies are indeed reaching them, and what is exciting is the first time that *you* witness them, irrespective of whether someone else has before you (it could, after all, be your partner or a relative or friend who does).

Organisation will be vital in managing your return to work. In the week before you start, write a list of your babies' feeding and sleeping habits, their likes and dislikes, their activities and anything else you think might be useful for the person or nursery that is taking over the care of your babies. If you are employing a nanny and you arrange for them to start a few days before you go back to work, they can have the chance to get to know your babies while you are still around to provide additional information, although it is a good idea to gradually make yourself scarce as the week goes on so that they can all get used to being together without you being present.

Once you start work, you and your partner will need to be organised and to communicate effectively with each other and with your childcare provider in order for daily life to run smoothly. If one of you needs to work late, for example, let the other one know *in advance*, so that you know who has to be home in time (*see* Chapter 7, p. 214–16 for more on childcare).

The first few weeks are a transition time when everyone is getting used to a new way of life, so do not worry if things do not always run smoothly. Try to remain open to suggestions and flexible about how you manage your return to work. If, after a while, you sense that your childcare arrangements are not working or that your babies do not seem happy and settled, do not be afraid to discuss the situation with the person/people concerned and, if necessary, change the arrangement. On the other hand, as is more likely, if your babies develop a close bond with the person/people who look after them, you should be extremely grateful. Finally, remember that babies know who their parents are and, however wonderful your childcare might be, they will never love anyone more than you.

Index

Useful Resources

General

Websites for parents of multiples:
MBF (Multiple Births Foundation)
www.multiplebirths.org.uk
An organisation led by professionals with a range
of publications, advice and support for families.

TAMBA (Twins and Multiple Births Association)
www.tamba.org.uk
A parent-led range of publicatoins and helpline.

Twins clubs in the UK are listed on the following sites:
www.twinsclub.co.uk
www.twinsonline.org.uk
www.twinsuk.co.uk

Parenting forums
www.netmums.com
www.mumsnet.com

Chapter 2

Antenatal depression:
www.mind.org.uk
www.pndsupport.co.uk

Work legislation (*see* Chapter 8 listings)

Maternity clothes:
www.jojomamanbebe.co.uk
www.asos.com
www.boden.co.uk
www.thegap.co.uk
www.hm.com
www.mamasandpapas.com
www.mothercare.com
www.topshop.com

Chapter 3

Questions to ask your hospital:
www.cqc.org.uk

Deciding whether to have tests and scans:
Fetal Anomaly Screening Programme (FASP) http://
fetalanomaly.screening.nhs.uk/, www.downs-syndrome.org.uk

Birth choices:
www.birthchoiceuk.com

Selective termination:
www.arc-uk.org

Chapter 4

Back pain:
www.osteopathy.org.uk

Miscarriage and stillbirth:
www.miscarriageassociation.org.uk
www.tommys.org
www.childbereavement.org.uk
www.uk-sands.org

Pre-eclampsia:
www.apec.org.uk

Chapter 5

Doulas:
www.doula.org.uk

Chapter 6

Premature and sick babies:
www.bliss.org.uk
www.tommys.org
www.epicure.ac.uk

Milk banking:
www.ukamb.org

When babies die:
www.childbereavement.org.uk
www.uk-sands.org
www.winstonswish.org.uk
www.childhoodbereavementnetwork.org.uk
www.cruse.org.uk

Chapter 7

Equipment for hire:
www.thebabyloft.co.uk
www.minilodgers.co.uk
www.beha.co.uk

Breastfeeding support:
www.nct.org.uk
www.laleche.org.uk
www.thetruthaboutbreastfeeding.com
www.letsbreastfeed.com
www.breastfeedingnetwork.org.uk
www.abm.me.uk
www.breastfeeding.co.uk

Expressing:
www.expressyourselfmums.co.uk

Breast pumps:
www.boots.com
www.ameda.com

Nappy laundering:
www.wen.org.uk
www.goreal.org.uk
There are cloth nappy incentive schemes
run by many local authorities

Crying:
www.cry-sis.org.uk

Sudden infant death syndrome:
www.lullabytrust.org.uk

Help and childcare:
www.doula.org.uk
www.childcare.co.uk
www.home-start.org.uk
www.oneparentfamilies.org.uk
Each local athority has a Family Information Service
who can provide a list of all Ofsted registered providers
in the area.

Chapter 8

General safety:
www.mothercare.com
www.rhs.org.uk/Gardening/Sustainable-gardening/
pdfs/c_and_e_harmful

Breastfeeding when you return to work:
www.healthpromotionagency.org.uk
See other websites in Chapter 7

Child health:
www.bestbeginnings.org.uk

Meningitis:
www.meningitis-trust.org

Maternity leave:
www.dwp.gov.uk
www.direct.gov.uk
www.maternityaction.org.uk
www.adviceguide.org.uk
www.adviceuk.org.uk
www.childrenslegalcentre.com

Returning to work:
http://tlc.howstuffworks.com/family/programs-for-
working-parents3.htm
www.gov.uk/browse/benefits/families
www.payingforchildcare.org.uk

Postnatal depression:
www.mind.org.uk
www.pni.org.uk
www.pndsupport.co.uk
www.pandasfoundation.org.uk
www.mama.bm

Acknowledgements

Many thanks to the women and their babies I have had the privilege to look after over the years.
MARK KILBY

Professor Mark Kilby is an obstetrician and fetal medicine specialist who is an internationally renowned expert on multiple pregnancies. He brings not only medical expertise but years of experience of advising and supporting women and their partners through the additional complexities of multiple births. Victoria Marshallsay is the mother of twins who encouraged us both to produce this book to provide the information which she struggled to find during her own pregnancy. Her enthusiasm and commitment have been invaluable. Between us, I hope we have achieved our goal.
JANE DENTON

Consultants

Many thanks to the consultants and medical professionals who have contributed to this book:

Caroline King BSc SRD, Paediatric Dietitian (Neonatal Specialist)
Department Nutrition & Dietetics
Imperial College Healthcare NHS Trust

Sunit Godambe, Consultant Neonatologist
Imperial College Healthcare NHS Trust

Jo Dafforn, Lead Physiotherapist/Clinical Specialist
Women's Health Physiotherapy
Imperial College Healthcare NHS Trust

Gillian Weaver, Milk Bank Manager
Queen Charlotte's and Chelsea Hospital Milk Bank
Imperial College Healthcare NHS Trust

Annie Aloysius, Senior Clinical Specialist Speech and Language Therapist (Neonatology)
Imperial College Healthcare NHS Trust

Becky Armstrong, Clinical Psychologist
Clinical Psychology Department to Imperial Neonatal Units and Hammersmith Hospital Paediatrics
Imperial College Healthcare NHS Trust

Henry Leese, Professor of Biology
Professor Emeritus
Hull York Medical School

Brenda Leese, Honorary Fellow MBF
Honorary Research Fellow in the Faculty of Health and Social Care at Hull University.

Julia Kilby, Physiotherapist

Multiple Births Foundation staff:
Margie Davies, Midwifery Advisor
Rosie Ticciati, Health Visitor and Counsellor
Katrina Alcock, Manager

Photographs

Many thanks Queen Charlotte's & Chelsea Hospital Neonatal Unit staff and patients.

Many thanks to the parents and babies who kindly allowed themselves to be photographed for this book:

Anne and Nick Caine
Elizabeth and Benjamin Anandarajah
Audrey and Paul Kelly
Claire and James Matthias
Katharine and Stuart Schofield
Maelle and Camille Gutapfel

Personal stories

Many thanks to parents who have contributed their personal stories:

Ruth Field, Trine Adler, Alexandra Garfield, Victoria Marshallsay, Emily Collins, Tasha Airey, Katharine Schofield

Dragonfly

Lucy Bowden, Lucinda Hicks, Hannah Shrives, Iain Walmsley

Shine 360

Frances Adams, David Christopher, Lori Heiss, Kathryn Holland, Ben Liebmann

Disclaimer
No responsibility for any loss, harm and/or damage occasioned to any person acting
or refraining from action as a result of the material in this publication can be accepted
by the authors or the Publishers or Shine 360 and any company within the Shine Group.
This book is not intended as a substitute for professional medical advice, and you are
advised to consult a medically qualified practitioner about you and your symptoms.

Editorial Director Anne Furniss
Creative Director Helen Lewis
Original Concept Victoria Marshallsay
Project Editors Victoria Marshallsay and Pauline Savage
Design Jim Smith
Illustrations Annamaria Dutto
Photography Tiffany Mumford
Production Director Vincent Smith
Production Controller Leonie Kellman

First published in 2013 by
Quadrille Publishing Ltd
Alhambra House
27–31 Charing Cross Road
London WC2H OLS
www.quadrille.co.uk

British Library Cataloguing-in-Publication Data.
A catalogue record of this book is available from the British Library.

ISBN: 978 184949 316 1

Printed in China